The Challenge of Stability and Security in West Africa

The Challenge of Stability and Security in West Africa

Alexandre Marc, Neelam Verjee, and Stephen Mogaka

A copublication of the Agence Française de Développement and the World Bank

Africa Development Forum Series

The **Africa Development Forum Series** was created in 2009 to focus on issues of significant relevance to Sub-Saharan Africa's social and economic development. Its aim is both to record the state of the art on a specific topic and to contribute to ongoing local, regional, and global policy debates. It is designed specifically to provide practitioners, scholars, and students with the most up-to-date research results while highlighting the promise, challenges, and opportunities that exist on the continent.

The series is sponsored by the Agence Française de Développement and the World Bank. The manuscripts chosen for publication represent the highest quality in each institution and have been selected for their relevance to the development agenda. Working together with a shared sense of mission and interdisciplinary purpose, the two institutions are committed to a common search for new insights and new ways of analyzing the development realities of the Sub-Saharan Africa region.

Advisory Committee Members

Agence Française de Développement
Jean-Yves Grosclaude, Director of Strategy
Alain Henry, Director of Research
Guillaume de Saint Phalle, Head of Research and Publishing Division
Cyrille Bellier, Head of the Economic and Social Research Unit

World Bank
Francisco H. G. Ferreira, Chief Economist, Africa Region
Richard Damania, Lead Economist, Africa Region
Stephen McGroarty, Executive Editor, Publishing and Knowledge Division
Carlos Rossel, Publisher

West Africa Subregion and Members of the Ecomonic Community of West African States (ECOWAS)

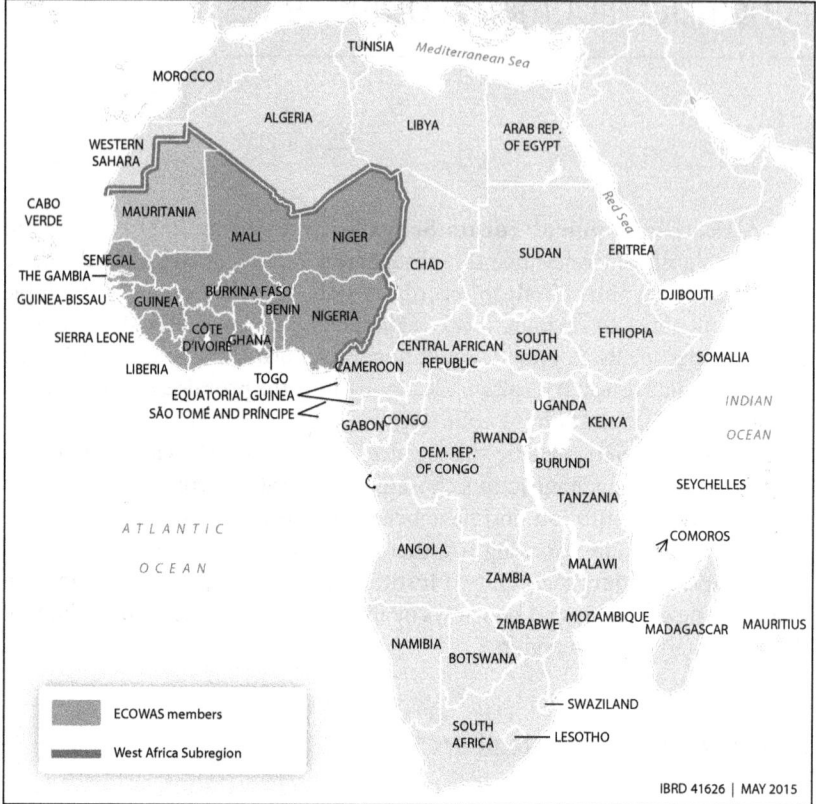

TUNISIA
Mediterranean Sea
MOROCCO
ALGERIA
LIBYA
ARAB REP. OF EGYPT
WESTERN SAHARA
CABO VERDE
MAURITANIA
MALI
NIGER
Red Sea
SENEGAL
THE GAMBIA
GUINEA-BISSAU
GUINEA
BURKINA FASO
BENIN
NIGERIA
CHAD
SUDAN
ERITREA
DJIBOUTI
SIERRA LEONE
CÔTE D'IVOIRE
GHANA
CENTRAL AFRICAN REPUBLIC
SOUTH SUDAN
ETHIOPIA
SOMALIA
LIBERIA
TOGO
CAMEROON
EQUATORIAL GUINEA
SÃO TOMÉ AND PRÍNCIPE
GABON
CONGO
UGANDA
KENYA
INDIAN
OCEAN
RWANDA
DEM. REP. OF CONGO
BURUNDI
SEYCHELLES
TANZANIA
ATLANTIC
OCEAN
COMOROS
ANGOLA
MALAWI
ZAMBIA
ZIMBABWE
MOZAMBIQUE
MADAGASCAR
MAURITIUS
NAMIBIA
BOTSWANA
SWAZILAND
SOUTH AFRICA
LESOTHO

ECOWAS members

West Africa Subregion

IBRD 41626 | MAY 2015

Titles in the Africa Development Forum Series

Africa's Infrastructure: A Time for Transformation (2010) edited by Vivien Foster and Cecilia Briceño-Garmendia

Gender Disparities in Africa's Labor Market (2010) edited by Jorge Saba Arbache, Alexandre Kolev, and Ewa Filipiak

Challenges for African Agriculture (2010) edited by Jean-Claude Deveze

Contemporary Migration to South Africa: A Regional Development Issue (2011) edited by Aurelia Segatti and Loren Landau

Light Manufacturing in Africa: Targeted Policies to Enhance Private Investment and Create Jobs (2012) by Hinh T. Dinh, Vincent Palmade, Vandana Chandra, and Frances Cossar

Informal Sector in Francophone Africa: Firm Size, Productivity, and Institutions (2012) by Nancy Benjamin and Ahmadou Aly Mbaye

Financing Africa's Cities: The Imperative of Local Investment (2012) by Thierry Paulais

Structural Transformation and Rural Change Revisited: Challenges for Late Developing Countries in a Globalizing World (2012) by Bruno Losch, Sandrine Fréguin-Gresh, and Eric Thomas White

The Political Economy of Decentralization in Sub-Saharan Africa: A New Implementation Model (2013) edited by Bernard Dafflon and Thierry Madiès

Empowering Women: Legal Rights and Economic Opportunities in Africa (2013) by Mary Hallward-Driemeier and Tazeen Hasan

Enterprising Women: Expanding Economic Opportunities in Africa (2013) by Mary Hallward-Driemeier

Urban Labor Markets in Sub-Saharan Africa (2013) edited by Philippe De Vreyer and François Roubaud

Securing Africa's Land for Shared Prosperity: A Program to Scale Up Reforms and Investments (2013) by Frank F. K. Byamugisha

Youth Employment in Sub-Saharan Africa (2014) by Deon Filmer and Louis Fox

Tourism in Africa: Harnessing Tourism for Growth and Improved Livelihoods (2014) by Iain Christie, Eneida Fernandes, Hannah Messerli, and Louise Twining-Ward

Safety Nets in Africa: Effective Mechanisms to Reach the Poor and Most Vulnerable (2015) edited by Carlo del Ninno and Bradford Mills

Land Delivery Systems in West African Cities: The Example of Bamako, Mali (2015) by Alain Durand-Lasserve, Maÿlis Durand-Lasserve, and Harris Selod

Enhancing the Climate Resilience of Africa's Infrastructure: The Power and Water Sectors (2015) edited by Raffaello Cervigni, Rikard Liden, James E. Neumann, and Kenneth M. Strzepek

Africa's Demographic Transition: Dividend or Disaster? (2015) edited by David Canning, Sangeeta Raja, and Abdo S. Yazbeck

The Challenge of Stability and Security in West Africa (2015) by Alexandre Marc, Neelam Verjee, and Stephen Mogaka

All books in the Africa Development Forum series are available for free at
https://openknowledge.worldbank.org/handle/10986/2150

Contents

Figures

Maps

Tables

Foreword

West Africa has come of age. The last decade has seen the subregion make tremendous strides in democratic consolidation and advance the cause of regional cooperation, while enjoying a surge in economic growth. Battered by civil war and political strife during the 1980s and 1990s, and undermined by poor governance, the subregion has emerged into the new millennium with a renewed sense of purpose and identity.

Economic growth has been on a rising trend since the middle of the last decade, powered by high commodity prices across natural resource-rich countries. The push toward greater openness is reinforced by an increasingly youthful citizenry, educated and impatient for change and clamoring to have their voices heard. The advent of social media, technological innovations, and globalization has multiplied avenues and opportunities for expression and participation that previous generations could only have dreamed of, all the while fostering greater accountability and transparency.

Despite its remarkable progress, the subregion still faces formidable challenges from various quarters. The emergence of new threats, such as narco-trafficking, maritime piracy, and religious extremism, as seen in Mali and northern Nigeria, presents a significant test for the institutions and capacities of the worst affected countries.

The devastation of the Ebola epidemic has also underscored the institutional weakness of postwar countries such as Liberia and Sierra Leone, as well as the impact of political instability in Guinea. It highlights the legacy of conflict, and its consequences for future generations, as well as the herculean effort required to rebuild institutions and infrastructure in the wake of conflict, regain the trust of the public, and regenerate social cohesion.

Drivers of fragility in West Africa are represented in the lack of clarity around land ownership, the neglect and the marginalization of peripheral regions, which are also often border regions, and the demographic challenge posed by an increasingly youthful population demanding greater inclusion, in particular through jobs and livelihood opportunities. There is also the rapid development of the extractives industry, which, if not well managed, creates opportunities for rent capture and generates more grievances than benefits at the local level.

As with many of the region's potential conflict triggers, some sources of tension also represent the potential and vitality of the subregion. For instance, West Africa has one of the most mobile populations in the world; the migratory populations that have at times been seen as contributing to instability and conflict as a result of competition over land, resources, and jobs are also a key motor that drives the economies of the subregion.

This study offers a very timely overview of the trends and dynamics of conflict and fragility in West Africa, as well as an analysis of some of the major drivers of fragility and conflict in the subregion. It is important to improve our understanding of how development policy can contribute to peace and stability and how we can better address the new challenges that are obstructing the impressive progress that West Africa has made in recent times.

Makhtar Diop
Vice President, Africa Region
World Bank

Acknowledgments

This volume is part of the African Regional Studies Program, an initiative of the Africa Region Vice Presidency at the World Bank. This series of studies aims to combine high levels of analytical rigor and policy relevance, and to apply them to various topics important for the social and economic development of Sub-Saharan Africa. Quality control and oversight are provided by the Office of the Chief Economist of the Africa Region.

This report has been prepared by the Fragility, Conflict, and Violence Group at the World Bank. It integrates the findings, and some of the analysis, of six thematic papers prepared by high-level experts on the West Africa subregion and commissioned by the World Bank. A member of the World Bank staff managed each paper, and Alexandre Marc led the overall study. This report was written by Alexandre Marc, Neelam Verjee, and Stephen Mogaka, and edited by Lauri Scherer.

The paper on trafficking and organized crime was prepared by an internal team from the World Bank that included Côme Dechery and Laura Ralston, with inputs from Mathieu Pellerin from the Institut Francais des Relations Internationales. International Alert prepared the paper on youth dynamics, employment, and generational gaps under the guidance of Alys Willman at the World Bank. The paper on the responses to the new security threats and the security sector was prepared by the Institute of Security Studies and Dr. David Zounmenou and was overseen by Roland Lomme at the World Bank. Professor Francis Stewart and Professor Arnim Langer prepared the paper on horizontal inequalities and regional imbalances, under the guidance of Alexandre Marc at the World Bank. The paper on land conflicts, migration, and citizenship was prepared by Kerry Maze of the International Organization for Migration, under the guidance of Peter Van der Auweraert of the International Organization for Migration and Deborah Isser at the World Bank. Dr. Roy Maconachie and Nicholas Menzies prepared the paper on mining and extractive industries, under the guidance of Radhika Srinivasan at the World Bank.

The report has benefited from being peer reviewed by Lynne Sherburne-Benz, Bernard Harborne, Bryan Christopher Land, Nadia Fernanda Piffaretti, and Michael Woolcock, all of the World Bank. The overall study has benefited from the advice of Alys Willman of the World Bank. The authors are grateful to Francisco H. G. Ferreira of the World Bank for his comments and his support.

About the Authors

Alexandre Marc is the chief specialist for the Fragility, Conflict, and Violence Group of the World Bank. He was the cluster leader for the Social Cohesion and Violence Prevention team within the Social Development Department of the World Bank from 2009 to 2012. He has extensive experience in the areas of conflict and fragility and has worked on related themes across four continents over the past 22 years. He joined the World Bank in 1988 in the Africa Region. From 1999 to 2005, he was sector manager for social development in the Europe and Central Asia Region of the World Bank and was responsible for postconflict reconstruction programs in eastern Europe. In addition to his World Bank experience, he was director of the Roma Education Fund from 2006 to 2007; in 2005, he was a visiting fellow at the Centre d'Études et de Recherches Internationales in Paris, responsible for research on cultural diversity and public policy. Marc was chair of the Global Experts Team on Conflict and Fragility and was a contributor to the World Bank's *World Development Report 2011: Conflict, Security, and Development*. He holds a doctorate in political science from the Paris Institute of Political Science (Sciences Po). Before joining the World Bank, Marc undertook research and consulting on Africa at Oxford University (St. Antony's College) and for the Société d'Études Économiques et Sociales in Paris. His most recent publications are *Societal Dynamics and Fragility: Engaging Societies in Responding to Fragile Situations* (World Bank 2013) and *Violence in the City: Understanding and Supporting Community Responses to Urban Violence* (World Bank 2010).

Neelam Verjee has worked for the Fragility, Conflict, and Violence Group of the World Bank since December 2013. She has a master's degree in public administration from the School of International and Public Affairs at Columbia University, where she focused on security studies and conflict, and a bachelor of science degree in social policy and government from the London School of Economics. Previously, she worked as program manager at Sisi Ni Amani, a Kenyan-based nongovernmental organization that developed technology as a tool for peace building, and on capacity-building projects at the World Policy

Institute in New York. Verjee has written extensively for the print media; she spent five years as a business reporter and features writer for the *Times* newspaper in London, as well as worked as a features writer for *Mint* newspaper in Mumbai, India, where she covered the entertainment industry and Bollywood. She is a contributor to Quartz, the online global news publication of Atlantic Media, and has done stints with television and radio.

Stephen Mogaka works with the Fragility, Conflict, and Violence Group of the World Bank. He is a political scientist by background, with a bachelor's degree in political science from the University of Delhi in India and a master's degree in political science from the University of Nairobi in Kenya. Mogaka has a wealth of experience in research on and analysis of issues related to conflict and postconflict recovery. His areas of expertise concern politics in Africa, particularly related to identity-based conflicts; democratic transitions; civil-military relations; and the politics around the emergence of extractives across the continent, with a focus on East Africa and the Horn of Africa.

Abbreviations

ACLED	Armed Conflict Location and Event Dataset
AQIM	Al-Qaeda in the Islamic Maghreb
ECOWAS	Economic Community of West African States
EITI	Extractive Industry Transparency Initiative
GDP	gross domestic product
IMF	International Monetary Fund
MUJAO	Movement for Oneness and Jihad in West Africa
NGO	nongovernmental organization
RUF	Revolutionary United Front
UN	United Nations
UNODC	United Nations Office on Drugs and Crime

Introduction

The rise in violence and conflict in West Africa since 2010 has sparked concerns that emerging threats could derail hard-won economic gains and undermine future development. Upheaval in Mali and in Nigeria shows that West Africa is still prone to violence. Drug trafficking and maritime piracy have taken root, locking some countries into fragility traps.

The surge in violence and conflict comes as the subregion has registered some of the most impressive growth rates seen on the continent in years. West Africa is the fastest-growing subregion in Sub-Saharan Africa, having grown 6.7 percent in 2013 and 7.4 percent in 2014 (ADB and others 2013). Paradoxically, some of the development gains in West Africa have provoked tensions and instability. Rapid growth has widened inequities, as accelerated development in the extractives industry and higher agricultural prices have spawned social tensions, and a better-educated population has heightened expectations for rapid improvements in living conditions and greater inclusion in power structures. Some of the drivers of fragility can thus be regarded as the flip side of progress.

Despite recent violence in the Sahel and Nigeria, and the devastating impact of the Ebola epidemic, West Africa reduced fragility and conflict over the past decade, increasing the inclusiveness of politics and democratization, which helped reduce tensions over the medium term. West Africa is home to some of Africa's most stable countries (Ghana, Senegal), and several countries (Côte d'Ivoire, Liberia, Sierra Leone) successfully transitioned from war to peace. Despite the Biafran War and the violence that affected the countries of the Mano River Basin in the 1990s, West Africa experienced fewer fatalities from violence and conflict than any other subregion of Sub-Saharan Africa. It therefore offers lessons on the dynamics of fragility and conflict that can be useful for countries around the world.

The Ebola outbreak had claimed more than 11,000 lives, mostly in Guinea, Liberia, and Sierra Leone as of May 2015 (CDC 2015). The crisis brings into sharp relief the legacy and consequences of conflict for a country's social, political, and economic fabric. Ebola overwhelmed the health sectors of Liberia and Sierra Leone, where the destruction of physical infrastructure as a result of civil

1

wars, combined with the flight of trained doctors and health care providers, has had a lasting impact on social services. The crisis is a reminder of the debilitating inheritance of protracted conflict and the scale of investment required to ensure that institutions truly recover from conflict.

This book has three purposes:

- It explains the major drivers of fragility and violence in West Africa and identifies dynamics of resilience that have allowed some countries to come out of protracted conflict and fragility.

- It examines the regional dimension and the external dynamics that influence these factors.

- It identifies possible policy and programmatic responses and directions for policy dialogue at the national and international levels.

It also identifies areas of further investigation that will fill the vast data and research gaps that exist on many of the topics it addresses.

The book draws on existing analysis and an in-depth literature review, particularly the six papers prepared by some of the world's leading experts on West Africa. It builds on an analytical framework that reflects the findings of *The World Bank Development Report 2011: Conflict, Security, and Development* and the analysis carried out in *Societal Dynamics and Fragility*, a 2012 study by the World Bank's Social Development Department. It bases its methodological framework on recent research on development interventions in conflict settings, in particular *Contesting Development: Participatory Projects and Local Conflict Dynamics in Indonesia* (Barron, Diprose, and Woolcock 2011) and *War and Conflict in Africa* (Williams 2011).

The *World Development Report* posits that fragility and conflict are born from external and internal stresses that local and regional institutions are unable to contain or mitigate (World Bank 2011). In some cases, the stresses (or accelerating factors) are so intense that even strong institutions are unable to contain them. In other cases, the institutions themselves are so weak and ineffective that even low-intensity stresses create instability and violence that can spin out of control.

One factor seems essential: the way in which institutions reflect and incorporate various social norms across society (World Bank 2012). To be legitimate and effective, institutions must be in sync with what individuals and groups accept as legitimate. Leaders, politicians, or groups of individuals can create institutions, but institutions can be effective only if the society believes that they are useful and legitimate. Effective institutions must display at least some success in resolving the issues social groups face, such as marriage, security, and land use. The manner in which institutions interact with one another—and the quality of these interactions—is also important, especially in dealing with conflicts (World Bank 2012). Strong institutions also shape social groups' norms and behaviors and frame the collective behavior of members; they can foster cohesion or lead to further fragmentation. Elites often use institutions to impose norms on various members of society, especially young people, women, and minority groups. There is a constant interaction between institutions and a society's social dynamics: institutions both shape and are shaped by social dynamics.

Another important factor is how institutions operate and adapt. Institutions constantly need to adapt to make sure they are in sync with the social needs, norms, and demands of the individuals who comprise a society. Institutions can be internally transformed or even disappear if they fail to adapt quickly enough. When social structures change quickly and norms are rapidly transformed, institutions usually face issues of legitimacy and efficiency. In periods of rapid social and economic transformation, they face heavy pressure to transform. However, because institutions are created to provide a framework of predictability for individuals' collective behaviors, they usually resist change, which weakens them and can reinforce ineffective relations among institutions and between institutions and society. Periods of rapid and deep social transformation are usually characterized by increased fragility of institutions and accompanied by heightened internal stress.

Africa has experienced deep and rapid social and economic transformation, which explains in large part why the continent is more prone to conflict and violence than others. As Lant Pritchett and Frauke de Weijer (2010, 3) put it:

> Transformation is a shift in the overall "rules systems," the established patterns, norms of behavior, and expectations, in which individuals as agents are embedded. This means that during transitional periods individuals will be embedded in multiple, potentially conflicting, rules systems which creates stress and conflict. It also means that the transition is far from painless or easy, and that "success" is not inevitable.

This book's main hypothesis is that the rapid pace at which societies in Africa are changing puts enormous strain on its institutions, pushing them to transform rapidly but also risking rendering them illegitimate and ineffective. Relations between various types of institutions—especially state institutions (which try to answer a society's global needs) and customary institutions (which dominate at the local level and deal locally with a variety of social needs)—are particularly problematic. Many institutions in Africa are strained by these rapid changes and are increasingly out of sync with social groups' expectations and needs. For instance, an increasing number of people, especially youth, do not recognize the legitimacy of either local customary institutions or national and global institutions. The changing role of women in the economy has not yet been accompanied by institutions that have adapted to support this social evolution. Customary institutions still reflect rural norms and have not yet adapted to the needs or increasing numbers of urban dwellers. And political institutions are responding very slowly to calls for a larger share of power and resources from an increasingly educated population.

In trying to understand the drivers of fragility and the factors of resilience, this book looks first at stresses. Across West Africa, stresses that increase the risk of conflict stem largely from global factors, including the rapidly growing youth population; increases in the movement of populations within countries and across borders; growing inequalities and fast evolving regional disparities inside countries; the accelerated development of the extractives industry; and the explosion of various forms of trafficking and criminal activities, especially involving drugs. (Other sources of stress, such as climate change and rapid urbanization, are also important, but they are reflected largely through issues of land scarcity and migration. They are not specific to West Africa but are experienced by many countries.)

This books examines the ability of institutions to manage these stresses. It focuses on three institutions that play particularly important roles in fragility and conflict: political institutions, which deal with the way power is managed and organized; institutions that deal with land and, in a broader sense, natural resources; and institutions that deal with security and conflict management.

Separating stresses from institutions is a useful analytical device, but for policy makers, the two are very much connected and interrelated. For instance, land scarcity reflects increasing demographic pressures, climate change, and ineffective institutions. Demography and climate change are stresses, whereas the ability of local and national institutions to deal with land management is an institutional issue. Policy makers must deal with both.

To prepare this book, the authors commissioned six papers from organizations or individuals that have conducted in-depth academic research in this area.[1] The papers addressed six themes:

- Trafficking and organized crime
- Youth dynamics, employment, and generational gaps
- Responses to new security threats and the security sector
- Regional and horizontal inequalities
- Land conflicts, migration, and citizenship
- Mining and extractive industries

The book also analyzes various datasets on violence and conflict in West Africa, including the Armed Conflict Location and Event Dataset (ACLED), the Uppsala Conflict Data Program (UCDP), and Conflict Trends in Africa 1946–2004.

The book is divided into three parts. Part I (chapter 1) analyzes trends in and the dynamics of violence and conflict in West Africa and compares it to other subregions in Sub-Saharan Africa. Part II (chapters 2–7) analyzes the drivers of conflict and fragility by looking at both stresses and institutions; it draws on the six papers prepared for this book. Part III (chapters 8–9) looks at the factors of resilience, based on an analysis of countries that successfully exited from conflict. It also suggests ways in which donors and development agencies can improve the ways in which they support stability and the reduction of fragility.

Note

1. The papers are available at https://openknowledge.worldbank.org/. The topics were identified from the fragility assessments carried out by the World Bank in preparing strategies for 10 countries in West Africa between 2012 and 2014 (Burkina Faso, Côte d'Ivoire, Guinea, Guinea-Bissau, Liberia, Mali, Mauritania, Niger, Nigeria, and Sierra Leone). Each analysis included an in-depth review of the literature on the country and, in many cases, the results of consultations and seminars with in-country experts.

References

ADB (African Development Bank), OECD (Organisation for Economic Co-operation and Development, UNDP (United Nations Development Programme), and UNECA (United Nations Economic Commission for Africa). 2013. *African Economic Outlook 2013: Regional Edition/Western Africa*. Abidjan. http://www.africaneconomicoutlook .org/fileadmin/uploads/aeo/PDF/Regional_Edition/West_Africa_2013_en.pdf.

Barron, P., R. Diprose, and M. Woolcock. 2011. *Contesting Development: Participatory Projects and Local Conflict Dynamics in Indonesia*. New Haven, CT: Yale University Press.

CDC (Centers for Disease Control and Prevention). 2015. "2014 Ebola Outbreak in West Africa—Case Counts." March. http://www.cdc.gov/vhf/ebola/outbreaks/2014 -west-africa/case-counts.html.

Pritchett, L., and F. de Weijer. 2010. "Fragile States: Stuck in a Capability Trap." Background paper for the *World Development Report*, World Bank, Washington, DC.

Williams, P. D. 2011. *War and Conflict in Africa*. Cambridge: Polity Press.

World Bank. 2011. *World Development Report 2011: Conflict, Security, and Development*. Washington, DC: World Bank.

———. 2012. *Societal Dynamics and Fragility: Engaging Societies in Responding to Fragile Situations*. Washington, DC: World Bank.

Chapter 1

An Overview of Conflict and Violence in West Africa

Recent events in West Africa have pivoted the world's attention back to the risk of conflict and fragility in the region. Upheaval in Mali and Nigeria, as well as the recent coups in Burkina Faso and Guinea-Bissau, shows that West Africa is still prone to violence. This violence notwithstanding, the subregion has suffered fewer conflict events and fatalities from conflicts over the last 60 years than any other subregion on the continent.[1]

In the decade after 1960—the year in which most West African countries gained independence (dates range from 1957 [Ghana] to 1975 [Cape Verde])—fatalities caused by regional conflict remained very low. As the majority of West African countries experienced a peaceful postcolonial handover of power, fatalities plummeted from the 2 million death toll that resulted from the separatist Biafran War in Nigeria (1967–70) to a near-zero figure in the 1970s. With the end of the Biafran War, West Africa enjoyed a period of relative tranquility until December 1989, when the Liberian civil war signaled the beginning of the subregion's slide into a crucible of political violence and internecine conflict.

The civil wars in Liberia and Sierra Leone, which together resulted in an estimated 800,000 fatalities, drew to a close in the early 2000s. The civil war in Guinea-Bissau, which contributed to a spike in casualties in 1998, ended a year later. The death toll from conflict nearly halved after 1999, continuing a gradual downward trajectory until 2006, albeit with a brief spike in 2003 in part because of the low-intensity civil war in Côte d'Ivoire. The number of fatalities from conflict events began a gradual climb once again after 2007 and accelerated in 2010 because of the outbreak of violence in Mali and Nigeria (Marshall 2005).

The last decade has seen a dramatic change in the character of violence in West Africa. Violence has shifted away from the large-scale conflict events and intrastate wars that characterized the postcolonial and post–Cold War periods toward an increase in low-level insurgencies and political violence by nonstate actors (table 1.1). The countries of the Mano River Basin conflict system—Côte d'Ivoire, Guinea, Liberia, and Sierra Leone—successfully emerged from conflict

Table 1.1 Selected Conflicts in West Africa

Name of conflict	Country	Years	Nature of conflict	Estimated fatalities
Guinea-Bissau War of Independence	Guinea-Bissau	1962–74	Insurgency	15,000
Biafran War	Nigeria	1967–70	Civil war	500,000–2,000,000
Casamance conflict	Senegal	1982–present	Insurgency	5,000
Mauritania and Senegal War	Mauritania and Senegal	1989–90	International conflict	500
First Liberian Civil War	Liberia	1989–96	Civil war	100,000–220,000
Tuareg rebellion	Mali	1990–95	Insurgency	—
Sierra Leone Civil War	Sierra Leone	1991–2002	Civil war	50,000–300,000
Guinea-Bissau Civil War	Guinea-Bissau	1998–99	Civil war	655
Second Liberian Civil War	Liberia	1999–2003	Civil war	150,000–300,000
First Ivorian Civil War	Côte d'Ivoire	2002–07	Civil war	3,000
Niger Delta conflict	Nigeria	2004–09	Insurgency	2,500–4,000
Tuareg rebellion	Niger	2007–09	Insurgency	270–400
Boko Haram uprising	Nigeria	2009–present	Insurgency	11,200
Second Ivorian Civil War	Côte d'Ivoire	2010–11	Civil war	3,000
Conflict in Northern Mali	Mali	2012–13	Insurgency	1,270

Source: Data on fatalities are derived from various sources, including Marshall 2005; ACLED 2014; Human Rights Watch 2011b; Nigeria Social Violence Dataset 2014; and Reuters 2009.
Note: — = not available.

and continue to demonstrate resilience, despite the high level of interconnectivity between them and the lack of resolution of some of the underlying causes of the initial political violence that rocked the region, such as land access and migration.

The push toward democratization that started in the 1990s has gradually seen elections replace military coups as the sole credible means of transferring power in the region. A counterintuitive consequence of this change has been the increase in election-related violence across the subregion, reflecting the new competition. The zero-sum stakes of many elections in several countries, and the manipulation of identities for political gain, make political violence particularly incendiary.

Drug trafficking, maritime piracy, and religious extremism have emerged as growing threats to stability. A spike in narcotics trafficking throughout the subregion has undermined governance and corroded state institutions, the surge in maritime piracy threatens the stability and economic development of the coastal states in the Gulf of Guinea, and a sharp increase in deadly attacks by Boko Haram against Nigeria's civilian population and the rise of extremist groups in the Sahel—such as Al-Qaeda in the Islamic Maghreb (AQIM) and Ansar Dine—risk plunging the region into a protracted period of instability.

Figure 1.1 State-Based Conflicts in Sub-Saharan Africa, by Subregion, 1960–2012

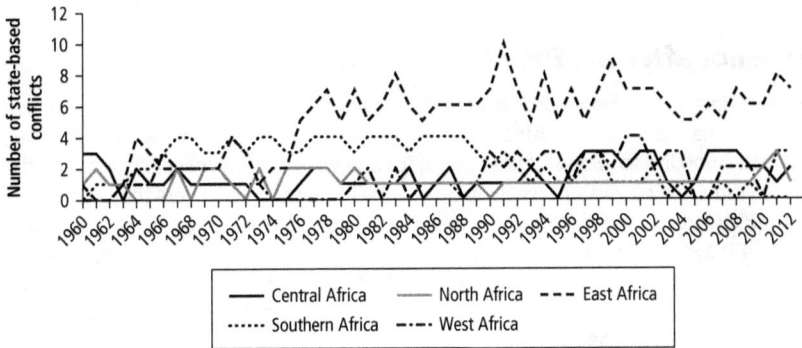

Source: Themnér and Wallensteen 2013.

Overall, West Africa has been affected by fewer conflicts and less violence than other regions in Africa (figure 1.1). The period of relative calm that accompanied the end of the Biafran War came to an abrupt end in the late 1980s, as a slew of post–Cold War civil wars wracked the region (Marshall 2005) (box 1.1 and figure 1.2). In the decade leading to 2004, the death toll climbed to about 150,000. During the same period, deaths from conflict across East Africa climbed steadily, to a peak of 1.6 million in 2004, while fatalities from conflict in Central Africa fell, from 200,000 in 1960 to close to zero in the 1980s before increasing again, to almost 1.6 million deaths by 2004 (Marshall 2005).

Data on deaths from conflict in West Africa also contrast with the trend in Southern Africa during the same period (figure 1.3), when countries waged protracted wars of independence against the colonial powers. The wars in Angola, Mozambique, Namibia, and South Africa, among others, saw the conflict-related death toll increase throughout the 1960s, before plateauing in the 1980s at 600,000 deaths per decade (Marshall 2005). It fell significantly only recently (Themnér and Wallensteen 2013).

The Nature of Violence and Conflict in West Africa

The multiple forms of violence in West Africa overlap to form an interlocking and mutating landscape of conflict across the region. Lines of potential fracture, such as religious, ethnic, cultural, or linguistic differences, which

BOX 1.1

Violence after the End of the Cold War

For two decades, competition between the United States and the Soviet Union helped maintain the status quo in Africa, as the great powers supported their client states, indirectly working to widen state-society gaps and weaken governance. France and the United Kingdom played a particularly critical role in West Africa, where they shaped the nature, evolution, and outcomes of various post–Cold War conflicts across the subregion (N'Diaye 2011). Support to states with very strong ties to the former colonial power—such as Houphouët-Boigny's Côte d'Ivoire, Samuel Doe's Liberia, and Gnassingbé Eyadéma's Togo—gave authoritarian leaders carte blanche to exercise repressive means of control.

The end of the Cold War triggered the collapse of central authority in many West African countries, either directly or indirectly. As unconditional backing ended overnight, the supply of arms, military assistance programs, funding, and other interventions dried up. The sea change left authoritarian states exposed, weakened, and stripped of their monopolies on violence (Luckham and others 2001), leaving them vulnerable to attacks from dissident groups. When conflicts did erupt after the end of the Cold War, there was no remaining imperative for external powers to intervene in defense of Western interests (N'Diaye 2011).

Figure 1.2 Fatalities from Organized Violence in West Africa, 1989–2012

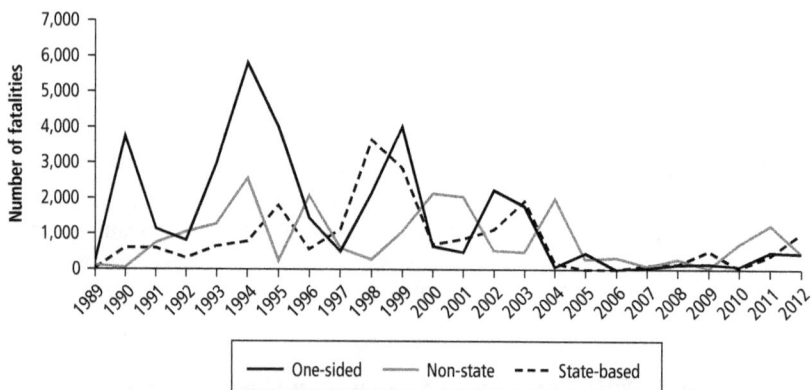

Sources: UCDP Battle-Related Deaths Dataset v. 5-2013 1989–2012; UCDP Non-State Conflict Dataset v. 2.5-2013 1989–2012; UCDP One-Sided Violence Dataset v 1.4-2013 1989–2012.

in and of themselves represent the countries' multiethnic make-up, have acted as incendiary devices in which perceptions of injustice, marginalization, and exclusion are manifested (figure 1.4 illustrates how drivers of conflict combined to create and sustain the conditions for civil war in Côte d'Ivoire).

The nature of violence has significantly changed in the period since independence, as swaths of the region display signs of stabilization even as they wrestle with new and insidious security threats. During this time, the subregion has also experienced an improvement in efforts to prevent conflicts, which has contributed to its overall stability.

Figure 1.3 Estimates of Fatalities from Organized Violence in East, Central, and Southern Africa, 1989–2012

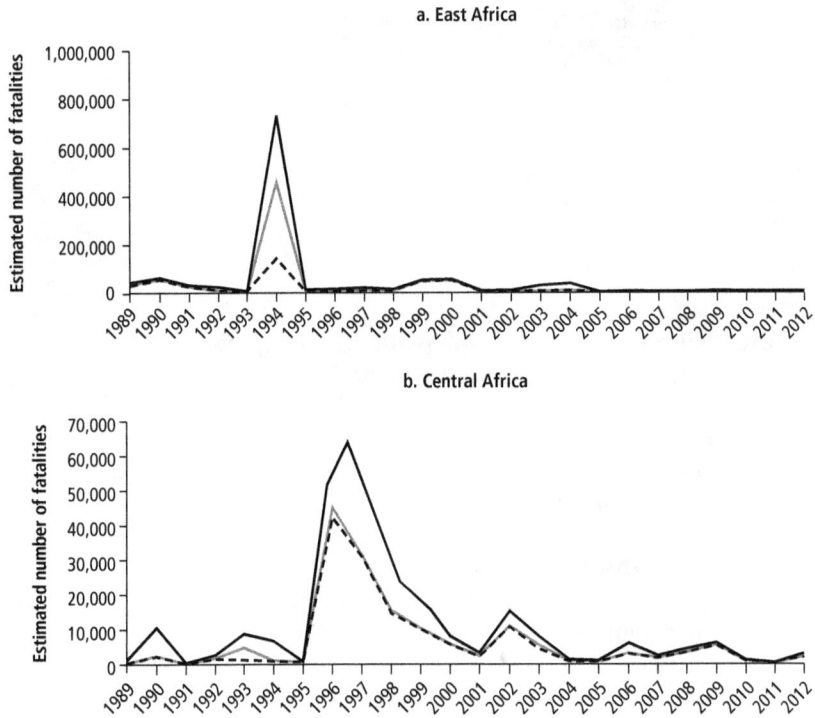

a. East Africa

b. Central Africa

(continued next page)

Figure 1.3 (continued)

c. Southern Africa

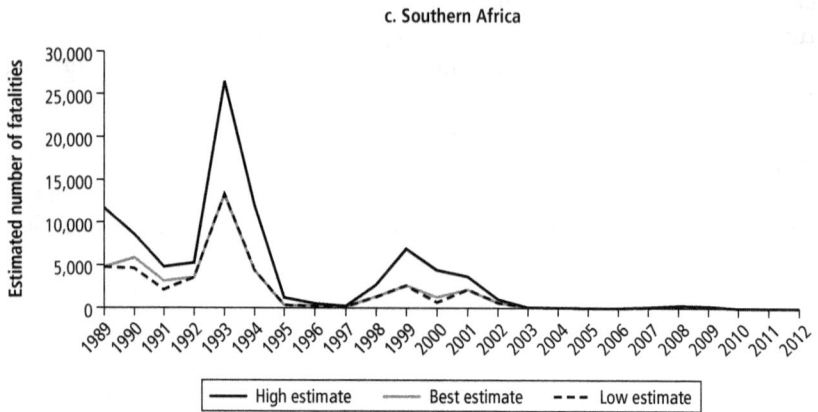

Sources: UCDP Battle-Related Deaths Dataset v. 5-2013 1989–2012; UCDP Non-State Conflict Dataset v. 2.5-2013 1989–2012; UCDP One-Sided Violence Dataset v 1.4-2013 1989–2012.
Note: Best estimate: Aggregate of most reliable numbers for all battle-related incidents during a year. If different reports provide different estimates, an examination is made into which source is most reliable. If no such distinction can be made, as a rule, UCDP includes the lower figure. Low estimate: Aggregated low estimates for all battle-related incidents during a year. If different reports provide different estimates and a higher estimate is considered more reliable, the low estimate is also reported if deemed reasonable. High estimate: Aggregated high estimates for all battle-related incidents during a year. If different reports provide different estimates and a lower estimate is considered more or equally reliable, the high estimate is also reported if deemed reasonable. If there are incidents in which there is some uncertainty about which parties were involved, they are also included in the high estimate.

Limited Number of Armed Independence Struggles

The run-up to independence and the political transition from colonialism to self-rule was a largely peaceful period for West Africa, with the subregion's countries the first on the continent to shake off the colonial shackles. The only nation in the region to fight a war for its independence was Guinea-Bissau, which waged an armed struggle against Portugal (box 1.2).

Dominance of Intrastate Conflicts

The vast majority of the armed conflicts in West Africa after independence have been intrastate conflicts. In only two cases were the parties sovereign states: the war between Mali and Burkina Faso in April 1985 and the war between Senegal and Mauritania in April 1989. In both cases, active combat lasted no longer than a week (Souaré 2010).

During its short postcolonial history, West Africa has recorded five large-scale civil wars and at least seven other conflicts of more localized unrest (M'Cormack 2011), in addition to a significant number of military coups (box 1.3).

Figure 1.4 Combination of Drivers That Created and Sustained Conditions for Civil War in Côte d'Ivoire

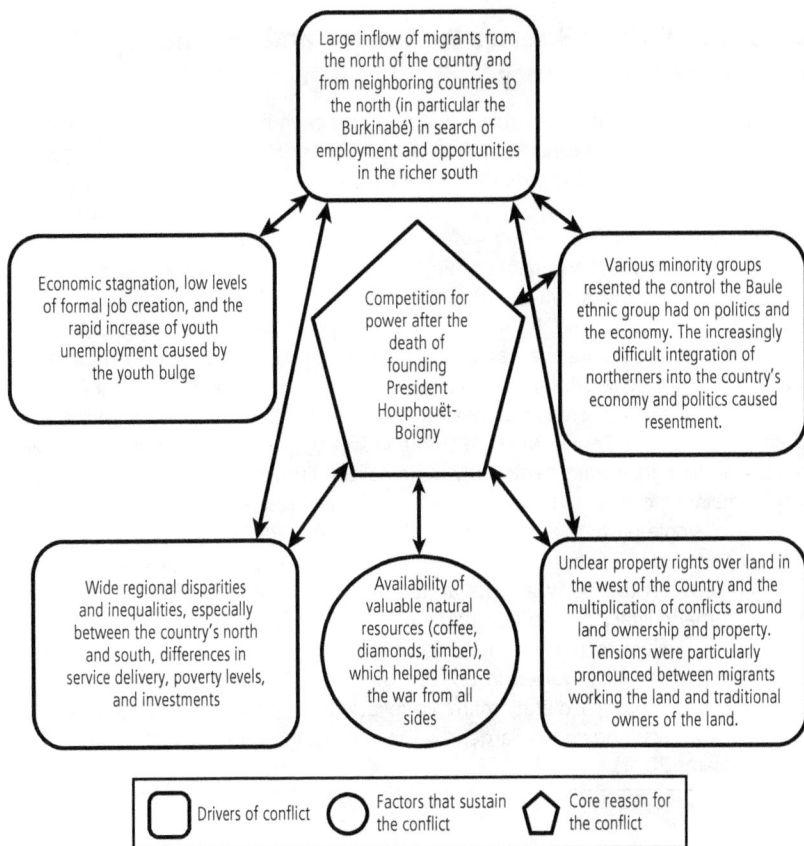

The Biafran War (1967–70) was the subregion's first large-scale civil war. The other civil wars, which took place following the end of the Cold War, were in Liberia (1989–96 and 1999–2003), Sierra Leone (1991–2002), Guinea-Bissau (1998–99), and Côte d'Ivoire (2002–07 and 2010–11).

In terms of scale and impact, conflicts other than the Biafran War cost nearly 827,000 lives, with Liberia's civil wars alone resulting in about 520,000 deaths.[2] The impact on the civilian population was extensive, with the conflicts in Liberia and Sierra Leone alone generating about 1 million refugees and internally displaced persons (IDPs) (Luckham and others 2001). Sexual and gender-based violence against both men and women was pervasive in all conflicts, the psychological and physiological trauma of conflict

BOX 1.2

Legacy of Guinea-Bissau's Protracted and Violent Anticolonial Insurgency

The legacy of an anticolonial insurgency has a long-term impact on institutional development. Countries that experienced major rural uprisings tend to be more autocratic and unstable, whereas countries that experienced a political anticolonial struggle with low levels of violence tend to be more democratic and less conflict ridden (Wantchékon and García-Ponce 2013).

A prime example of this relationship is Guinea-Bissau, where continued instability has been linked to the drawn-out rural armed struggle for independence from Portugal waged between 1963 and 1974. The rural insurgency during the fight for independence helped perpetuate the use of violence as both a means of expression and a method of conflict resolution. The intervention and involvement of Guinea-Bissau's military in the political arena has been a constant feature of life in the coastal state since independence. Former guerrilla commanders, often with limited education, who came in large part from a particularly marginalized ethnic group, used the army as a way to maintain control over the country's politics and resources.

In the single-party political regime led by the PAIGC (Partido Africano da Independência da Guiné e Cabo Verde) following independence, there was no distinction between the party and its armed wing and the state. This lack of clarity between the military and other parts of the state was enshrined in the 1984 constitution. Failure to redefine the military's role and reform the army has enabled the military to remain involved in politics. Between 1974 and 2012, Guinea-Bissau experienced four coups d'état, many coup attempts, and a high level of political instability that was engineered largely by the military, with the support of the political class (Williams 2011).

and violence was severe, and the economic and social costs of war were significant.

West Africa has also seen conflicts of lesser magnitude. The Casamance separatist insurgency in Senegal has been ongoing since 1982, and Ghana experienced land disputes in the north in the mid-1990s that manifested as ethnic tensions. Mali and Niger saw Tuareg uprisings, and there have been crises of security and governance in Burkina Faso and Guinea. Nigeria has suffered from overlapping forms of political, communal, ethnoreligious, election-related, and resource-related strife for many years (box 1.4).

Despite the artificial borders imposed by the colonial powers, the quasi absence of interstate conflicts can be explained by the sanctity of territorial boundaries. This concept found resonance across West Africa following independence. It was bolstered by the inclusion of an article in the Organization of

BOX 1.3

Theories of Civil War and Political Violence: Greed versus Grievance

Theories about the onset of civil war and political violence—often couched as "greed versus grievance" theories—question whether economic incentives or broader social and political motives drive societies to violence (World Bank 2011). Collier and Hoeffler (2002) find a strong association between civil conflict and both exports of primary commodities (which provide the means for rebellion) and the lack of opportunities for young men (which reduce the opportunity cost of rebellion). This evidence supports the greed hypothesis. Collier and Sambanis (2005) find that the proxies used for grievance as a driver of conflict are "insignificant," with ethnic dominance alone showing adverse effects, implying that conflict is more likely in a highly polarized environment.

Critics of the greed hypothesis argue that it fits specific conflicts (such as the civil wars in Liberia and Sierra Leone) better than others (such as the civil war in Cote d'Ivoire) and that it fails to account for historical transformations in the character and dynamics of conflict. Another criticism is that the distinctions used to distinguish greed from grievance are simplistic. Fearon and Laitin (2001) argue that conditions that favor insurgency, such as poverty, are better at identifying countries at risk of civil war than are measures of grievance, such as the lack of democracy. There is agreement that grievance factors may be at the source of conflicts whereas greed factors tend to prolong conflicts.

BOX 1.4

Overlapping Forms of Violence in Nigeria

Nigeria underwent a successful transition from military to civilian rule in 1999. Since then it has held four elections. There is a sense that the country has crossed the Rubicon as far as civilian rule is concerned.

The transition has not been peaceful. Within four years of the transition to civilian rule, an estimated 10,000 people died in communal violence across the country (Isaacs 2004).

Violence has taken various forms. The north has experienced high levels of religious and ethnoreligious violence, a trend that began in the 1980s but increased significantly in recent years with the rise of Boko Haram (ICG 2010). The Niger Delta region has experienced a local insurgency that has mutated into criminality and maritime piracy (ICG 2012; Nwankpa 2014). Urban violence has erupted in several locales (Oruwari and Owei 2006). The Middle Belt region has experienced high levels of ethnoreligious conflict as well as clashes between farmers and pastoralists (Sayne 2012).

The drivers of conflict vary. But throughout the country, violence is seen as arising from a "common matrix" that encompasses, among other factors, "multiple crises of authority, patterns of human insecurity, sociopolitical exclusion, and a deep-seated crisis of youth" (World Bank 2012, 6).

African Unity (OAU) Charter of 1963 in support of territorial integrity (Zacher 2001). In line with the principles of pan-Africanism, countries of the subregion respected territorial boundaries in the postcolonial period despite the arbitrary nature of borders and the common linguistic and cultural heritages shared by transnational ethnic groups. An additional dimension was the weakness of states at the time of independence. The incomplete process of nation building had left countries struggling to establish order, security, and stability. In this light, borders and international boundaries acted as "external shells" that no party was willing to challenge—a state of being that can be described as "negative peace" (Kacowicz 1997). With the end of the Cold War, there appears to have been a shift in sentiment, as the allure of pan-Africanism faded and took a backseat to the multiple triggers and causes of conflict and violence. As a result, the past decades have seen several instances of regional spillovers of conflict across porous and mutable boundaries.

Since the beginning of the new millennium, the incidence of civil war in West Africa has dramatically dropped off, suggesting that large-scale political violence is on the wane (Straus 2012). Guinea-Bissau, Liberia, and Sierra Leone all entered a postconflict phase and successfully conducted multiparty elections; after a brief relapse in 2010 following its elections, Côte d'Ivoire has once again returned to stability. This trend represents a watershed in the political stabilization of the region, even as emerging threats and alternative forms of political violence have come to replace large-scale conflicts and civil wars. Guinea-Bissau remains very unstable, and the coup of 2012 set the clock back, but it did so without igniting major violence (box 1.5). Indeed, the country has made some progress since, holding peaceful elections in 2014.

Evidence for this stabilization is also seen in the decline in battle deaths across the continent as a whole, which, according to the Armed Conflict Location and Event Data Project (ACLED) (Marshall 2005), have been on a steady downward path over the past two decades. Part of this trend can be attributed to the move toward democratization and multiparty elections, which permits grievances to be expressed at the ballot box instead of on the battlefield. Credit also goes to the role played by regional mechanisms for dispute resolution and conflict prevention and management such as the Economic Community of West African States (ECOWAS), which helped bring about a fragile peace and draw a close to the festering civil wars of the Mano River Basin.

Longstanding Ethno-National Conflicts
Despite the major shift in the nature of violence, longstanding ethno-national conflicts are still present in the region. The unresolved issue of the economic marginalization and political exclusion of the Tuareg people has been a bone of contention and a cause of violence in the Sahel since colonial times. French-drawn national boundaries interrupted caravan routes and cut off access to

BOX 1.5

Guinea-Bissau's Fragility Trap

A "fragility trap" is a situation in which a fragile or conflict-affected country is caught in a slow-growth/poor-governance equilibrium that stems from the weakness of its institutions and policies. It is characterized by political instability and violence, insecure property rights, and unenforceable contracts (Mcloughlin 2012).

Guinea-Bissau is an example of a country caught in a fragility trap. Political instability has undermined the capacity of successive governments to guarantee control of the territory, deliver basic public services and infrastructure, and create a climate conducive to economic investment. The structural antecedents of the problem lie in the inability of postcolonial governments to "fundamentally transform the institutions inherited at independence" (Andriamihaja, Cinyabuguma, and Devarajan n.d).

The 1998 civil war damaged the country's physical capital and reduced national income by 25 percent (Andriamihaja, Cinyabuguma, and Devarajan n.d). Although growth rates have since picked up—to 0.3 percent in 2013 and 2.5 percent in 2014, according to the World Bank—years of political instability, weak governance, poor economic management, and corruption have taken their toll on the country's institutional resilience (Pouligny 2010). Indeed, the Institute of Security Studies lists Guinea-Bissau as one of 10 countries in Sub-Saharan Africa that is at risk of remaining stuck in a fragility trap beyond 2050 (Cilliers and Sisk 2013). The elections of 2014 seem to have changed this dynamic.

---

traditional pasture grounds. Tuaregs and Arabs were grossly underrepresented in postindependence cabinets, the army, and the senior civil service (Bakrania 2013). Perceptions of injustice run high in the north of Mali, which has experienced economic marginalization and unequal access to health and education provision. These perceptions have been reinforced by environmental stresses, including desertification, drought, and the scarcity of land and water, as well as the weakening of traditional institutions that helped mediate conflict among members of these groups.

Although the crisis in Mali in 2012 caught observers by surprise, the long history of Tuareg rebellion (Antil and Mokhefi 2014) in the Sahel dates back to the 1890s, when French colonial incursions into the northern areas of present-day Mali were met with armed resistance (Thurston and Lebovich 2013). Numerous violent uprisings have taken place since, including against the French colonial state in 1916, in 1963 following independence, and in 1990. The outbreak of violence between 2006 and 2009 gave momentum to the notion of a Tuareg homeland. The most recent uprising, in 2012, which led to the collapse of the state, was distinguished by its strong Islamist overtones. Tuareg uprisings cumulatively comprise the longest-running insurgency in West Africa.

Although the number of casualties has been relatively small, the conflict represents a major source of fragility for the Sahel.

A number of other low-intensity conflicts in the subregion that are based on ethnicity and issues of inclusion, and access to land, could flare up at any time. They include the conflict in Casamance, tensions with the Mandingo in Liberia and Sierra Leone, stresses over land in western Côte d'Ivoire, unrest in Nigeria's Middle Belt, the ethnic polarization of politics in Guinea, and stratification between socioeconomic groups in Mauritania (Bertelsmann Stiftung 2014).

Subregional Conflict Systems and the Imperative for Regional Approaches

The frequency of regional spillovers of internal conflicts in West Africa highlights the close level of interconnectivity between countries. Localized conflicts can trigger region-wide conflict systems and destabilize neighboring countries. Conflicts that emerge from a single conflict system may have diverse causes and varying durations, with some more lethal than others. They are interlinked, however, and therefore necessitate region-wide approaches to conflict resolution and management (Diallo 2009).

The theory of conflict systems posits that conflicts can spill across borders and are in fact shaped and sustained by strong transnational connections between countries (Buhaug and Gleditsch 2008). Conflict systems are characterized by an epicenter, or a source, as well as a dynamic that accounts for the evolution, spread, and regression of conflict (Diallo 2009). Diverse transnational links facilitate the spread and spillover of conflicts. Borders are porous, and communities on either side maintain close ties based on ethnicity, language, culture, and trade. Shared grievances, such as environmental or socioeconomic factors, or marginalization based on a common identity, find ideological support across borders. Porous borders and common ties also facilitate the movement of people—militias, workers, and refugees—as well as arms, drugs, and contraband (Kacowicz 1997). The movement of large numbers of refugees across borders can contribute to the spillover of conflict while facilitating arms smuggling and increasing the pool of rebels for recruitment (Blattman and Miguel 2009).

The complexity and depth of ties between countries whose boundaries were drawn in an arbitrary fashion means that it is almost inevitable that conflict will spread. In some cases, countries share the internal dimensions of a conflict and are therefore exposed to the same stresses. In Liberia and Sierra Leone, for example, deteriorating economic performance in the 1980s under the aegis of repressive and authoritarian governments resulted in lower household income and social spending and declining access to health care and education. In other cases, cross-border linkages and porous borders make neighbor states vulnerable to the contagion effect of conflict events (N'Diaye 2011). Although Guinea did not experience the same intensity of conflict as its neighbors in the Mano River Basin during the 1990s, it was affected by the large flow of refugees as well as unrest in the south (Jörgel and Utas 2007). The "bad neighborhood" effect, where violence in one country can affect the prospects of neighboring countries, suggests that countries can lose 0.7 percent of their annual GDP for every neighbor involved in a war (World Bank 2011).

West Africa has also been susceptible to cross-border influences from North Africa. Libya has played a role in the region's political development for several decades. Armed with petro-dollars, Libya's leader Muammar Gaddafi meddled in the region's political movements and rebel uprisings, funding leaders and backing ventures such as Charles Taylor's exploits in the Mano River Basin and Foday Sankoh's Revolutionary United Front. After the fall of the Gaddafi regime, thousands of impoverished and unemployed migrant workers, as well as armed men who had fought for Gaddafi, returned south to their homes. They contributed to an uprising against the government of Mali.

Another destabilizing factor from North Africa has been the spillover of international ideological groups into the Sahel from Libya and Algeria. These groups have grafted extremist ideology onto local grievances in Mali, escalating and internationalizing the conflict there (World Bank 2011).

Within West Africa, there are a number of conflict systems (map 1.1). The most destabilizing has been the Mano River Basin conflict system, which includes Côte d'Ivoire, Guinea, Liberia, and Sierra Leone (box 1.6). To date, the fallout from the other conflict systems has been of a lower magnitude, but they nonetheless have had profound impacts on their regional convergences. Although tensions in some systems have abated, there is potential for them to flare up again.

The southern Senegambia conflict system covers Senegal, The Gambia, and Guinea-Bissau. The uprising for self-determination in the Casamance region of Senegal is rooted in the grievances of the Diola people regarding perceptions of political underrepresentation and economic disadvantage (M'Cormack 2011). Links of kinsmanship between the secessionists and President Yahya Jammeh of The Gambia led to claims that he played an active role in aiding the rebels, as did various governments of Guinea-Bissau (Fall 2010). The Casamance uprising triggered the civil war in Guinea-Bissau from 1998 to 1999, after officers from the armed forces were found to have aided Casamance separatists.

Other conflict systems in West Africa include the tensions and outbreaks of violence between the governments of Mali and Niger and between the Tuareg rebels and other ethnic groups from the northern parts of both countries, which has had some resonance in Mauritania. The Tuaregs are found across multiple states, including Algeria, Burkina Faso, Libya, Mali, and Niger. Their traditional lifestyles have come under pressure since independence, and drought, coupled

BOX 1.6

Subregional Conflict Systems: The Example of the Mano River Basin

The political entrepreneurship of Charles Taylor lit the match of a region-wide conflict system in the Mano River subregion in 1989 after he and his lumpen forces launched the civil war in Liberia from inside Côte d'Ivoire (Sawyer 2004). The conflict set in motion the civil war in Sierra Leone (1991–2002) and a second civil war in Liberia (1999–2003), stirred up sectarian violence in Côte d'Ivoire in 2002, and threw Guinea into a period of significant political instability (M'Cormack 2011).

The personalized and predatory systems of governance in Guinea, Liberia, and Sierra Leone repressed and marginalized tracts of the population. Failure of governance, common grievances, and economic crisis set the stage for the collapse into conflict. Porous borders, refugee flows, and the existence of cross-border communities contributed to instability and facilitated the spillover of conflict from one country to another.

Several reactivated Liberian networks contributed to violence after the 2010 disputed elections in Côte d'Ivoire (ICG 2014). Taylor's armies of marauding child soldiers added to tensions, as did members of the Revolutionary United Front, who were drawn from various countries and moved freely across boundaries to mete out horrific levels of violence on unarmed civilians.

Map 1.1 Conflict Systems in West Africa

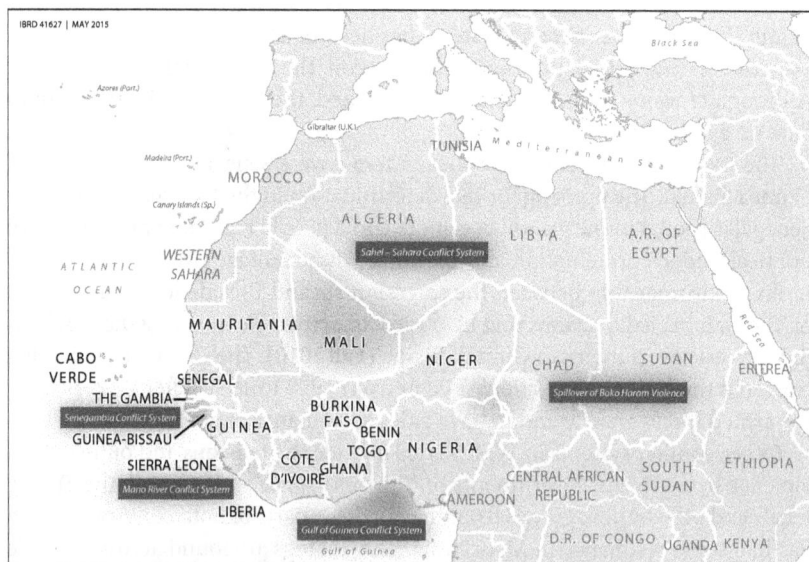

Source: GSD IBRD 41108.
Note: The area shaded as part of each conflict system is not meant to be based on specific or exact geographic coordinates but instead serves as a visual representation of the way conflicts cluster across borders.

with economic, political, and social marginalization, have triggered recurring rebellions in both Niger and Mali (N'Diaye 2011).

The insurgency in Nigeria's Delta Region is affecting the security of the Gulf of Guinea countries of Benin and Togo, particularly through maritime piracy. A wide range of militias emerged from the conflict in the Niger Delta. They engaged in theft and sabotage, with the aim of undermining the oil industry. Their activities paved the way for the spread of piracy beyond Nigerian territory (UNODC 2013).

Violence from the Boko Haram insurgency in northeast Nigeria is also spilling over to other countries. Although the insurgency is "ultimately a Nigerian crisis," its militants have crossed over into Cameroon, Chad, and Niger, where borders drawn by colonial powers at the end of the 19th century had "little social relevance against the cultural unity of the old empire of Kanem-Bornu" (Pérouse de Montclos 2014, 8). The group has established camps on islands in Lake Chad, and in May 2014, suspected Boko Haram militants attacked a police station and camp run by a Chinese engineering company in Cameroon. At the May 2014 Paris Summit, neighboring countries committed to deepening their cooperation on security, with Benin, Cameroon, Chad, Niger, and Nigeria pledging to revive the Lake Chad Basin Multilateral Force.

Ebola: The Long-Term Impacts of Conflict

The wildfire spread of Ebola through West Africa in 2014 exposed the underlying fragility of the postconflict countries of Liberia and Sierra Leone. Both countries, which endured decade-long civil wars through the 1990s and early 2000s, found their capacity to address and halt the spread of the virus critically compromised by the cumulative impact of protracted conflict on health care systems and infrastructure. Guinea, which was also affected by the Ebola crisis, did not suffer from open-ended violent conflict, but it experienced an extended period of political isolation and suffered from major political tensions that resulted in significant institutional fragility. The response to the Ebola crisis has been further hampered by the deficit of trust in public authorities and institutions, which is also tied to the long-term impacts of conflict, as well as to the legacy of political instability, as seen in Guinea. Despite assistance and support from donors and development partners to rebuild capacity in the initial postconflict years, the two countries, as well as Guinea, have seen their health care systems overwhelmed and have been forced to call on international assistance to bring the current outbreak under control.

As of May 2015, the death toll stood at more than 11,000 (CDC 2015). Donor assistance in the decade after the end of the civil war had helped significantly boost Liberia's health care system and show improved outcomes. From 2006 to 2012, the percentage of Liberians residing within five kilometers of a health facility rose from 31 percent to 71 percent. Infant mortality and mortality among children under the age of five declined dramatically as well (Glassman 2014). Despite such improvements, health systems have remained fragile and largely underdeveloped. Along with the destruction of physical infrastructure such as health care facilities, laboratories for diagnosing and testing, clinics, and hospitals, is the dearth of human capital to combat the spread of Ebola. In another legacy of conflict on the institutional and social fabric of Liberia and Sierra Leone, the shortage of trained medical staff has greatly hindered an effective response.

The two countries, which have borne the brunt of the impact of Ebola in terms of casualties, have among the lowest doctor-patient ratios in West Africa. For a population of 4.4 million, Liberia counted 51 doctors and "fewer than two thousand underpaid nurses" (Epstein 2014); for a population of 6.2 million, Sierra Leone counted 136 doctors. These figures compare with the 3,000 doctors Liberia is estimated to have had before its civil wars—a figure that had collapsed to 40 by the time the civil wars drew to a close (BBC News Africa 2014). In terms of infrastructure, Liberia had 293 public health facilities before its plunge into civil war. After the conflicts, 242 of these facilities were deemed nonfunctional because of destruction and looting (Kruk and others 2010).

Another constraining factor has been inequity in the supply of health care services between urban and rural areas, which has had implications for disease surveillance (MacKinnon and MacLaren 2012). The first suspected victim of Ebola died in December 2013, but the first correct diagnosis was determined only three months later (Grady and Fink 2014). Indeed, with no laboratory capable of testing for Ebola, Liberia sent blood samples to France in February. By the time the results were returned, in late March, Ebola had spread in Liberia (Epstein 2014).

Guinea has a more favorable doctor-patient ratio than Liberia or Sierra Leone—at 1 doctor for every 11,000 people, or a total of 940 doctors for a population of 10.6 million—but it, too, has found its health care systems overwhelmed by the virus. Although Guéckédou, in the south, was at the epicenter of the outbreak, Guinea has suffered fewer casualties than its neighbors. However, it is experiencing the effects of years of political instability, which undermined institutions as well as trust in the state and public authorities, as exemplified by the massacre of eight health workers in a village in rural Guinea as they tried to raise awareness of Ebola. Distrust and suspicion of government and public authorities is such that health workers are suspected of spreading the disease (BBC News Africa 2014).

It has been said that the Ebola crisis is at heart a governance crisis. The postconflict gains in Liberia and Sierra Leone as well as robust economic growth of recent years disguised the underlying fragility of institutions and concealed a deficit of accountability and capacity (Thomas 2014). Lack of trust in the authorities also reflects disillusionment with the political elite (Boisvert 2014). Large tracts of the Liberian population prefer to get their information from community networks rather than through official channels (Thomas 2014).

In Liberia, civil society groups have blamed decades of corruption, deep-rooted mistrust of the government, and weak public services for hastening the spread of Ebola. Poor communication between the government and citizens has been an additional obstacle. Successful examples from elsewhere on the continent of the fight against Ebola highlight the importance of strong channels of communication between the government and the people.

What began as a complex health care emergency has morphed into a humanitarian one. The ripple effects of Ebola on the health care systems left people with non-Ebola-related diseases or conditions, such as malaria, dysentery, and even pregnancy, without adequate medical attention (Worthington 2014). Ebola has jeopardized critical human development gains, such as efforts to fight malaria (Dreaper 2014) and improve education (Hamilton 2014). Ebola has also risked exacerbating food insecurity, disrupting economic activity, breaking down law and order, and delivering a body blow to development and economic growth. The World Bank (2015) has warned that the fallout from the epidemic will push Guinea and Sierra Leone into recession in 2015, with the total cost to both countries as well as to Liberia in terms of curtailed investment and lost business amounting to about $1.6 billion, or more than 12 percent of their combined gross domestic product (GDP). In the most extreme scenario, it estimates that economic growth in 2015 could be cut by 4.5 percent in Guinea, 3.8 percent in Liberia, and 10.9 percent in Sierra Leone. Already Ebola is estimated to have shaved $500 million from the finances of the governments of the three hardest-hit countries, equating to nearly 5 percent of their combined GDP.

Mali, Nigeria, and Senegal also experienced cases of Ebola, as the result of transmission from Guinea, Liberia, and Sierra Leone. Isolated cases were also recorded in Spain and the United States.

Management of the Ebola crisis in Nigeria and Senegal has been singled out for praise, with the World Health Organization (WHO) citing Nigeria for "world-class epidemiological detective work" (Dixon 2014). News of the first Nigerian case in Lagos, in July 2014, raised fears of the likely impact of an outbreak in the densely populated metropolis. Nigerian authorities confounded fears of an apocalyptic scenario by rapidly containing the spread of the disease. The country was declared Ebola-free on October 20, with a total of 20 reported cases and a death toll of 8.

A number of factors contributed to the effective management of the crisis in Nigeria and Senegal. Both countries rapidly launched effective public awareness campaigns encouraging people affected to seek treatment. They also neutralized the insidious impact of rumors and misinformation that impedes the containment of the virus (Dixon 2014). Both countries have better health care systems—in terms of their ratio of doctors to population and their capacity for rapid detection of the virus—than Liberia and Sierra Leone. They were thus better able to respond quickly and introduce measures to prevent the spread of the virus. In addition, Nigeria tapped into a network of health personnel and infrastructure that was already in place to combat polio and other diseases. It provided a platform from which to trace people who had been exposed to the virus. According to the U.S. Centers for Disease Control and Prevention (CDC), the Nigerian health authorities contacted and monitored nearly 900 people as part of this process. Senegal also moved quickly to identify and monitor the 74 people who had come into contact with the country's sole Ebola patient while heightening surveillance at ports of entry. The authorities in both countries established strategic relationships with international actors with expertise in health care emergencies, thereby benefiting from advice and expertise from institutions such as the WHO, Doctors without Borders, and the CDC.

The experiences of other countries in West Africa suggests that the rapid spread of Ebola in Liberia and Sierra Leone is directly linked to the long-term impact of the devastating conflicts both countries experienced. The contrast reinforces the importance of long-term efforts to rebuild institutions in the wake of conflict.

The Rapidly Changing Nature of Violence in West Africa

The nature of violence in West Africa has changed significantly over the last decade. Conventional and large-scale conflict events, and civil wars, have receded in scale and intensity, replaced by a new generation of threats. Election-related violence is on the rise, and extremism and terror attacks, drug trafficking, maritime piracy, and criminality have spiked. In addition, wars are increasingly being fought on the periphery of the state by armed insurgents who are both factionalized and in some cases militarily weak (Straus 2012), as evidenced by the campaign carried out by Boko Haram in Nigeria and the Tuareg and Arab uprisings in Mali.

Election-Related Violence

The wave of democratization in the 1990s that signaled waning tolerance for military coups marked a turning point for governance in the region, but it also brought new challenges in the form of election-related violence. Historically coup-prone countries such as Benin, Ghana, and Nigeria began to see a shift in civil-military relations, amidst a wave of multiparty elections across West Africa, including in Cape Verde, Côte d'Ivoire, Mali, Senegal, and Sierra Leone, with Benin leading the charge in 1990 (Kacowicz 1997). The end of the Cold

War saw the onset of civil wars, but it also enabled new political openings. Although this process of political liberalization has had mixed results, it marks a milestone in the political maturation of the region.

The frequency and legitimacy of multiparty elections has meant that power is increasingly transferred via the ballot box instead of down the barrel of a gun. The increase in the number of elections in West Africa since 1990 has been accompanied by a corresponding rise in internal struggles and election-related violence. Burkina Faso, Côte d'Ivoire, Nigeria, Sierra Leone, and Togo have experienced varying degrees of turmoil and political violence before, during, or after elections. In Nigeria, election-related violence has intensified with each subsequent poll, with protests around the 2011 elections degenerating into communal violence that resulted in some 800 deaths, according to Human Rights Watch (2011a).

The acceptance of elections as the standard for legitimate power transfers has led political rivals to view the process as a zero-sum game, largely because the stakes of the outcome are so high, with control of the state equating to very strong control over the economy and associated trappings, often for private gain (Souaré 2010). Elections provide political entrepreneurs with an opportunity to strengthen their position and issue "extremist appeals" to mobilize their ethnic or religious constituencies, which can ramp up violence. In this way, elections have the potential to act as a "precipitating rather than an underlying" (Leonard 2010, 3) cause of violence. Other variables include the type of elections, vested interests, and the expectations from the outcome of the polls (Souaré 2010). Violence over the stakes of political competition can overlap and interlink with other types of political violence, such as violence associated with tensions over access to land and resources, as in the case of Côte d'Ivoire (Straus 2012). Where no incumbent is vying for reelection, the chances of election-related violence are generally lower (Souaré 2010).

Drug Trafficking

The scale of drug trafficking through West Africa became apparent between 2005 and 2007, with the seizure of more than 20 shipments involving thousands of kilograms of cocaine from South America that was destined for Europe (UNODC 2013). Trafficking through West Africa has become a major threat to security. South American drug cartels favor the coastal states as transit routes because of their porous borders, sparsely inhabited off-coast islands, state weakness and political instability, corruption, poor surveillance, and proximity to Europe. In addition to cocaine, West Africa has become a transit hub for methamphetamines and heroin. The discovery of methamphetamine labs in Liberia in May 2010 and in Nigeria in 2011 indicates that the region is no longer merely acting as a transit point but has also become a supplier (UNODC 2013).

The implications and consequences of trafficking are manifold. They include the potential to compromise government officials and security agents, destabilize the government and weaken the state, erode the region's social fabric and economic development, and, as in the case of Guinea-Bissau, influence elections (Souaré 2010).

Trafficking increases overall criminality and laundering, as avenues are sought to channel illicit funds. There have been reports that terrorist groups such as AQIM, rebel groups, insurgents in the Sahel, and other organized criminal groups have all exploited the instability of fragile states such as Guinea-Bissau to fund their activities (O'Regan and Thompson 2013). Another danger to stability is the risk that a consuming society will emerge in West African countries that have been exposed to the drug trade (Security Council Report 2011).

There are signs of narcotics trafficking and links to trafficking networks in some of the more resilient and politically stable West African countries, too, including The Gambia, Ghana, and Senegal (O'Regan and Thompson 2013). The institutional resilience and strong political governance of these states may better equip them to withstand the destabilizing effects of drug trafficking than weaker states. But the example of Mali—where cocaine trafficking helped weaken an emerging democracy and model of stability, leaving it susceptible to militia, criminal, and terrorist networks—suggests that even stronger states need to be vigilant (O'Regan and Thompson 2013).

Maritime Piracy and Criminality

Maritime piracy in the Gulf of Guinea overtook piracy in the Gulf of Aden in 2012, according to the International Maritime Bureau. This threat has evolved over the past decade from initially targeting Nigerian fishing boats and local vessels to spreading along the coast to countries such as Benin, Côte d'Ivoire, and Togo and shifting focus to large oil tankers, according to ACLED. Many of Sub-Saharan Africa's oil-producing nations are located in the Gulf of Guinea. Linkages have been made between piracy and armed groups. The money flowing from these activities creates vectors of instability and acts as a disincentive to peace talks (UNODC 2013).

The consequences of piracy are far-reaching. Directly, proceeds can be used to arm rebels; indirectly, piracy adversely affects the domestic economy and political stability, as well as the flow of foreign direct investment and trade (Security Council Report 2011).

Transnational organized crime networks have also exploited the weak border control and rule of law systems across many West African countries (Center for International Peace Operations 2012), resulting in an increase in banditry, human smuggling, and cigarette smuggling. The proliferation of small arms in the region and the smuggling of arms through porous borders is a threat, which can contribute to instability and increase criminal activity, as it has, for example, in Mali.

Religious Extremism and Terrorism

Religious extremism has emerged as a growing threat in West Africa, with groups such as Boko Haram targeting civilians in increasingly deadly attacks. Nigeria has by far the largest number of documented events involving violent Muslim-identified militias in Africa (128 between 1997 and 2012). Violent activity by Islamist militias increased significantly after 2010, having climbed from 5 percent of all political violence in Africa in 1997 to 13.5 percent in 2012, according to ACLED (Dowd 2013).

Mali has also seen an increase in Islamist militia activity since 2011, as Ansar Dine, a domestic Tuareg-based movement, affiliated itself with the broader Al Qaeda movement. AQIM has committed far less violence against civilians in Mali, Mauritania, and Niger than Boko Haram has in Nigeria. The goal of the international terrorist network in the recent war in the north of Mali was to leverage the credibility and presence of Ansar Dine and gain traction on the ground to overthrow the national regime and impose an alternative one. In contrast, Boko Haram tends to focus on regional or subnational goals, as it lacks the capacity to overthrow the government or even the desire to mount such a challenge and establish an alternative regime (Dowd 2013). Despite its international profile, just 14 percent of violence by AQIM in Mali constitutes violence against civilians, compared with more than 50 percent by Boko Haram. Boko Haram also has a higher average fatality per event rate (5.6) than AQIM (3.1), topping that of Al-Shabaab in the Horn and East Africa (3.0), according to ACLED.

Extremist groups in West Africa move with ease between states. The fighting forces resemble "mobile armed bands" with bases in numerous territories rather than traditional, organized armies (Straus 2012). They draw support and funding from international terrorist networks. In Mali, for example, AQIM first appeared in 2009 and has since built up a presence. By 2013, it had notched up higher activity rates in Mali than in Algeria, where it had a longer-established presence, according to ACLED. AQIM has an on-and-off presence in Mali, Mauritania, Niger, and possibly parts of Burkina Faso.

Notes

1. This report relies on fatalities as a result of conflict as a key indicator of violence. There are some limitations to this measure. Data may not always be reliable, and using fatality figures does not capture the full cost of conflict, including nonlethal forms of violence or the long-term costs of violence.
2. These estimates are high estimates (see note to figure 1.1).

References

ACLED (Armed Conflict Location and Event Data Project). ACLED Version 4 (1997–2013). http://www.acleddata.com/data/version-4-data-1997-2013.

Andriamihaja, N., M. Cinyabuguma, and S. Devarajan. n.d. *Avoiding the Fragility Trap in Africa: The Case of Guinea Bissau.* World Bank, Washington, DC. http://siteresources .worldbank.org/INTDEBTDEPT/Resources/468980-1218567884549/5289593-12247 97529767/5506237-1300891972867/DFSG05GuineaBissauFR.pdf.

Antil, A., and M. Mokhefi. 2014. "Managing the Sahara Periphery." World Bank, Sahara Knowledge Exchange Series, Washington, DC.

Bakrania, S. 2013. "Conflict Drivers, International Responses, and the Outlook for Peace in Mali: A Literature Review." GSDRC Issues Paper, Governance and Social Development Resource Centre, University of Birmingham, United Kingdom.

BBC News Africa. 2014. "Liberia's Ellen Johnson Sirleaf Urges World Help on Ebola." October 19. http://www.bbc.com/news/world-africa-29680934.

Bertelsmann Stiftung. 2014. *BTI 2014: Mauritania Country Report.* Bertelsmann Stiftung: Gütersloh, Germany. http://www.bti-project.de/uploads/tx_itao_download/BTI _2014_Mauritania.pdf.

Blattman, C., and E. Miguel. 2009. "Civil War." NBER Working Paper 14801, National Bureau of Economic Research, Cambridge, MA. http://www.nber.org/papers/w14801 .pdf.

Boisvert, M.-A. 2014. "Building Public Trust Is a Key Factor in Fighting West Africa's Worst Ebola Outbreak." Inter Press Service, August 26. http://www.ipsnews.net/2014/08 /building-public-trust-is-a-key-factor-in-fighting-west-africas-worst-ebola-outbreak.

Buhaug, H., and K. S. Gleditsch. 2008. "Contagion or Confusion? Why Conflicts Cluster in Space." *International Studies Quarterly* 52 (2) 215–33.

CDC (Centers for Disease Control and Prevention). 2015. "2014 Ebola Outbreak in West Africa—Case Counts." March. http://www.cdc.gov/vhf/ebola/outbreaks/2014 -west-africa/case-counts.html.

Center for International Peace Operations (ZIF). 2012. *The West African Region: Between Peace Dividends and the Road to Recovery.* Berlin.

Cilliers, J., and T. D. Sisk. 2013. "Assessing Long-Term State Fragility in Africa: Prospects for 26 'More Fragile' Countries." ISS Monograph 188, Institute for Security Studies, Pretoria. http://www.issafrica.org/uploads/Monograph188.pdf.

Collier P., and A. Hoeffler. 2002. "Greed and Grievance in Civil War." Working Paper, Center for the Study of African Economies, Oxford. http://www.csae.ox.ac.uk /workingpapers/pdfs/2002-01text.pdf.

Collier, P., and N. Sambanis, eds. 2005. *Understanding Civil War.* Washington, DC: World Bank.

Diallo, M. 2009. "Conflict Systems in West Africa: Introducing Conflict Systems with a View towards a Regional Prevention Policy." Workshop on Conflict Systems and Risk Assessment in West Africa, ECOWAS/SWAC Joint Work Programme, Bamako.

Dixon, R. 2014. "Ebola-Free Nigeria Hailed as 'Success Story' in Battling Outbreak." *Los Angeles Times*, October 20. http://www.latimes.com/world/africa/la-fg-nigeria-ebola -20141020-story.html#page=1.

Dowd, C. 2013. "Tracking Islamist Militia and Rebel Groups." Research Brief 8, Climate Change and African Political Stability (CCAPS) and Armed Conflict Location and Event Data Project (ACLED), Austin, TX.

Dreaper, J. 2014. "Fears That Ebola Crisis Will Set Back Malaria Fight." BBC News, October 26. http://www.bbc.com/news/health-29756066.

Epstein, H. 2014. "Ebola in Liberia: An Epidemic of Rumors." *New York Review of Books*, December 18. http://www.nybooks.com/articles/archives/2014/dec/18/ebola -liberia-epidemic-rumors.

Fall, A. 2010. "Understanding the Casamance Conflict: A Background." KAIPTC Monograph 7, Kofi Annan International Peacekeeping Training Centre, Accra. http:// www.kaiptc.org/publications/monographs/monographs/monograph-7-aissatou.aspx.

Fearon, J. D., and D. D. Laitin. 2001. "Ethnicity, Insurgency, and Civil War." Working Paper, Stanford University, Stanford, CA. http://web.stanford.edu/group/ethnic /workingpapers/apsa011.pdf.

Glassman, A. 2014. "Letter from Liberia: Ebola Is Not a Failure of Aid or Governance." Center for Global Development, Washington, DC. http://www.cgdev.org/blog/letter -liberia-ebola-not-failure-aid-or-governance.

Grady, D., and S. Fink. 2014. "Tracing Ebola's Breakout to an African 2-Year-Old." *New York Times*, August 9. http://www.nytimes.com/2014/08/10/world/africa/tracing -ebolas-breakout-to-an-african-2-year-old.html.

Hamilton, J. 2014. "Ebola Today Could Mean Illiteracy Tomorrow in West Africa." Morning Edition, National Public Radio, Washington, DC. http://www.npr.org/blogs /goatsandsoda/2014/11/10/362302778/ebola-today-could-mean-illiteracy-tomorrow -in-west-africa.

Human Rights Watch. 2011a. "Nigeria: Post-Election Violence Killed 800." May 17. http://www.hrw.org/news/2011/05/16/nigeria-post-election-violence-killed-800.

———. 2011b. *They Killed Them Like It Was Nothing: The Need for Justice for Côte d'Ivoire's Post-Election Crimes*. New York: Human Rights Watch. http://www.hrw.org/sites /default/files/reports/cdi1011WebUpload.pdf.

ICG (International Crisis Group). 2010. "Northern Nigeria: Background to Conflict." Africa Report 168, ICG, Brussels. http://www.crisisgroup.org/~/media/Files/africa /west-africa/nigeria/168%20Northern%20Nigeria%20-%20Background%20to%20 Conflict.pdf.

———. 2012. "The Gulf of Guinea: The New Danger Zone." Africa Report 195, ICG, Brussels. http://www.crisisgroup.org/~/media/Files/africa/central-africa/195-the-gulf -of-guinea-the-new-danger-zone-english.pdf.

———. 2014. "Côte d'Ivoire's Great West: Key to Reconciliation." Africa Report 212, ICG, Brussels. http://www.crisisgroup.org/en/regions/africa/west-africa/cote-divoire/212 -cote-divoire-s-great-west-key-to-reconciliation.aspx.

Isaacs, D. 2004. "Analysis: Behind Nigeria's Violence." BBC News, May 4. http://news .bbc.co.uk/2/hi/africa/1630089.stm.

Jörgel, M., and M. Utas. 2007. "The Mano River Basin Area: Formal and Informal Security Providers in Liberia, Guinea and Sierra Leone." Report FOI-R--2418--SE, Swedish Defense Research Agency, Stockholm. http://www.foi.se/ReportFiles /foir_2418.pdf.

Kacowicz, A. M. 1997. "'Negative' International Peace and Domestic Conflicts, West Africa, 1957–1996." *Journal of Modern African Studies* 35 (3): 367–85.

Kruk, M. E., P. C. Rockers, E. H. Williams, S. T. Varpilah, R. Macauley, G. Saydee, and S. Galea. 2010. "Availability of Essential Health Services in Post-Conflict Liberia." *Bulletin of the World Health Organization* 80 (7): 481–560. http://www.who.int /bulletin/volumes/88/7/09-071068/en.

Leonard, D. K. 2010. "Elections and Conflict Resolution in Africa." In *When Elephants Fight: Preventing and Resolving Election-Related Conflict in Africa*, ed. K. Matlosa, G. M. Khadiagala, and V. Shale, 37–50. Johannesburg: Electoral Institute for the Sustainability of Democracy in Africa.

Luckham, R., I. Ahmed, R. Muggah, and S. White. 2001. "Conflict and Poverty in Sub-Saharan Africa: An Assessment of the Issues and Evidence." IDS Working Paper 128, Institute of Development Studies, University of Sussex, Brighton, United Kingdom.

MacKinnon, J., and B. MacLaren. 2012. "Human Resources for Health Challenges in Fragile States: Evidence from Sierra Leone, South Sudan and Zimbabwe." North-South Institute, Ottawa. http://www.nsi-ins.ca/wp-content/uploads/2012/11/2012-Human -Resources-for-Health-Challenges-in-Fragile-States.pdf.

Marshall, M. G. 2005. "Conflict Trends in Africa, 1946–2004: A Macro-Comparative Perspective." Report prepared for the Africa Conflict Prevention Pool, Government of the United Kingdom, London.

Mcloughlin, C. 2012. "Topic Guide on Fragile States." Resource Guide, Governance and Social Development Resource Centre, University of Birmingham, United Kingdom. http://www.gsdrc.org/docs/open/con86.pdf.

M'Cormack, F. 2011. *Conflict Dynamics in West Africa*. Helpdesk Research Report, October 17, Governance and Social Development Resource Centre, University of Birmingham, United Kingdom.

N'Diaye. B. 2011. "Conflicts and Crises: Internal and International Dimensions." In *ECOWAS and the Dynamics of Conflict and Peacebuilding*, ed. T. Jaye and S. Amadi. Dakar: CDD West Africa, Consortium for Development Partnerships, and Council for the Development of Social Science Research in Africa (CODESRIA).

Nigeria Social Violence Project Database. 2014. "Connect SAIS Africa." SAIS Africa, Johns Hopkins University, Baltimore, MD. http://www.connectsaisafrica.org/research /african-studies-publications/social-violence-nigeria.

Nwankpa, M. 2014. "The Politics of Amnesty in Nigeria: A Comparative Analysis of the Boko Haram and Niger Delta Insurgencies." *Journal of Terrorism Research* 5 (1).

O'Regan, D., and P. Thompson. 2013. "Advancing Stability and Reconciliation in Guinea Bissau: Lessons from Africa's First Narco-state." ACSS Special Report 2, Africa Center for Strategic Studies, Washington, DC.

Oruwari, Y., and O. Owei. 2006. "Youth in Urban Violence in Nigeria: A Case Study of Urban Gangs from Port Harcourt." Niger Delta Economies of Violence Working Paper 14, Institute of International Studies, University of California–Berkeley. http://oldweb.geog.berkeley.edu/ProjectsResources/ND%20Website/NigerDelta/WP/14-Oruwari.pdf.

Pérouse de Montclos, M.-A. 2014. "Nigeria's Interminable Insurgency? Addressing the Boko Haram Crisis." Chatham House, London. http://www.chathamhouse.org/sites/files/chathamhouse/field/field_document/20140901BokoHaramPerousedeMontclos_0.pdf.

Pouligny, B. 2010. "Resistance, Trauma, and Violence." Background paper for *Societal Dynamics and Fragility: Engaging Societies in Responding to Fragile Situations*, World Bank, Washington, DC.

Reuters. 2009. "Niamey et les rebelles touaregs s'engagent en faveur de la paix." April 8. http://www.maliweb.net/category.php?NID=42798&intr=.

Sawyer, A. 2004. "Violent Conflicts and Governance Challenges in West Africa: The Case of the Mano River Basin Area." *Journal of Modern African Studies* 43 (3): 437–63.

Sayne, A. 2012. "Rethinking Nigeria's Indigene-Settler Conflicts." USIP Special Report 311, United States Institute of Peace, Washington, DC. http://www.usip.org/sites/default/files/SR311.pdf.

Security Council Report. 2011. "Emerging Security Threats in West Africa." Special Research Report, New York. http://www.securitycouncilreport.org/special-research-report/lookup-c-glKWLeMTIsG-b-6740225.php.

Souaré, I. K. 2010. "A Critical Assessment of Security Challenges in West Africa." Situation Report, October 18, Institute of Security Studies, Paris.

Straus, S. 2012. "Wars Do End! Changing Patterns of Political Violence in Sub-Saharan Africa." *African Affairs* 111 (443): 179–201.

Themnér, L., and P. Wallensteen. 2013. "Armed Conflicts, 1946–2012." *Journal of Peace Research* 50 (4): 509–21.

Thomas, K. 2014. "Mistrust of Government Spurs Ebola Spread." IRIN Africa, September 24. http://www.irinnews.org/report/100568/mistrust-of-government-spurs-ebola-spread.

Thurston, A., and A. Lebovich. 2013. "A Handbook on Mali's 2012–2013 Crisis." Working Paper 13-001, Institute for the Study of Islamic Thought in Africa, Northwestern University, Evanston, IL.

UCDP (Uppsala Conflict Data Program). UCDP Battle-Related Deaths Dataset, v. 5-2013, 1989–2012. http://www.pcr.uu.se/research/ucdp/datasets/ucdp_battle-related_deaths_dataset.

———. UCDP Non-State Conflict Dataset, v. 2.5-2013, 1989–2012. http://www.pcr.uu.se/research/ucdp/datasets/ucdp_non-state_conflict_dataset_.

———. UCDP One-Sided Violence Dataset, v. 1.4-2013, 1989–2012. http://www.pcr.uu.se/research/ucdp/datasets/ucdp_one-sided_violence_dataset.

UNODC (United Nations Office on Drugs and Crime). 2013. *Transnational Organized Crime in West Africa: A Threat Assessment*. Vienna: UNODC.

Wantchékon, L., and O. García-Ponce. 2013. "Critical Junctures: Independence Movements and Democracy in Africa." Working paper, Princeton University, Princeton, NJ.

Williams, P. D. 2011. *War and Conflict in Africa*. Cambridge: Polity Press.

World Bank. 2011. *World Development Report 2011: Conflict, Security, and Development*. Washington, DC: World Bank.

———. 2012. "Conflict, Public Authority and Capability in Nigeria: Rethinking Causes, Consequences and Prospects." Background paper to country partnership framework consultations, World Bank, Washington, DC.

———. 2015. "Ebola: Most African Countries Avoid Major Economic Loss but Impact on Guinea, Liberia, Sierra Leone Remains Crippling." Press release, Washington, DC. https://www.worldbank.org/en/news/press-release/2015/01/20/ebola-most-african -countries-avoid-major-economic-loss-but-impact-on-guinea-liberia-sierra-leone -remains-crippling.

Worthington, S. A. 2014. "Ebola—a Fragile Health Care System's Ripple Effects." *Huffington Post*, September 24. http://www.huffingtonpost.com/samuel-a -worthington/ebola-a-fragile-healthcar_b_5871080.html.

Zacher, M. W. 2001. "The Territorial Integrity Norm: International Boundaries and the Use of Force." *International Organization* 55 (2): 215–50.

Chapter 2

Addressing Emerging Threats: Trafficking, Maritime Piracy, and Religious Extremism

The last decade has seen West Africa catapulted to global notoriety for its role as a key transit point in the trafficking of narcotics between Latin America and Europe. The competitive advantage generated by the region's weak state capacity and rule of law, the existence of well-developed smuggling networks, and its geographic location all heighten its appeal to drug trafficking cartels and criminal gangs.

Drug trafficking is not new to the subregion. It dates back to as early as 1952, when Lebanese smugglers used West Africa as a transit point for heroin to the United States (Ellis 2009). However, the scale of the flow of contraband since the turn of the millennium is such that it threatens the stability and security of the region.

In a few short years, the continent that had avoided terrorism and religious extremism over the last decades has become a hotbed of radicalization, particularly in East Africa and West Africa. Although Al-Qaeda in the Islamic Maghreb (AQIM) is still very much influenced by North Africa, Boko Haram and other militant groups in the subregion are in large part home-grown movements that are expanding, terrorizing populations in Northern Nigeria and neighboring countries. Meanwhile, the rise of maritime piracy threatens to compromise the stability and economic development of the region's coastal states, particularly in light of recent discoveries of offshore hydrocarbon deposits and the geostrategic importance of the Gulf of Guinea.

The Scourge of Narcotrafficking

Trafficking, which combines the illicit character of smuggling with the illegal nature of a crime, has the potential to interlink with fragility and accelerate conflict in a number of ways (Dechery and Ralston 2014). The insidious effects of trafficking range from providing a source of funding to rebel movements and extremists to pitting elites against one another in competition over drug-related rents and undermining institutions and weakening governance.

A combination of protracted conflicts, corruption, and weak state capacity has fueled the evolution of trafficking into a full-fledged criminal enterprise in West Africa (Reitano and Shaw 2013). Criminal networks have taken advantage of both West Africa's location halfway between the Andean producing nations and the European consumer market, and its fragile political institutions, relying on coercion and patronage to build their own political capital or tap into that of local elites (Cockayne 2013). The region's integration with the global economy—through better communications, improved transportation, and access to new markets—has created further opportunities for international criminal syndicates to thrive.

The lion's share of narcotics transiting through West Africa is cocaine, which commands the highest markup. With the long-term decline of demand for cocaine from the United States, the focus has shifted to the European market, where the volume of cocaine used doubled between 2004 and 2010 (UNODC 2010). Traffickers capitalize on the fact that West Africa is a viable and less monitored route to Europe than Central America and the Caribbean (map 2.1).

Map 2.1 Flow of Cocaine from Latin America via West Africa to Europe

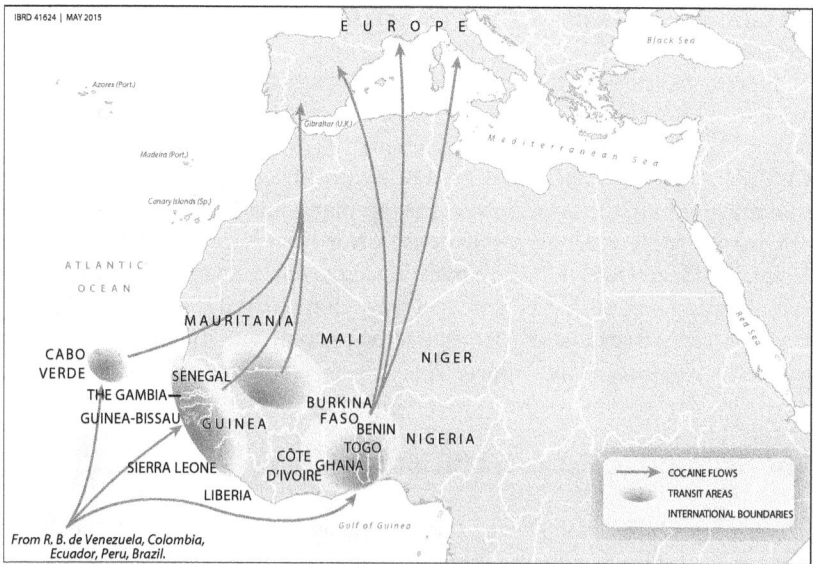

Source: UNODC 2013.

It is estimated that 17 percent of all cocaine consumed in Europe—21 tons—passed through West Africa in 2011, for a retail value of $1.7 billion (table 2.1).[1]

In addition to being a transshipment route, West Africa displayed signs at the turn of the decade of becoming a producer of narcotics, in particular methamphetamine (UNODC 2013). Labs were discovered in Nigeria in 2011–12 and in Liberia in 2010.

West Africa is also a transit route for other narcotics and contraband, including cannabis resin, methamphetamines, heroin, cigarettes, and fraudulent medicines, and it is a source and channel for the trafficking of migrants and firearms. The subregion has seen an increase in the flow of small arms and light weapons, as instability in northern Africa has allowed weapons to enter through the Sahel

Table 2.1 Estimated Value of Flows of Some Trafficked Goods in West Africa
(millions of dollars)

Good	Value	Mark-up (difference between revenue and cost)	Source
Oil	$4,168[a]	$1,146[b]	UNODC (2008b); British Petroleum (2013); Katsouris and Sayne (2013)
Cocaine	$1,764[c]	$1,176[d]	UNODC (2011)
Cannabis	$595[e]	—	UNODC (2008a)
Human trafficking	$226[f]	—	UNODC (2008b)
Methamphetamines	$225[g]	—	UNODC (2013)
Firearms	$167[h]	—	UNODC (2008b)
Total	$7,145		

Note: — = not available.
a. Estimated by multiplying the estimated numbers of barrels stolen in 2012 according to Katsouris and Sayne (2013) by the average spot price of a barrel of Nigerian crude oil for the year, as reported in the BP Statistical Review.
b. Estimated by applying the best estimate of the discount rate at which local traffickers sell their oil (72.5 percent).
c. Estimated by multiplying the size of the flow (21 tons) by the wholesale value of a kilogram of cocaine in Europe ($84,000). Using the retail value would yield an even greater figure but would be inconsistent with the methodology generally used by UNODC.
d. Estimated by taking the difference between the wholesale price in Europe ($84,000 per kilogram) and West Africa ($28,000 per kilogram), times the size of the flow (21 tons). According to UNODC, only a third of the traffic is conducted by African groups, which would put their gross profits at $392 million. We include the mark-up of all traffickers, as regardless of nationality, their proceeds affect West Africa (through corruption, violent competition for control, and so on).
e. Estimated by multiplying regional production (3,500 tons) by the average regional retail price ($0.17 per gram). The retail price is the West African retail price, as West Africa virtually exports none of its cannabis, growing it mainly for local consumption.
f. Estimated by taking the midpoint of UNODC's estimates for the annual flow of humans trafficked for sexual exploitation out of West Africa (4,750) times the midpoint UNODC estimate of the price for one individual ($47,500). Estimates for the flow were originally obtained by looking at the numbers of victims detected in Europe and assuming that 1 out of 30 trafficked humans was detected on average.
g. Estimated by taking the mean of the estimated values of the flow according to UNODC, which took the possible sizes of the flow (750–3,000 kg)—extrapolated from the number of seizures in 2010—times the midpoint estimate for the wholesale price in the end markets ($120,000 per kilogram).
h. Estimated by extrapolating the legal imports of ammunitions and firearms in West Africa and assuming that rebel and criminal groups at least match the government's purchases.

(Aning and Pokoo 2014). The United Nations Office on Drugs and Crime (UNODC 2013) estimates that up to 12,000 arms—including 9,000 assault rifles—may have been stolen from Muammar Gaddafi's arsenal after the fall of his regime in Libya; these arms could be destined for any number of rebel or criminal groups in West Africa. Most arms in West Africa are trafficked by land and traded at well-known hubs, particularly in the Sahel. Security forces, former and current militants, and mercenaries all partake in the trade (UNODC 2013).

In parts of West Africa, the state has been captured by elites (politicians, businessmen, members of the security establishment) who seek to neutralize law enforcement and enable criminal activities from which they can profit. Drug trafficking can reshape relational dynamics between and among security and political actors, the business community, and the citizenry, both within and beyond borders (Aning and Pokoo 2014). In Burkina Faso, a local diplomat assisted a heroin trafficking ring by providing diplomatic passports to associates (Lacher 2012). In Guinea, the son of former president Lansana Conté was linked to the shipment of drugs from South America by plane, and seized cocaine has routinely disappeared from custody (*New York Times* 2011). In Sierra Leone, the minister of transportation was forced to resign after his cousin was found to have used an aircraft to ship 700 kilograms of cocaine (UNODC 2013).

The scale of the threat is so great that it prompted the 2009 launch of the West Africa Coast Initiative (WACI), a multiagency initiative involving the United Nations Office for West Africa (UNOWA), the UNODC, and INTERPOL, among others, to support the "ECOWAS [Economic Community of West African States] Regional Action Plan to Address the Growing Problem of Illicit Drug Trafficking, Organized Crime and Drug Abuse in West Africa" (Kavanagh 2013). The initiative has been piloted in Côte d'Ivoire, Guinea-Bissau, Liberia, and Sierra Leone, where the agencies are on standby to offer advice in their area of expertise. WACI has also established transnational crime units (TCU) in the four countries. The initiative has reported progress, with the Sierra Leone TCU having secured 25 convictions midway through 2011. However, obstacles remain, including the lack of political will in some countries (Shaw 2012).

Guinea-Bissau is a particularly poignant example of a country in the throes of the debilitating effects of narcotrafficking. This coastal state, with its numerous uninhabited islands and archipelagoes, served for some time as an important beachhead for trafficking into the region. One of the poorest countries in the world, it has a long history of fragility, a highly politicized military, weak institutions, and political elites bent on controlling the state to extract revenues (O'Regan and Thompson 2013). State capacity is so weak that at one point Guinea-Bissau did not have a single prison, and a single ship patrolled its 350-kilometer coastline and archipelago of 82 islands (Vulliamy 2008). The onset of cocaine trafficking has magnified these weaknesses, as the high returns from the drug trade mean that traffickers find ready partners in politicians, businessmen, and military leaders (Kemp, Shaw, and Boutellis 2013). With annual growth of just 0.4 percent over the past three decades,[2] cocaine represented a very lucrative source of income for some of the elite (Reitano and Shaw 2013). In 2012, UNODC estimated that $500 million earned from the narcotics trade had either remained in or been laundered through West Africa (Lebovich 2013).

Trafficking has reinforced the disruptive effect of the military on politics in Guinea-Bissau while fueling competition among political elites. Violence has erupted where governments and security officials have competed for access to drug trafficking–related rents (Aning and Pokoo 2014). It has been widely argued that the collusion of trafficking and politics led to the assassination of President João Bernardo Vieira and his chief of staff in 2010 and played a significant role in the military coup that ensued. The announcement in May 2014 that José Mário Vaz, the former finance minister, had won the presidential elections is seen as an opportunity for the former Portuguese colony to draw a line under the coup of 2012 and repair frayed relations with regional and international partners (Dabo 2014).

Another example of the interplay between trafficking and fragility is found in Mali, which had been considered a beacon of democracy in the region until it suffered a military coup in March 2012. Although smuggling has traditionally been regarded as a resilience strategy and plays an important role in the country's economy, the rise in trafficking of cocaine and other forms of contraband in the Sahel is seen as a key factor in the erosion of state institutions and the spread of corruption (Dechery and Ralston 2014). The trade offered political and military elites lucrative opportunities for personal enrichment and gave former president Amadou Toumani Touré a means to manage instability in Mali's north (Lebovich 2013). To contain violence linked to a 2006 Tuareg rebellion, his government created informal alliances with some intermediaries, local leaders, and businessmen, as well as Arab and Tuareg militias with ties to traffickers. This arrangement enabled Touré to exert some influence in the north of the country, but it also provided the intermediaries with the opportunity to exploit their position in a way that undermined local governance and state presence.

Mali is at the center of the Sahelian trafficking corridor between West Africa and the Maghreb, which is a channel for cocaine and cannabis resin to Algeria, the Arab Republic of Egypt, Libya, and onward. The north of the country encompasses swaths of desert and arid lands that local law enforcement cannot effectively monitor and where government provision of goods and social services is sparse. The protection given by the state to some local elites and influential businessmen, as well as to local armed groups that were involved in trafficking in order to maintain influence in the north, is often cited as one of the reasons for the rapid spread of trafficking in the region. This protection enabled traffickers to launder money through development projects, property, infrastructure, and the acquisition of livestock (Global Initiative against Transnational Organized Crime 2014), giving them unparalleled local influence and legitimacy. Individuals and networks involved in trafficking gradually converted their wealth into political influence and military power. As a consequence, they were able to help fund conflicts and localized violence, "hollowing out the Malian state, undermining institutions, and eroding the legitimacy of official systems of governance" (Reitano and Shaw 2013, 1).

Concerns have surfaced about interdependence between drug trafficking and extremist groups in northern Mali and throughout the Sahel, leading to warnings of the dangers of narcoterrorism. Although local armed groups such as AQIM and the Movement for Oneness and Jihad in West Africa (MUJAO) have been linked to drug deals across the subregion (Savage and Shanker 2012), the narcoterrorism label is misleading and counterproductive, according to Lacher (2013). He argues that it risks diverting attention away from the key perpetrators of the trade, including "state agents and members of local elites in organized crime" (Lacher 2013, 9). Kidnappings for ransom represent a more lucrative source of income for extremist groups in the Sahel than does drug trafficking. Various Western governments are estimated to have spent $40–$65 million on ransom payments between 2008 and 2012, contributing to the war chests of AQIM and MUJAO. Rather than being a factor behind drug trafficking, the rise of such groups has had "common cause with the growth of narcotics smuggling across the region" (Lacher 2013, 4). The flow of heavy and sophisticated weapons from Gaddafi's vast arsenals in Libya also considerably aided the rebels, militia groups, and extremists in Mali and the Sahel (Gow, Olonisakin, and Dijxhoorn 2013).

Competition between rival trafficking networks who wield significant political and military influence (Lacher 2013) is a further vector of instability. It encourages the acquisition of the violent skills required for criminal activities. Trafficking can also lead to the development of a local drug market and gang criminality. Although West Africa has yet to develop secondhand criminality of this nature on a large scale, UNODC warns that certain criminals in trafficking networks are paid in kind and not cash, which could lead to the creation of domestic cocaine markets (Dechery and Ralston 2014). West Africa is at particular risk from this form of criminality. Youth in many countries display the risk factors for gang membership: social marginalization, lack of social and economic opportunities, troubled families, academic failure, street socialization, histories of trauma, and the ready availability of drugs in the neighborhood (Martinez and others 2013). The combination of the availability of small arms in urban centers, massive underemployment, and purchasing power could make the emergence of a local market a formidable threat in the future. Urban violence prevention programs are urgently needed to prevent this scenario.

Trafficking does not necessarily translate into fragility, instability, and conflict. Cabo Verde, Ghana, and Senegal have managed to keep their political processes insulated from trafficking, even though the drug trade has coopted their transport infrastructure and financial institutions (Dechery and Ralston 2014). Their resilience stems from judicial systems that enable the prosecution and conviction of high-profile targets and from the political will their governments have demonstrated in tackling organized crime.

Maritime Piracy in the Gulf of Guinea

The rise of maritime piracy in the Gulf of Guinea—fueled by a fourfold increase in the spot price of a barrel of oil between 2000 and 2012 (BP 2013)—represents one of the major emerging threats in West Africa. It undermines the stability of the coastal states while compromising economic development by putting pressure on livelihood practices such as fishing and maritime trade.

Several factors have contributed to the rise of maritime piracy, including weakness and general inadequacy of the maritime policies of the Gulf of Guinea states, the lack of cooperation between coastal countries, porous borders, and the opportunistic maneuvers of criminal networks that harness the needs and grievances of local communities (ICG 2012). Abuse of Nigeria's fuel subsidies has helped boost a cash-based black market, and thriving illegal trade of refined petroleum products has created strong incentives for piracy. The proliferation of small arms in the region has contributed to the frequency and intensity of conflicts and criminality, including piracy. Neglect of maritime security forces, such as navy and coast guards, has left countries ill equipped to defend their waters (Onuoha 2012).

The recent discovery of offshore hydrocarbon deposits has increased the geostrategic importance of the Gulf of Guinea (ICG 2012). Criminality and violence from the Niger Delta have spilled over and reinforced piracy, fueled by poverty, high unemployment, inequality, and contestations over the way in which oil wealth is distributed in Nigeria, which recorded oil revenues of $52 billion in 2011 (UNODC 2013). Seaborne armed groups from the Bakassi peninsula and the Niger Delta have resorted to kidnappings, maritime attacks, and piracy. Profit is the dominant motive, but these groups also have political interests (ICG 2012).

In 2011, pirates shifted their focus away from Nigeria to neighboring countries, with a spate of attacks executed off the coast of Benin, many of which were aimed at vessels transporting petroleum products (map 2.2). As a result, the Joint War Committee, which comprises Lloyd's and IUA Company Markets, reclassified Beninese waters as high risk (Lloyd's Market Association n.d.). Port traffic declined 70 percent, reducing taxes on trade and raising the cost of living because of the reduction in imports (UNODC 2013). In 2012, Togo became the new hotspot for attacks

Map 2.2 Piracy Incidents in the Gulf of Guinea, 2012

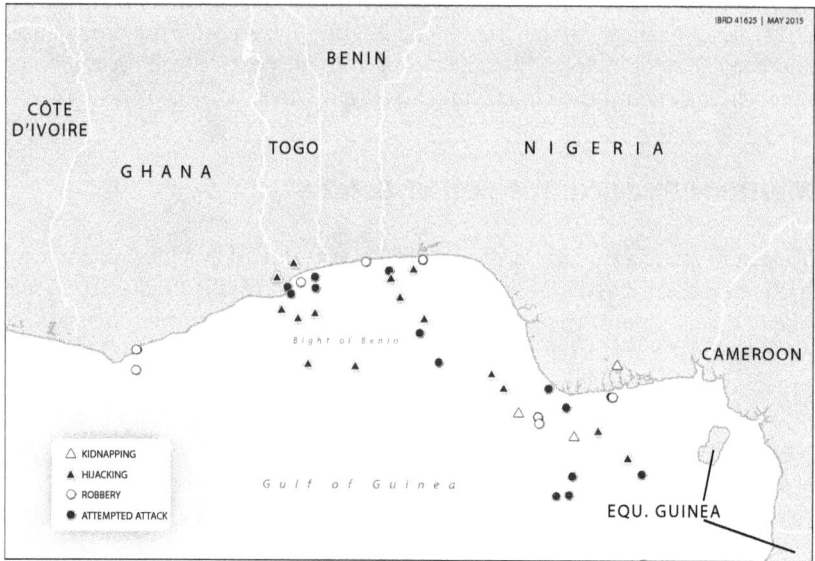

Source: UNODC 2013.

on oil tankers (UNODC 2013). Ghana risks becoming a target for its newly discovered reserves.

A significant risk is that if the black market for fuel opens up sufficiently, piracy could attract dissidents and participants from beyond Nigeria; tankers far offshore could become targets, too. The International Maritime Bureau estimates that the real number of monthly pirate attacks is at least twice the official number of 50 (UNODC 2013), three-quarters of which are simple robberies that net little for pirates. The amount taken per attack is about $10,000–$15,000, which means that if the pirates succeeded in securing the entire value, they would gain up to $1.3 million a year from maritime attacks (UNODC 2013). The theft of refined petroleum tends to be more lucrative, with estimates of losses ranging from $2 million to $6 million for these attacks, according to Lloyd's. The pirates would likely realize around half of this value, at up to $30 million a year.

Like drug trafficking, maritime piracy is a criminal activity that transcends borders. States with weak institutions and rule of law are most vulnerable to predation by transnational criminal networks, which find ready partners in elites, local businessmen, security forces, and ordinary citizens. Although they challenge a state's security and judicial capabilities, these threats are not traditional in nature. They therefore require nonconventional security responses that are regional in scope and demand collaboration and cooperation between organizations such as ECOWAS, the African Union (AU), and the United Nations, as well as national governments. As in other parts of the world, these emerging threats are complex, and not state specific. They require a multi-pronged approach to counter and address their root causes.

The Rise of Religious Extremism in West Africa

From the rise of extremist movements in the Sahel—such as Ansar Dine (Defenders of the Faith) and MUJAO—to the escalating violence of Nigeria's Boko Haram, the emergence of religious radicalism across West Africa has presented a growing threat, helping cast it as the new frontline in the "global war" against extremism. The seizure of more than half of Mali's land area by radical groups (Østebø 2012), along with kidnappings, incursions, and the mounting savagery of Boko Haram attacks, which killed more than 2,000 people in 2014 alone (Associated Press 2014), have brought the extent of the threat into sharp relief and triggered fears of contagion and spillover to other parts of the region (Guichaoua 2014).

As the national, regional, and international focus zeroes in on containment and eradication of the menace within the frame of the global threat of extremism, the danger is that radical groups in West Africa could be miscast and treated as homogenous. Doing so would misdiagnose the root causes of the phenomenon. Along with tackling insecurity, the authorities need to address the injustices and marginalization that drive some of the radicalization and violence, in order to mitigate the risk of extremist groups taking deeper root and plunging the region into a period of protracted instability. Indeed, to date the threat has been viewed primarily as a global security one, with the United States moving to establish the Pan Sahel Initiative (PSI) and the Trans-Sahara Counter Terrorism Initiative (TSCTI) to build capacity and train specialist forces (Obi 2006). The kidnappings of schoolgirls by Boko Haram in 2014 prompted various offers of assistance from Canada, China, France, the United Kingdom, and the United States (CBC News 2014).

Although militant Islamist movements in West Africa have drawn some external support and doctrinal influence from the Middle East and South Asia, there is substantial evidence that the origins and character of radical groups such as Ansar Dine in the Sahel and Boko Haram in Nigeria are overwhelmingly homegrown. They have their roots in a combination of "real governance, corruption, impunity, and underdevelopment grievances" (ICG 2014, i); an intergenerational crisis; the disillusionment of young men; and friction between differing schools of Islamic thought. Although Islamist militancy in West Africa remains interlinked with broader ideological currents of foreign influence, local circumstances have played a critical role in its emergence and trajectory (Østebø 2012). As Gow, Olonisakin, and Dijxhoorn (2013) note, "domestic factors, rather than external influences, were more important in causing radicalization and violence, and external influences were only 'excuses' for domestic agitation." This development is particularly concerning, as Islam in West Africa was traditionally regarded as very tolerant, as a result of the strong influence of the large Sufi brotherhoods, such as Qadiriyya and Tijaniyya.

Foreign radical groups—in particular AQIM, which morphed out of the Algerian Groupe Salafiste pour la Predication et le Combat (GSPC) and retreated to Mali following its suppression by the Algerian state—have extended tactical assistance, weapons, and ideological support to homegrown groups (Onuoha and Ezirim 2013). AQIM has built up a presence in the north of Mali since 2003, grafting itself onto Tuareg and other communities through intermarriage. It has brought a new degree of professionalism to organized crime and drug smuggling in the Sahel (Kühne 2013). It has infiltrated local communities by taking advantage of the state's weaknesses and the frustrations of the population while fitting its wider narrative into domestic grievances. AQIM and its sleeper cells have been behind several kidnappings; the murder of Western tourists, aid workers, and soldiers; and attacks on government targets and foreign diplomatic missions (Onuoha and Ezirim 2013). The group is reported to have netted about $70 million in ransom payments between 2006 and 2011 and has lent its kidnapping expertise to its Nigerian affiliate, Ansaru. Like Boko Haram, it relies on some involvement in narcotics trafficking and bank robberies to generate funds.

Boko Haram has reportedly benefited from its relationships with various radical groups, including AQIM and Al Qaeda. It moves seamlessly through the forested porous border areas between Niger, Chad, and Cameroon and has tried to establish a rear base in Niger (ICG 2014). It recruits from the dominant regional ethnic group, the Kanuri, whose members straddle the border regions. Although Boko Haram's agenda remains focused on domestic goals and it is not bent on attacking Western interests (Walker 2012), it has accepted financial resources, military arsenals, and training facilities from AQIM (ICG 2014), and collaboration between AQIM, MUJAO, and Boko Haram has been reported.

More significant drivers of radicalization and violence in West Africa are socioeconomic factors such as poverty, unemployment, and illiteracy, which have particularly profound effects on youth (Gow, Olonisakin, and Dijxhoorn 2013). Corruption, poverty and alienation, and perceived marginalization have led many youth to identify with groups looking for more extreme ways to change the status quo. It is in this context that Boko Haram emerged in 2002. It set out to rid northern Nigerian politics of the "corrupt, false Muslims" (Walker 2012, 2) who were seen as commandeering it and to create a "pure"

Islamic state ruled by Sharia law, with the eventual goal of taking over the whole territory. Under the leadership of the charismatic Mohammed Yusuf, it initially carried out low-level attacks against police armories and other targets (ICG 2014). Following a brutal crackdown by security forces and the execution of its founder by the police, it reemerged in 2009 in a more deadly guise, with a desire for vengeance, having been influenced through its collaboration with Al Qaeda franchises. The response by the security forces, and poor respect for the rule of law by law enforcement agencies, helped swell its ranks and radicalized the group further. It targeted government installations and security forces, but its campaign soon began to feature pure terrorism, with attacks on secular schools, bars, Christians, critical Muslim clerics, traditional leaders, the UN office in Abuja, polio vaccination health workers, and perceived symbols of Western influence. The group funds its operations by robbing banks, cash-in-transit convoys, and businesses; there is also some evidence that it receives donations from wealthy individuals (Walker 2012).

In Mali, extremist Islamist factions have taken advantage of socioeconomic grievances and the void left by the state in the north. The influx of militants from Northern Africa, the return of Tuaregs who had fought on behalf of Gaddafi, and heavy weaponry from Libya all tipped the delicate balance between the Tuareg and other communities in the north and the government. Although religious radicalization did not trigger the uprising in Mali, the coup enabled extremist groups to strengthen their hold and infiltrate the gaps left by a weak state and poor governance. Strong rivalry among the leadership of the Ifoghas Tuaregs (Antil and Mokhefi 2014) exacerbated the situation. Political instability and marginalized youth "lacking prospects of hope for a better future" have made for "easily mobilized militias," demonstrating that a tradition of a secular state is no guarantee against radical elements (Gow, Olonisakin, and Dijxhoorn 2013). The complexity of three intertwined but distinct conflicts in Mali has muddied the picture somewhat and forged unlikely alliances between the flag bearers of a movement for an independent homeland in the north, Islamist groups (some of which have adopted radical ideas out of expediency), and criminal organizations involved in drug trafficking. Some of the rebel groups in the north thus do not represent radical Islam. Rather they are made up of people who feel disenfranchised and not sufficiently supported by the government in Bamako, as well as local elites looking for influence and recognition (Gow, Olonisakin, and Dijxhoorn 2013).

The rise of extremist groups in Mali raised the specter of the threat spreading to Niger, which has faced its own Tuareg rebellions and has been confronted with violence and hostage taking by AQIM in its northern regions (Gow, Olonisakin, and Dijxhoorn 2013). These fears appear to have been realized in May 2013, when the country suffered a double terrorist attack, one on a military barracks in Agadez and another on a plant owned by the French company Areva in Arlit, for which MUJAO and Signatories in Blood, founded by a former AQIM leader, took credit (Zounmenou, Toupane, and Lidawo 2013). Niger also lost 22 inmates during a prison break in June 2013 in an attack led by MUJAO (BBC News 2013).

Radical Islam has become more prominent in Niger as a product of social and economic hardships and the associated dissatisfaction of ethnic groups. Although the primary drivers of radicalization are domestic, the arrival of radical elements and extremist narratives have played into existing perceptions of the government and uranium miners in the north, enabling groups like AQIM to leverage the local context and launch kidnappings and terror attacks (box 2.1) (Gow, Olonisakin, and Dijxhoorn 2013).

A limitation to the expansionist ambitions of radical groups includes the prism through which religious identity is filtered, such as ethnicity or caste.

BOX 2.1

Niger: Holding Fast in a Troubled Neighborhood

Located on the fringes of the Sahara, Niger faces external security threats similar to the ones that contributed to destabilizing its neighbor Mali. It must also contend with exposure to the lawless Sahara interior through its shared border with Libya, and with Boko Haram, which has repeatedly encroached into its territory from Nigeria.

Despite these challenges, Niger has maintained stability within its borders for a number of reasons. The combination of local factors that foster cohesion and a more inclusive and forward-looking government have helped Niger manage tensions between its communities and therefore avert the danger of conflict.

Niger has a strong sense of national unity that stems from President Mahamadou Issoufou's emphasis on grassroots rural development. This focus has helped consolidate the state's legitimacy at the local level (Pérouse de Montclos 2014). Niger also has a centralized government and a small population. Its army is well trained, protects civilians, and has not alienated local populations. The government and the Nigerien opposition work together to develop responses to terrorist threats, as they did when fending off the Tuareg rebellion of 2007–08. Niger also successfully avoided conflict in 2012, as the return of migrant workers and armed fighters from Libya helped destabilize Mali and contributed to an insurrection there. Its success was attributed to its long-standing tradition of integrating political elites from marginalized regions into the political process, the Niger Sahel Strategy to improve the lives of people in the country's north, and decentralization at the local level. Intermarriage between communities and a low degree of fragmentation among northern groups have also contributed to cohesive social dynamics at the local level (Antil and Mokhefi 2014). Despite historically rooted grievances of certain communities in the north, the north-south divide is not felt as strongly in Niger as it is in Mali (ICG 2013).

In Mauritania, where two explosives-laden trucks detonated in Nouakchott in February 2011 (Goita 2011), Islamist movements such as AQIM have struggled to recruit black Africans, who have historically been marginalized, a factor that restricted AQIM's reach into the Moorish community. Similarly, historical rivalries between clans in Mali mean that as one clan adopts a new doctrine, others immediately reject it (Jourde 2011). There are claims that ethnic boundaries are complicating relations between militants from Mali and the Algerian-dominated AQIM (Østebø 2012). In Senegal, which is also susceptible to the spread of extremism, the Sufi brotherhoods of Islam and Mouridism are perceived as being a "shield against foreign extremist influences," despite the existence of a minority discourse that favors "reformist" strains of thought, particularly in the urban periphery among the youth (Sambe and Bah 2013). In postconflict Sierra Leone, a predominantly Muslim country but not an Islamic state, there is "virtually no evidence of Islamist radicalization or related violent extremism," for a number of reasons (Gow, Olonisakin, and Dijxhoorn 2013). Religious tolerance and freedom are enshrined in the constitution and vigorously defended by the government, and given the country's recent history, its population is more focused on peace, security, and development than the desire to engage in violent extremism. The complexity of society in Sierra Leone, and the wide number of Islamic organizations, tribal affiliations, and ethnic identities, serve as a buffer against extremism (Gow, Olonisakin, and Dijxhoorn 2013).

Islam in West Africa has traditionally taken the guise of Sufi orders such as Tijaniyya, which have proven to be a source of resistance against the encroachment of radical thought in countries such as Senegal and Sierra Leone. In Mali and Niger, although Tijaniyya remains the dominant order, the process of democratization in the 1990s enabled the entry of local anti-Sufi groups, such as Izala, as well as foreign-funded extremist groups, which promoted a more radical interpretation of the faith and targeted both Sufi practices and Western political elites as part of a political "reformist" agenda (Gow, Olonisakin, and Dijxhoorn 2013). The tensions between these strands of theological thought have been a further driver of radicalization and violence in the region, as have the massive evangelization exercises undertaken by Christians in Nigeria's Middle Belt in the 1980s and 1990s, which triggered religious riots. Indeed, some of the most violent forms of radicalization have been seen along the Christian-Muslim divide.

Recommendations for Addressing Emerging Threats

West Africa has experienced an upsurge in violent extremism in recent years. But despite the fact that many countries in the region have sizable Muslim populations, the phenomenon has affected only a few countries—namely,

Mali, Niger, Nigeria, and Mauritania—in any significant way. Religious extremism in West Africa remains largely homegrown and driven by local dynamics, even if foreign actors have provided doctrinal influence, financial support, and training. Although the triggers of radicalization are complex, manifold, and unique to each context, the threat has implications for regional stability and therefore necessitates a regional response, which enables West Africa to benefit from the successful experiences of other countries. It also requires a focus on the need to better integrate minorities, improve local governance, ensure more equitable subregional development, and strengthen the security and justice sectors.

Development organizations are in a strong position to help governments address emerging threats such as narcotics trafficking, maritime piracy, and violent extremism, which prey on states with weak institutions and poor governance. Such threats are prone to contagion and pose a challenge to the stability of the entire region.

Recommendations to address these drivers of conflict and fragility include the following:

- Encourage a shift in thinking and policy to approach these threats holistically by adopting a region-wide strategy while building the capacity of ECOWAS to deal with such nonconventional threats. Conduct more research and investigation in order to improve the understanding of the economic and social impact of these new threats.

- Encourage regional collaboration and initiatives and support regional organizations such as ECOWAS, in close collaboration with UNODC, to address these threats. Trafficking, piracy, and terrorism threats require solid regional initiatives and strong coordination with countries from outside the region (from North Africa, Latin America, Europe, and the United States).

- Use anti–money laundering mechanisms. Donors and development agencies have fostered relatively effective mechanisms of control, which should be applied to the region. Additionally, support regional initiatives such as the ECOWAS Inter-Governmental Action Group against Money Laundering in West Africa.

- Improve the understanding of the social and economic underpinnings of the new security threats. Understand the mechanisms by which youth and others are drawn into criminal activities (by identifying push and pull factors, for example). Improve the understanding of governance issues, and in particular, how corruption fuels these new threats. Both regional and country-level analyses are needed in order to craft effective policies.

- Encourage the sharing of and learning from successful examples from other parts of the world, particularly in relation to urban crime control, narcotics (from Latin America and the Caribbean), and antipiracy activities (from East Africa and East Asia).

Notes

1. This estimate was made by multiplying the size of the flow (21 tons) by the wholesale value of a kilogram of cocaine in Europe ($84,000). Using the retail value would yield an even greater figure but would be inconsistent with the methodology generally used by the United Nations Office on Drugs and Crime.
2. Efforts since 2010 boosted growth until the coup of 2012.

References

Aning, K., and J. Pokoo. 2014. "Understanding the Nature and Threats of Drug Trafficking to National and Regional Security in West Africa." *International Journal of Security and Development* 3 (1): 1–13.

Antil, Alain, and Mansourieh Mokhefi. 2014. "Managing the Sahara Periphery." World Bank, Sahara Knowledge Exchange Series, Washington, DC.

Associated Press. 2014. "Boko Haram Killed Hundreds in North-East Nigeria, Witnesses Say." *Guardian.* June 5. http://www.theguardian.com/world/2014/jun/05/boko -haram-killed-hundreds-north-east-nigeria.

BBC News. 2013. "Niamey Prison Break: Niger Confirms 22 Escaped." June 2. http:// www.bbc.com/news/world-africa-22749230.

BP (British Petroleum). 2013. *British Petroleum Statistical Review of World Energy.* London.

CBC News. 2014. "Canada Part of Effort to Free 300 Nigerian Schoolgirls." May 13. http://www.cbc.ca/news/politics/canada-part-of-effort-to-free-300-nigerian-schoolgirls -1.2641842.

Cockayne, J. 2013. "Chasing Shadows: Strategic Responses to Organised Crime in Conflict-Affected Situations." *RUSI Journal* 158 (2): 10–24.

Dabo, A. 2014. "Vaz Wins Guinea-Bissau Presidential Vote, Loser Rejects Result." May 20. Reuters. http://uk.reuters.com/article/2014/05/20/uk-bissau-election -idUKKBN0E01PQ20140520.

Dechery, Côme, and Laura Ralston. 2014. "Trafficking and Fragility in West Africa." World Bank, Fragility, Conflict, and Violence Group, Washington, DC.

Ellis, S. 2009. "West Africa's International Drug Trade." *African Affairs* 108 (431): 171–96.

Global Initiative against Transnational Organized Crime. 2014. "Illicit Trafficking and Instability in Mali: Past, Present and Future." Geneva.

Goita, M. 2011. "West Africa's Growing Terrorist Threat: Confronting AQIM's Sahelian Strategy." Africa Security Brief 11, Africa Center for Strategic Studies, Washington, DC.

Gow, J., F. Olonisakin, and E. Dijxhoorn. 2013. *Militancy and Violence in West Africa: Religion, Politics, and Radicalisation.* London: Routledge.

Guichaoua, Yvan. 2014. "Transformations of Armed Violence in the Sahara." World Bank, Sahara Knowledge Exchange Series, Washington, DC.

ICG (International Crisis Group). 2012. "The Gulf of Guinea: The New Danger Zone." Africa Report 195, ICG, Brussels. http://www.crisisgroup.org/~/media/Files/africa /central-africa/195-the-gulf-of-guinea-the-new-danger-zone-english.pdf.

———. 2013. "Niger: Another Weak Link in the Sahel?" Africa Report 208, ICG, Brussels. http://www.crisisgroup.org/~/media/Files/africa/west-africa/niger/208-niger-another -weak-link-in-the-sahel-english.pdf.

———. 2014. "Curbing Violence in Nigeria (II): The Boko Haram Insurgency." Africa Report 216, ICG, Brussels. http://www.crisisgroup.org/~/media/Files/africa/west -africa/nigeria/216-curbing-violence-in-nigeria-ii-the-boko-haram-insurgency.pdf.

Jourde, C. 2011. "Sifting through the Layers of Insecurity in the Sahel: The Case of Mauritania." Africa Security Brief 15, Africa Center for Strategic Studies, Washington, DC.

Katsouris, C., and A. Sayne. 2013. Nigeria's Criminal Crude: International Options to Combat the Export of Stolen Oil. London: Chatham House.

Kavanagh, Camino. 2013. "International and Regional Responses to Drug Trafficking in West Africa: A Preliminary Overview." WACD Background Paper 6, West Africa Commission on Drugs, Geneva. http://www.wacommissionondrugs.org/wp -content/uploads/2013/10/International-and-Regional-Responses-to-DT-in-West -Africa-Kavanagh-Walker.pdf.

Kemp, W., M. Shaw, and A. Boutellis. 2013. The Elephant in the Room: How Can Peace Operations Deal with Organized Crime? New York: International Peace Institute.

Kühne, W. 2013. "West Africa and the Sahel in the Grip of Organized Crime and International Terrorism: What Perspectives for Mali after the Elections?" Policy Brief, Johns Hopkins School of Advanced International Studies (SAIS) and the Center for International Peace Operations. http://www.zif-berlin.org/fileadmin/uploads/analyse /dokumente/veroeffentlichungen/ZIF_Policy_Briefing_Winrich_Kuehne_Aug_2013 _ENG.pdf.

Lacher, W. 2012. "Organized Crime and Conflict in the Sahel-Sahara Region." Carnegie Endowment for International Peace, Washington, DC.

———. 2013. "Challenging the Myth of the Drug Terror Nexus in the Sahel." WACD Background Paper 4, West Africa Commission on Drugs, Geneva.

Lebovich, A. 2013. "Mali's Bad Trip: Field Notes from the West African Drug Trade." Foreign Policy. March 15. http://www.foreignpolicy.com/articles/2013/03/15/mali _s_bad_trip.

Lloyd's Market Association. n.d. Lhttp://www.lmalloyds.com/Web/market_places /marine/JWC/Joint_War.aspx.

Martinez, J., J. Tost, L. Hilgert, and T. Woodard-Meyers. 2013. "Gang Membership Risk Factors for Eighth-Grade Students." Nonpartisan Education Review 9 (1): 1–31.

New York Times. 2011. "A Selection from the Cache of Diplomatic Dispatches: A Well-Connected Drug Trafficker in Guinea." June 19. http://www.nytimes.com/interactive /2010/11/28/world/20101128-cables-viewer.html#report/drugs-08CONAKRY163.

Obi, C. I. 2006. "Terrorism in West Africa: Real, Emerging or Imagined Threats?" African Security Review 15 (3): 87–101.

Onuoha, F. C. 2012. "Piracy and Maritime Security in the Gulf of Guinea." Al Jazeera Center for Studies, Doha, Qatar. http://studies.aljazeera.net/en/reports/2012/06 /2012612123210113333.htm.

Onuoha, F. C., and G. E. Ezirim. 2013. "'Terrorism' and Transnational Organised Crime in West Africa." Al Jazeera Center for Studies, Doha, Qatar. http://studies.aljazeera .net/en/reports/2013/06/2013624102946689517.htm.

O'Regan, D., and P. Thompson. 2013. "Advancing Stability and Reconciliation in Guinea-Bissau: Lessons from Africa's First Narco-State." Special Report, Africa Center for Strategic Studies, Washington, DC.

Østebø, T. 2012. "Islamic Militancy in Africa." Africa Security Brief 23, Africa Center for Strategic Studies, Washington, DC.

Pérouse de Montclos, M.-A. 2014. "Nigeria's Interminable Insurgency? Addressing the Boko Haram Crisis." Chatham House, London. http://www.chathamhouse.org/sites /files/chathamhouse/field/field_document/20140901BokoHaramPerousedeMontclos _0.pdf.

Reitano, T., and M. Shaw. 2013. "The Evolution of Organised Crime in Africa: Towards a New Response." Institute for Security Studies, Pretoria.

Sambe, B., and D. Bah. 2013. "Overview of Religious Radicalism and the Terrorist Threat in Senegal." ECOWAS Peace and Security Report 3, Institute for Security Studies, Pretoria.

Savage, C., and T. Shanker. 2012. "U.S. Drug War Expands to Africa, a Newer Hub for Cartels." New York Times, July 21. http://www.nytimes.com/2012/07/22/world/africa /us-expands-drug-fight-in-africa.html.

Shaw, Mark. 2012. "Leadership Required: Drug Trafficking and the Crisis of Statehood in West Africa." Policy Brief 37, Institute for Security Studies, Pretoria. http://www .issafrica.org/uploads/No37Oct2012Drugs.pdf.

UNODC (United Nations Office on Drugs and Crime). 2008a. Drug Trafficking as a Security Threat in West Africa. Vienna: UNODC.

———. 2008b. Transnational Trafficking and the Rule of Law in West Africa: A Threat Assessment. Vienna: UNODC.

———. 2010. World Drug Report 2010. Vienna: UNODC.

———. 2011. Estimating Illicit Financial Flows Resulting from Drug Trafficking and Other Transnational Organized Crimes. Vienna: UNODC.

———. 2013. Transnational Organized Crime in West Africa: A Threat Assessment. Vienna: UNODC.

Vulliamy, E. 2008. "How a Tiny West African Country Became the World's First Narco State." Guardian. March 8. http://www.theguardian.com/world/2008/mar/09 /drugstrade.

Walker, A. 2012. "What Is Boko Haram?" Special Report, U.S. Institute of Peace, Washington, DC. http://www.usip.org/sites/default/files/SR308.pdf.

Zounmenou, D., P. M. Toupane, and K. Lidawo. 2013. "Under Attack? Niger Faced with Religious Extremism and Terrorism." ECOWAS Peace and Security Report 7, Institute for Security Studies, Pretoria.

Chapter 3

Tackling the Complex Challenges of Youth and Migration

One of West Africa's defining challenges in the coming decades will be its skyrocketing youth population. Young people represent a tremendous asset and a potential catalyst for growth and progress in the subregion. This potential needs to be channeled, however, and the expectations and energy of youth carefully managed in order to mitigate conflict risks.

Migration also presents significant opportunities for the subregion as an economic driver and source of resilience. But it has the potential to be disruptive and to drive conflict over issues such as competition for resources and questions over land rights. Like the challenge of youth, it requires careful management and appropriate structures.

The Challenge of Youth Inclusion: Promise or Peril?

Youth are the future of Africa: they represent massive potential for the continent. Enormous challenges confront them, however, linked to the poor quality of education, growth that creates fewer and fewer formal employment opportunities, and the very rapid transformation of the institutions that integrate youth into society.

Youth have been key actors in much of the conflict and violence experienced across West Africa since independence, from the decade-long civil wars in Liberia and Sierra Leone to the conflict in Côte d'Ivoire, the subnational violence in Nigeria since 1999, and the violence in northern Ghana between the Nanumbas and Konkombas. Youth have participated in the insurgency in the Casamance region of Senegal and the Tuareg rebellions in Mali and Niger. They have contributed to both urban and politically motivated violence across the region and filled the ranks of extremist groups.

Youth-Led Violence and Conflict in West Africa
The triggers of youth violence in West Africa are manifold. They tap into reservoirs of resentment caused by several factors, including the failure of corrupt

and patrimonial states to function on behalf of youth, the associated absence of opportunity, a sense of frustration and alienation, a desire for recognition and esteem, an intergenerational crisis, and elites' manipulation of youth.

Fear of future youth-led conflagrations stems from the rapid increase in the number of young people in the population. West Africa's population more than quadrupled between 1950 and 2007, from approximately 70 million to 315 million (de Verdière and others 2009). One-third of the population is between the ages of 15 and 24, and 60 percent are under the age of 25 (de Verdière and others 2009; Hervish and Clifton 2012). One-third of the more than 30 countries in Sub-Saharan Africa experiencing "youth bulges" are in West Africa (Olonisakin 2008), where the number of youth is expected to grow through 2035 and plateau around 2050 (UNECA 2011), by which time the region's population will have doubled to about 700 million (Ikelegbe and Garuba 2011).

The extent to which this phenomenon presents a security and stability threat or opportunity or combination of both has been much debated. What is clear is that unless the economy, including the informal sector, can absorb the influx of youth and provide them with a source of revenue, the growth of the youth cohort has the potential to contribute to regional instability. "As the number of schooled youth outpaces job growth, it risks leaving even those who are educated facing significant challenges to make a living, as well as feeling frustrated and resentful of those who enjoy the opportunities they lack" (Olonisakin 2008, 20). Although not in themselves a cause of armed conflict, these problems can facilitate the recruitment of young people into militias, extremist networks, political gangs, and insurgent organizations, which become de facto employers of young men and "the main avenues of political mobility in weaker countries" (Olonisakin 2008, 20).

Attempts to address this problem are complicated by the fact that rapid economic growth across West Africa has not been accompanied by high levels of job creation. Meanwhile, the limited capacity of the formal sector to absorb the growing youth population is associated with increasing inequalities (Filmer and Fox 2014). The scarcity of good jobs has widened the gap between aspirations and reality, entrenching intergenerational differences (Fortune, Ismail, and Stephen 2014). The prospects for educated youth integrating into an urban economy and earning decent incomes are considerably lower than they were for previous generations, creating enormous frustrations.

The multiple motivations for the engagement of youth in violence and conflict in West Africa need to be understood in terms of the context (Walton 2010). Weak economic and political structures across much of the region have had a debilitating effect on youths' lifestyles and living conditions, as well as on their social and political culture (Keen 2002, 2005). The drivers of violence and atrocities perpetuated by youth combine diverse dynamics that encapsulate economic exclusion and grievances related to limited access to education, jobs, and health care, in addition to intergenerational tensions that drive a search for "respect through the barrel of a gun" (Keen 2002, 5; Keen 2005). The need for status and visibility are key reasons why young people become involved in violence. The drivers of violence are thus related to the transition to adulthood (Fortune, Ismail, and Stephen 2014).

Social and political grievances have played a central role in motivating youth violence, with perceptions of an unjust or corrupt society or political system underpinning frustration. Linked to such grievances is the perception that social norms prevent young people from successfully transitioning to adulthood—being able to support a household and contribute to community well-being. Indeed, age-based definitions of youth in West Africa include people between the ages of 15 and 40, implying that young people are suspended in an indeterminate space between childhood and adulthood and may never become "social adults." West African youth may never attain the social goods and status associated with adulthood, such as a steady income, valuable skills, and a secure shelter (Jeffrey 2010; Honwana 2012). Blocked youth transitions, combined with the "corruption or hypocrisy of the local elite," have contributed to alienation (Walton 2010, 3).

The delayed transition to adulthood has resulted in the erosion of traditional norms, reducing the ability of men to fulfill traditional gender roles and provide for their families. As a result, many men feel humiliated and suffer from lower self-esteem, which in turn risks increasing child abuse and intimate partner violence (Alaga 2011).

The prevalence of single parenthood, particularly among urban women, has undermined kinship-based family structures. Increasing numbers of women are joining the labor force as they attempt to adapt to changes in educational status, employment, and in some cases, the decline in the pool of marriageable men (Bigombe and Khadiagala 2003). Although working outside the home enables women to take more control over their lives, it may leave them more vulnerable to sexual and other types of violence.

The control of resources by an entrenched elite drives youth grievances, rather than poverty and inequality per se. The act of taking up arms against the state or political elites provides a much sought after avenue through which to integrate into society or gain a sense of purpose and recognition that has otherwise proven elusive (Walton 2010).

The 1991–2002 civil war in Sierra Leone—which became synonymous with brutality meted out by marauding armies of child soldiers on hapless civilians and trade in "blood diamonds"—has been described as the "violent manifestation of a rational expression of a youth crisis" (Fraser and Hilker 2009, 26). The bulk of the leadership and the membership of both the Revolutionary United

Front (RUF) and the National Patriotic Front of Liberia (NPFL) were under the age of 35 (Ikelegbe and Garuba 2011). A key motivating factor for young recruits to the RUF was anger at an "unjust and patrimonial" system that excluded and alienated young people (Clapham 2003; Walton 2010). Youth violence was a reaction to exclusionary neopatrimonial practices and state decay (Richards 1996). It also reflected failures of the education system, lack of employment opportunities, and the "negative attitudes and practices" of the elders (Reno 2011). Richards (1996) describes the violence as a form of "political agency" in which young people seek to create an alternative future free from the shackles of patrimonialism. Violent conflict is thus the "registration of dissent and frustration and a challenge against the forms, practices, and conduct of the state and its officials and local elite" (Ikelegbe and Garuba 2011, 100). It was in this context that Charles Taylor's Small Boys Unit; the Gronna Boys in Liberia; the lumpen *rarray* boys in Sierra Leone; and the Area Boys in Lagos, the Egbesu Boys in the Niger Delta, and the Yan Daba in Kano, Nigeria, emerged (Ikelegbe and Garuba 2011).

The RUF leadership represented a young, excluded, intellectual elite (Fraser and Hilker 2009). In contrast, the rank and file foot soldiers were pulled into the movement by various factors, including the prospects of profit and plunder, coercion, drug use, indoctrination, ideology, leadership, and organizational dynamics. The appeal of being protected from violence by belonging to an armed group was another proximate factor. Grievances on the basis of social class, ethnic and political differences, personal dislocation, and frustrations have all led to participation in violence (Fraser and Hilker 2009).

The proliferation of small arms in West Africa has also been a significant factor in the perpetuation of violence. Weapons are recycled among the region's incidents of violence and conflict. They are durable, lightweight, and easily portable, enabling their use by child soldiers. Once conflicts end, the circulation of weapons has the potential to reignite hostilities, or weapons can be used for criminal activity and ethnic and political violence (Keili 2008). In addition, the porous borders of the Mano River Basin countries facilitate both the spread of small arms and the recruitment of child soldiers across conflicts, with more than 150 illegal crossings identified between Guinea, Liberia, and Sierra Leone. Hardened in the youth-dominated conflicts of Liberia and Sierra Leone, former combatants strengthened the ranks of both sides in the 2002 conflict in Côte d'Ivoire, as roving soldiers-for-hire became a fixture on the regional landscape (Gavin 2008). At least 40,000 young men and women—trained combatants—fought in the conflicts in Liberia and Sierra Leone. In 2000, Guinea trained and armed more than 3,000 youths, whom it failed to disarm and rehabilitate following the end of the insurgency. At least 8,000 young people were enlisted by both sides to fight in the conflict in Côte d'Ivoire (Alaga 2011).

The Economic and Social Legacy of the Conflict for Youth

One of the far-reaching consequences of youths' participation in violence and conflict in West Africa is the risk of excombatants slipping back into violence. Demobilizing young combatants and reintegrating them into civilian life is challenging and fraught with difficulties, not least the need to contend with the loss of power and feeling of marginalization because of prevailing intergenerational power differentials. Armed conflict and violence hurt young people's formal education prospects and leave many of them unskilled and unprepared for the job market. These factors risk exacerbating fragility and fueling a vicious cycle of conflict, as in Liberia, where young excombatants cited poverty as the most common reason for considering a return to violence, followed by lack of jobs and benefits or training (Walton 2010).

Fourteen years of civil war in Liberia devastated that country's institutions and infrastructure, leaving a generation of children without education or training, with girls particularly disadvantaged. In 2003, almost 60 percent of girls and 40 percent of boys had no formal schooling; data from 2007 show that more than 40 percent of adult women (and 20 percent of men) have no education at all (Adoho and others 2014).

In Côte d'Ivoire, where conflict reduced the educational attainment for children by 0.2–0.9 years, gender gaps were most pronounced in the north, which was cut off from basic public services after the conflict divided the country in half (Croke and Rees Smith 2013). Closures in the north during the postelection crisis meant that 800,000 children could not attend school. Many children born during the conflict never received birth certificates, which impedes their ability to attend school and access other basic services (Croke and Rees Smith 2013).

The conflicts in Liberia and Sierra Leone also featured sexual violence as a weapon of war. Indeed, the high incidence of sexual and gender-based violence has been a devastating consequence of conflict across West Africa. Sexual violence is a growing phenomenon in the subregion, but it has been particularly prevalent during and after conflict. It has involved mutilation, sexual slavery, and the gang rape of women and girls (Alaga 2011). More than 250,000 women were raped during the conflict in Sierra Leone, according to the United Nations Children's Fund, motivating President Ernest Bai Koroma to issue a public apology to women in March 2010 (Alaga 2011). The RUF alone was responsible for more than two-thirds of the 2,058 abductions of girls and women, as well as about three-quarters of all cases of sexual slavery in the Sierra Leone conflict (Ben-Ari and Harsch 2005). In Côte d'Ivoire, almost a third of girls reported having been forced or coerced into sexual relations during or after the conflict, according to a 2003 study by the United Nations Population Fund. Women were especially vulnerable at roadblocks, which were a constant presence throughout the conflict (McGovern 2011; Croke and Rees Smith 2013). In Liberia, it is estimated that 40 percent of the population—men, women, girls, and boys—were affected by sexual violence during the 14-year conflict there (Refugees International 2004). In Guinea-Bissau, Senegalese soldiers perpetrated acts of sexual violence against women at military checkpoints and barracks, according to Amnesty International (1998, 1999). Some women joined the rebel forces in an attempt to defend themselves from violence; others were abducted and forced to carry out armed operations (Ben-Ari and Harsch 2005).

The social stigma of rape has caused women to be marginalized and shunned by their own families, husbands, and communities (Ben-Ari and Harsch 2005). Domestic violence has also increased in the wake of conflict and violence (after the postelection crisis in Côte d'Ivoire, for instance). The phenomenon is ascribed to a breakdown in social norms and structures that is typical of post-conflict settings (Croke and Rees Smith 2013).

Youth have historically been agents of political and social change in West Africa. They played an important role in independence movements and were at the vanguard of the region's democratization movement, as it was students who first felt the pinch from cost-cutting as a result of structural adjustment. They have participated in regional, ethnic, religious, and civil society struggles, as they seek greater accommodation, inclusion, equity, justice, and accountability from the state (Ikelegbe and Garuba 2011). However, the exclusivity of the political arena, and the unwillingness of elites to create space and an outlet for energetic youth and their civic concerns, has at times escalated these struggles into violence. Violence with youth involvement in Nigeria after the 2011 elections began with the death of President Umaru Musa Yar'Adua. Youth have also been instrumentalized in political violence, as in parts of Nigeria, and there is evidence that powerful politicians have at times established youth militias to shore up their positions (Cambpell 2014).

Under these circumstances, youth have been viewed as the preferred demographic for enlistment as political foot soldiers, sometimes in return for payment and proximity to power, as in Guinea and Nigeria. An urban underclass has fed protests and violence in the region's urban centers, contributed to criminal activities, and been available for diverse kinds of mobilization (Ikelegbe and Garuba 2011). In some instances, the formation of militant party youth wings is explicit; in other cases, the link to the party is less apparent. Attempts by Sani Abacha to mobilize youth in a visible demonstration of support for his regime through the 1998 "two million man march" in Nigeria backfired, instead helping radicalize a generation after youth realized the discrepancy between the wealth in Abuja and the crushing poverty of the oil-producing communities in the Niger Delta (Gavin 2008). This realization empowered them to establish their own pressure groups and armed militias instead of relying on local chiefs and elites to negotiate with the government and oil companies on behalf of communities (Gavin 2008).

Unemployment and Conflict: Complex Interlinkages

In light of the region's recent past, debate surrounding the youth bulge in West Africa has reflected "more alarm than constructive engagement" (Sommers 2007). The rapid increase in the number of youth has frequently been presented as a threat to regional stability and security, based on the assumption of a linear relationship between a large youth cohort and high levels of unemployment and underemployment on the one hand and the incidence of conflict and violence on the other. Although West Africa's demographics can represent an opportunity for increased productivity and economic growth—enabled by a large, young, and healthy workforce and a relatively small dependent population—the tendency has been to view it as a ticking time bomb.

In fact, although youth unemployment may be a factor of violence, it is rarely a main or direct cause. The direct causal link between youth employment and violence has been debunked (Cramer 2010). The relationship between unemployment and violence is multifaceted and complex (Walton 2010). A focus on unemployment is problematic in that it treats youth as an undifferentiated mass, overlooking the fact that very few young people are unemployed in the sense that they are doing nothing (Fortune, Ismail, and Stephen 2014). It also assumes that the mismatch between employment aspirations and reality is a catalyst for youth violence. Finally, and critically, the focus on unemployment obscures the nuances of the social, economic, and security dynamics beyond unemployment and frustration that can coalesce to trigger youth-led violence. The evidence points to an intricate and diverse web of factors that lead young people to engage in violence, with a "complex transmission mechanism" connecting economic marginalization to engagement in violence (Batmanglich and Enria 2014).

The "panic" narrative, which situates young urban men as the problem and emphasizes formal sector development as the solution (Van der Geest 2010) has produced prescriptive policy responses and failed to reach a nuanced understanding of the diverse realities of different groups of young people. It risks fueling intergenerational misunderstandings and tensions by positioning youth as a destabilizing factor. Furthermore, it downplays the importance of the informal sector in creating livelihoods and spurring development and progress in West Africa (Sommers 2007).

West African youth have demonstrated their creativity, dynamism, and resourcefulness in the face of limited opportunities by seeking out livelihood activities in the informal sector (Fortune, Ismail, and Stephen 2014). Artisanal mining is gaining momentum and evolving as an industry, as increasing numbers of young people engage in it. Many young men find employment driving motorcycle taxis. Street trading is a survivalist entrepreneurial activity, and hairdressing and barbering represent effective coping strategies.

Drug trafficking is another common livelihood activity that enables young people to achieve wealth and social status, despite being associated with a range of significant negative social dynamics (see chapter 2).

Formal employment in Africa accounts for only about 16 percent of total jobs; about a third of 15- to 24-year-olds in Côte d'Ivoire, Ghana, Mali, and Nigeria participate in the formal labor force (Hervish and Clifton 2012). The remainder, categorized as "unemployed" according to official figures, work on small-scale family farms (63 percent) or in the informal economy (22 percent) (Van Gyampo and Obeng-Odoom 2013).

Across the continent, the informal sector is expanding. It accounts for 40–75 percent of gross domestic product (GDP) and employs 50–80 percent of the workforce across various countries (Jütting and de Laiglesia 2009). It accounts for about 60 percent of all urban jobs and was responsible for 90 percent of all new jobs created during the 1990s (Brown and Lyons 2010; Charmes 2012). In rural areas, the agricultural sector absorbs many young people as informal farm laborers. Nonfarm informal activities are also on the rise (Van der Geest 2010).

The rhetoric of governments and some development agencies still places too much emphasis on formal job creation. They think of a "job" solely as "a skilled position that provides a sustained and sufficient source of income for a family and lends status to individual and family" (Fortune, Ismail, and Stephen 2014). According to this definition, a job is characterized by a contract, a regular salary, social security and income tax, and perhaps benefits, which provide a level of security not found in more informal income-generating activities.

As a result of this narrative, people working in the informal economy often describe themselves as unemployed and experience a sense of failure that is rooted in the mismatch between employment aspirations and reality (Fortune, Ismail, and Stephen 2014). Evidence from Ghana identifies an additional source of frustration for unemployed and underemployed youth: the challenges they face when they do attempt to secure formal employment, such as a lack of relevant work experience and training for the demands of the labor market or the resources and support to pursue entrepreneurial activities.

Although governments across the region have adopted the rhetoric of youth empowerment and employment, their actions have failed to inspire the confidence of the youth (Fortune, Ismail, and Stephen 2014). More than two-thirds of people between the ages of 15 and 29 in Côte d'Ivoire, Ghana, Mali, and Nigeria indicate limited confidence in their government's ability to create jobs, with rural youth in Côte d'Ivoire and Mali particularly disappointed, according to Afrobarometer surveys. These figures reflect an urban bias in employment creation initiatives. The sense of broad-based disillusionment among youth regarding government inaction is reinforced by government performance, in particular regarding job creation policies (Fortune, Ismail, and Stephen 2014). Thousands of urban youth—mostly frustrated and unemployed excombatants—rioted in Liberia in 2004 following the end of the civil war. Their response reflected the fact that approaches to youth employment focus on the formal sector, despite the fact that youth increasingly look toward the informal sector for livelihood opportunities (Fraser and Hilker 2009).

Investment in the education sector has not been matched to the demands of the economy and labor markets. At the same time, these investments have helped create expectations of greater economic opportunities (UNECA 2011; Hervish and Clifton 2012; Esson 2013). In Ghana, for instance, education is thought to be the dominant channel by which a good life and improved prospects can be attained (Langevang 2008; Esson 2013). However, expectations that education will lead to a formal sector job are increasingly falling short, creating a surplus of graduates. Some young Ghanaians in rural areas have dropped out of school and moved to urban centers in search of opportunities (Esson 2013), rejecting education as a prerequisite for a more successful life.

In Mali, rural-to-urban migration is helping youth achieve their aspirations. It is producing a form of youth culture that is constructed around the idea of an "urban adventure," often including a foreign adventure. Mali has a long-established tradition that views migration as a rite of passage. In fact, in certain regions, young people are not allowed to marry until they have gone abroad (IRIN n.d.). The example of young Ghanaians and Malians seeking alternative pathways to adulthood reveals the capacity of young people to adapt and adjust to their circumstances in new and hybrid ways (Ferguson 1999; Philipps 2013). Social networks have also been credited for many of the creative strategies young people have developed under challenging circumstances. For example, some young men in urban areas have strategically used identity networks of ethnicity, tribe, and geography to their advantage (Vigh 2006; Hoffman 2011; Philipps 2013). Doing so helps them build the social networks that can help offset marginalization, frustration, anger, disillusionment, exposure to criminal gangs, and other risks (Ferguson 1999). Mobile phones and social media increase young people's connectivity and provide a channel for seeking support.

Recommendations on Youth Inclusion

West Africa is experiencing rapid growth in its youth populations that is not being matched by the creation of sufficient sources of livelihoods. Development actors should strive to engage with governments and other stakeholders on how to create more employment opportunities while managing expectations among youth regarding employment creation in the formal sector. The aspirations and demands of youth vary. Beyond jobs, they also demand a voice and place in the new institutions that define the modern state. Political inclusion is critical to channel their energy and create space for their expression and dissent.

Development actors should strive to change the conversation within the region by challenging the notion of youth as a homogenous category. More research and investigation are needed into how to best support the creation of informal sector livelihood opportunities for youth.

Recommendations to address this driver of conflict and fragility include the following:

- Refocus growth strategies on labor-intensive sectors, and encourage the development of the informal sector, the main future source of livelihood opportunities for unskilled and low-skilled labor. Further research is needed into how public investment can be more labor intensive and the extent to which it is possible to encourage the development of small businesses.

- Increase violence prevention programs, with a focus on gender-based violence and social inclusion programs. Social inclusion programs should focus on preventing substance abuse and petty crime. These programs are particularly important in peri-urban and slum areas, where gang culture is taking root. In this context, lessons from Latin America are very valuable.

- Improve access to and the quality of education, including technical training. In particular, ensure that the decline in the quality of education experienced in many countries is reversed and that the education system is ready to absorb the increase in students as a result of the youth bulge. Merely sustaining existing levels of education will require an enormous effort by governments; improving the quality and appropriateness of education will require massive investments in facilities, school books, and other teaching aids. Teaching methods and curricula should account for regional variations (in terms of both the level of skills of the labor force and regional identities).

- Improve understanding of the structural issues that constrain young peoples' opportunities and potential over the long term. More analysis is needed regarding where integration is occurring and which policies and programs can have a real impact. Such analysis is essential, especially where tensions are high.

Migration: A Subregion on the Move

Tensions surrounding migratory flows through West Africa—including discriminatory notions of citizenship and "foreigner," political and social marginalization, and competition over land, resources, and employment—have contributed to violence and conflict across the subregion. Regional migration represents both an important coping mechanism for many poor households and a valuable economic use of human capital. However, as a result of unclear property rights, political manipulation, and weak mechanisms for integration, migrants have frequently found themselves at the center of violent confrontation. Contestations over land, power, and resources have triggered violence in Nigeria's Middle Belt region between indigenous communities and the Hausa-Fulani people (ICG 2012). In Côte d'Ivoire, conflict has stemmed from an influx of migrants, as the indigenous Guere and migrant Diola communities clashed over land ownership in the west of the country (ICG 2014). Liberia saw tensions as returning refugees attempting to reclaim land came into conflict with excombatants in the northeastern city of Ganta who claimed customary rights over the land or demanded it as a reward for their war efforts (Rincon 2010, 2013).

Another source of potential instability is West Africa's rapid urbanization and the influx of migrants to urban centers. The expansion of informal settlements populated by unemployed youth and marginalized populations intensifies perceptions of inequality and unfairness, increasing the risk of violent crime, gang activity, and trafficking (Commins 2011).

Migrant Groups in West Africa

West Africa has served as an arena for intercrossing migratory routes for centuries. These population patterns can be traced back to the subregion's long history of nomadism and rich sociocultural connections that transcend borders. Historically, trade has played an important role in shaping West African migration patterns, with traders from the north moving goods and products to the south and the coast.

Before colonialism, local chiefs relied on migrants to cultivate their land. Forced labor practices during the colonial period saw the wholesale transfer of people across the region. Individuals and families were pushed from Burkina Faso, Guinea, Mali, Niger, and the Sahel to the cocoa and coffee plantations of Ghana and the forestry industries of Côte d'Ivoire, leaving generations to build their livelihoods as "outsiders" far from home.

Migration continues to be at the core of regional integration and economic development in West Africa. It also represents a coping mechanism, as demonstrated by the pastoralists inhabiting the harsh climes of the Sahel and the seasonal exodus of young men from Guinea and Mali to the groundnut production regions of The Gambia and Senegal.

West Africa boasts one of the most mobile populations in the world. Intraregional migrants constitute about 7.5 million people, or 3 percent of the total population (IOM 2014). Migration is predominantly intraregional (map 3.1). The level of migration is much higher than official figures, which do not capture undocumented migrants, internally displaced persons, internal rural migrants, and pastoralists.

Map 3.1 Intraregional Migration within the Economic Community of West African States (ECOWAS)

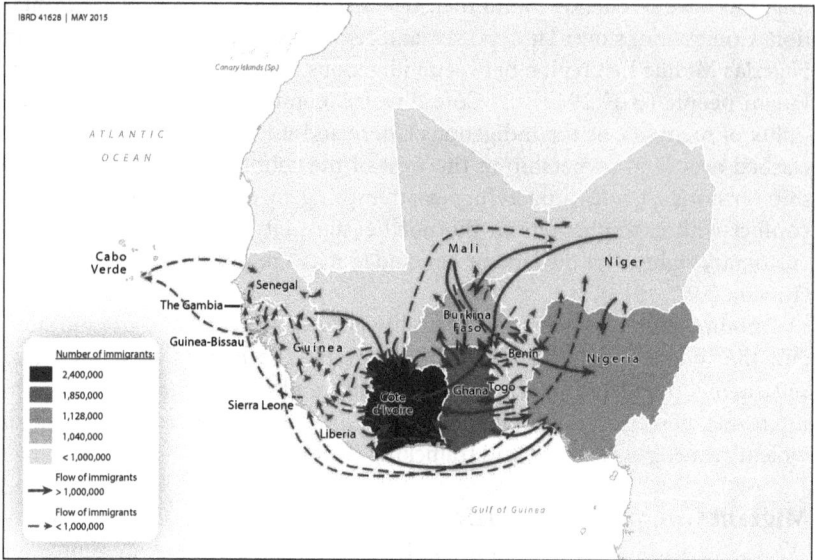

Source: Maze 2014.

The majority of migrants in West Africa are economic migrants; 70 percent of the movements in the subregion are linked to employment (IOM n.d.). Economic and labor migrants have historically been associated with the short-term migration of young single men journeying from the north or from the inland regions of Burkina Faso, Mali, and Niger toward the resource-rich coastal countries of Côte d'Ivoire and Nigeria. Traditionally, they then returned home to cultivate cotton and grain during the Sahelian rainy season (Konseiga 2005).

Mobility patterns have changed in the wake of high levels of unemployment (in particular among youth), increased levels of education, population growth, land scarcity, climate change, natural resource depletion, declining real incomes, and public sector cutbacks in response to structural adjustment programs (in Guinea, Nigeria, Senegal, Sierra Leone, and Togo, for example). In addition, advances in technology and remittance mechanisms enable migrants to explore longer-term migration opportunities farther from home while retaining stronger economic, social, and political ties (Shimeles 2010).

Many countries that traditionally sent or received people now contain mixes of immigrants, emigrants, or transiting migrants (Adepoju 2006), with remigration common. Families sponsor adult male members to go to cities to secure stable salaried jobs as an important alternative source of income.

Greater access to education has helped draw more women into migration streams, as seen in the case of Ghanaian women traveling to Côte d'Ivoire, Nigeria, and Togo (Cotula, Toulmin, and Hesse 2004). Economic migrants have come into conflict with indigenous populations in countries such as Côte d'Ivoire, Liberia, and Nigeria over ownership of assets, in particular land, as well as competition for jobs.

Pastoralists constitute another category of migrants that has frequently been caught up in conflict. Nomadic pastoralists rely on movement to cope with seasonal and climatic variations in West Africa's arid, semi-arid, and subhumid regions. They constitute a small portion of West Africa's livestock keepers and are randomly mobile depending on the rainfall (De Haan and others 2014). Transhumance pastoralists move seasonally between the rainy and dry seasons. In the Sahel, they represent a minority of the West African population, but they supply the bulk of livestock for domestic meat markets, contributing up to 10–15 percent of GDP in Burkina Faso, Mali, Niger, and Senegal (OECD-SWAC 2006).

Migrant pastoralists face a number of challenges, including very high poverty rates, instability, and insecurity of tenure. Despite their critical role in global food security, and their capacity to produce on land otherwise unsuitable for agriculture, pastoral communities in West Africa, including the Fulani, Tuareg, and the Moors, are in a persistent state of crisis (De Haan and others 2014).

Low-intensity conflicts between pastoralists and farmers, as well as among different pastoralist groups, have a long history that is becoming more intense in countries such as Burkina Faso, Ghana, Guinea, Mali, Mauritania, Niger, Nigeria, and Senegal (De Haan and others 2014). Although pastoral herders and farmers depend on mutually beneficial land and livestock arrangements and trading, competition over resources, encroachment of farms and projects on grazing lands and pastoral corridors, and tensions related to crop damage often lead to violence. Confrontations are particularly likely when coupled with political and social marginalization; the spillover from regional ethnic, religious, and political tensions; and the intensification of traditional cattle rustling practices because of the influx of weapons. For example, migrant Fulani herdsmen from neighboring countries have migrated to Ghana in search of grazing pasture, in the process destroying property in various villages there (Aning and Atta-Asamoah 2011). In northeastern Nigeria, competition between Fulani herdsmen and farmers over land use has spilled over into violence (Bello Tukur 2005). Challenges such as desertification, scarcity of resources, and other environmental issues have exacerbated this dynamic, as higher population growth means that the pastoral economy struggles to provide decent livelihoods to increasing numbers of people. As a result, pastoralists have suffered significant losses in livestock, plunging them deeper into poverty.

The vulnerability of pastoralists is exacerbated by their decreasing ability to supplement diminishing income from livestock-keeping activities, which has made illicit activities more attractive (De Haan and others 2014). In Mali, Tuareg perceptions of economic exclusion and marginalization by a state that favored sedentary populations over nomadic ones fed into grievances and helped trigger rebellions and conflict (World Bank 2013).

Conflict between herders and agriculturalists, and between various groups of pastoralists, is the most common form of land-based conflict in West Africa. Initiatives have been designed to prevent clashes between farmers and herders; in Mali, for example, a community radio station broadcasts customary tenure rules and harvesting times. These tensions can stoke deeper resentments and even escalate into large-scale conflicts, such as the war between Mauritania and Senegal.

Refugees and internally displaced persons make up a third critical set of migrants in West Africa. Forced displacement has been a consequence of regional conflict and violence, ranging from devastating civil wars, primarily in the Mano River Basin,[1] to simmering and sporadic low-intensity conflicts in Ghana, Nigeria, and Senegal, which are otherwise stable. Currently, Côte d'Ivoire and Mali have the highest number of internally displaced persons, but every country in the region except Cabo Verde is simultaneously hosting and producing refugees to varying degrees. Across West Africa, more than 120,000 displaced persons have returned, most of them to Côte d'Ivoire, Liberia, and Sierra Leone (IOM 2014). West Africa has also been a transit and staging post for refugees from northern Cameroon, the Central African Republic, Chad, Libya, and western Sudan.

The influx of refugees can strain host communities, as the flow of refugees from northern Mali into Mauritania has done. Communities already affected by the slowdown in cross-border trade and remittances and the disruption of seasonal pastoral migrations as a result of the conflict are dealt a further blow by the additional demands placed on land and water resources by the arrival of refugees, particularly where their numbers exceed those of the host community (Oxfam 2013).

One of the biggest factors impeding the return and reintegration of displaced populations is the uncertainty and insecurity stemming from land ownership. This problem is highlighted by the examples of the Guere people in Côte d'Ivoire, who returned following the electoral crisis of 2010–11 to find their land occupied by northerners, including Burkinabés, some of whom had been expelled from the same land years earlier or who had purchased the land from other Guere. In some cases, the land was considered to have been rightfully purchased, but the sale was conducted by individuals who did not have the authority to sell it. Land disputes and occupation or dispossession continue to be among the major reasons why many Guere are unable or unwilling to return.

In Sierra Leone, too, the process of reclaiming property has been so fraught with difficulties that it has threatened to obstruct the postwar recovery. Land disputes in Liberia, particularly in Lofa and Nimba counties, have played out between returnees from the Mandingo community and former combatants from the Gio community (NRC 2012).

Women are disproportionately affected by conflict-related displacement, which further erodes their land tenure security under customary systems. Property disputes make unmarried women and widows particularly suscep-tible to the loss of their land. Women with ongoing land disputes are more likely than men to be denied access to their land, although they report the same level of violence or risk associated with land disputes as do men. Displacement also causes women to lose the protection and support of their communities and families while depriving them of the necessary documenta-tion for land claims and physically removing them from their communities, where procedures for the recognition of customary rights are conducted (Croke and Rees Smith 2013).

Impact of Migration on Regional Stability

The benefits of migration include the provision of employment for about half of the subregion's economically active population, the generation of income through remittances, and the contribution of pastoral livestock to agricultural GDP. The boom of the cocoa and coffee industries in the Gulf of Guinea has been closely linked to the presence of migrant farmers and laborers there. For destination countries, migration helps maintain the stable labor market conditions that are conducive to economic growth. Migration positively affects the economy of origin through the flow of remittances and, in some cases, the transfer of skills and knowledge. In Senegal, where 30–50 percent of active men are absent from their villages, remittances are estimated to account for 30–70 percent of household budgets (Cotula and Toulmin 2004).

ECOWAS's Protocol on Free Movement of Persons and the Right of Residence and Establishment, ratified by member-states in 1980, grants migrants equal rights and protections as national citizens and safeguards them from "collective and arbitrary expulsion" (Addy 2005). Despite such measures, countries have sporadically moved to expel member-state citizens and restrict their access to certain economic activities. Nigeria expelled about a million irregular migrants, mostly from Ghana, in 1983 and 1985 in response to deteriorating economic conditions and rising unemployment (Adepoju 2005, 2006). Senegal expelled Moorish traders in 1989, following a border dispute with Mauritania. Côte d'Ivoire excluded its Burkinabé population from land rights in the 1990s.

Among the obstacles to upholding agreements regarding the treatment and protection of migrants is the difficulty of enforcing policies and sanctions against nonconforming states. Other hurdles include inadequate administrative and institutional capacity for effective migration policies and management, poor linkages between migration and development processes, lack of protections for migrant workers, and faltering political support (Robert 2004). The scarcity of formal documentation (such as identity cards or national passports) among West Africa's populations, in particular in rural areas, adds complexity to the precarious situation faced by migrants, which is compounded by corruption, poverty, and illiteracy (Adepoju, Boulton, and Levin n.d.).

Attempts have been made to regulate cross-border transhumance in the region. In 1998, ECOWAS agreed on a regional framework that defines the conditions for moving livestock, caring for animals, and hosting transhumant cattle (Abdoul 2011). Host country legislation must protect the rights of nonresident mobile herders, and herders must abide by the laws of the host country governing forests, wildlife, water points, and pastures (African Union 2013). Despite the framework, obstacles remain and conflicts continue over the movement of herds in the region. Red tape hinders cattle migration, and reports frequently emerge of major incidents in pastoral areas, sometimes including violence, caused by failure to comply with national and regional regulations, damage to fields and harvests, grazing in protected areas, and loss of animals (OECD-SWAC 2007).

Migration, Land Tenure, and Conflict

Grievances that sit at the intersection of migration and land tenure fuel many conflicts in West Africa. Conflicts in Côte d'Ivoire, Ghana, Mauritania, and Nigeria are in some way connected to migrants and to access to land. Historically, land chiefs relied on migrants to cultivate their lands and populate their villages as a way to shore up their political and economic power (Cotula, Toulmin, and Hesse 2004). In return for access to land through tenancies or tutorships, migrants were required to comply with local traditions and customs, abstain from political affairs, and offer respects to the landlord's family through regular gifts (Zongo 2010). Despite farming the land for generations, migrants could never assume full rights. They therefore depended on their patrons.

This traditional relationship between landholders and migrants has come under pressure from conflicting tenure systems, divergent interpretations over monetary transactions, sociogenerational change, and land scarcity. The descendants of migrants question the nature of transactions made by their ancestors, and the descendants of indigenous communities question the arrangements agreed to by their elders, calling on migrants to pay higher rates and make cash payments to avoid eviction. This tension has been observed across the region, on cocoa and plantation crop areas of southern Ghana and Côte d'Ivoire, irrigated plots in northern Nigeria and Senegal, areas of large in-migration in southwest Burkina Faso, and high-density and peri-urban zones in southern Benin and southeast Nigeria (IIED 2001). A complicating factor is the exchange of money, which indigenous landholders consider part of the lending transaction but migrants may view as conferring irrevocable ownership (Cotula, Toulmin, and Hesse 2004; Zongo 2010).

Along with population growth, sales of land outside the lineage have caused the fragmentation of large domestic landholding units into smaller family units, creating land shortages (IIED 2001). Landholders sharecrop or lease land belonging to immediate kin and further subdivide it out of economic necessity or the desire for personal profit, potentially triggering disputes, given the principle of inalienable rights to land. Migrants and women are among the most vulnerable to landlessness, as the Sahelian economic strategy of alternating out-migration with returning to farm the land is made possible only by virtue of membership in landholding communities and guaranteed access to land upon return (IIED 1999). The subdivision of holdings renders farming out-migrants vulnerable to losing land rights during their absence because of unauthorized sales or the inability to contest encroachment and competing claims (Maze 2014).

Rising land values are a key repercussion of land scarcity. When land was abundant and local landholders needed migrants to farm it, they negotiated mutually beneficial arrangements, including the outright sale of land, leasing and rental arrangements, sharecropping, and wage labor contracts (Maze 2014). In the Gulf of Guinea, much of the coastal forest is farmed under a mix of arrangements. With growing populations and less land available, migrants' negotiating powers have been greatly reduced. Moreover, landholders are increasingly aware of the value of their land, leading them to try and renegotiate the arrangements. Questions regarding the legitimacy of migrant farmers' land claims under the complex mixed systems complicate such efforts (IIED 1999).

Urbanization, Youth Violence, and Gangs

The population of West Africa was 320 million in 2010—10 times what it was four decades earlier—and is expected to reach about 500 million by 2030 (Bossard 2009). Half of the population is urban, and the figure is expected to rise to 60 percent by 2030, with Nigeria and the coastal countries along the Gulf of Guinea seeing the bulk of the influx. The capital cities of the Sahelian countries are also expected to double in size in the near future, with about 40 percent of the population living in towns of 5,000 or more by 2020 and 15–20 percent of Francophone Sahelians living outside their countries of origin.

The rapid rate of population growth over the past 30 years, along with the growth of urban centers, has implications for both in- and out-migration countries (Shimeles 2010). They include increased pressure on public services, land scarcity, reduced sizes of landholdings, disputes over migrant rights in land and property ownership, increased dependence on remittances, rising land values, and targeting of foreigners.

The growth of urban centers and cities is likely to be accompanied by the intensification of peri-urban issues (Maze 2014). The increase in land values will boost incentives to sell plots of customary land, which could negatively affect extended families and descendants. Governments might expropriate tracts of rural land for urban development, with inadequate compensation, taking from villagers and their descendants land they had farmed under customary arrangements.

The risks of urban-to-rural migration by landless but educated youth, which surges during periods of economic downturn and high unemployment, could place further stress on the land tenure system (Maze 2014). This phenomenon occurred in Côte d'Ivoire during the downturn of the 1990s, when youth returned to their communities to gain or rebuild a land-based livelihood and discovered that they no longer held rights or had access to family holdings. The marginalization of youth from land was a major grievance fueling the conflicts in Liberia and Sierra Leone, where the civil war that ravaged the country between 1991 and 2002 is often referred to as the "revolt of the youth" (Beall and Piron 2005).

The "combustible mix" of idle young men populating urban centers throughout West Africa—where crime, lawlessness, and insecurity overlap with socioeconomic grievances—can create a ready pool for recruitment into gangs, trafficking networks, and transnational organized crime syndicates, and it can contribute to political instability. Cities across the continent are growing by an estimated 15–18 million people a year. Cities—in which more than 40 percent of Africans under the age of 15 now live—have become "densely concentrated centers of unemployed young men" (Commins 2011, 1).

The high population densities of urban areas, which contain a mix of all the major ethnic groups in society and represent the site of competition for political power and resources, facilitates political mobilization, which could contribute to electoral violence (Commins 2011). In Conakry, Guinea, gangs of disenfranchised, unemployed young men have coalesced in urban areas, where they are available for hire for "demonstrating, campaigning, and acts of vandalism" (Philipps and Grovogui 2010, 4). Their presence increases the risk of political instability both before and after elections, because criminal gangs are often instrumentalized for "politically motivated acts of severe violence" (Philipps and Grovogui 2010, 5).

Some cities that have grown rapidly have experienced far less violence than others. They include Bamako, Lagos, Niamey, and Nouakchott. Although it is "slum-ridden" and "largely impoverished" (Kaplan 2014), Lagos—with its population of 21 million, which is expected to reach 40 million by midcentury—has seen a steady improvement in governance over the last decade and a "significant" (Filani 2012, 38) reduction in crime, as a result of greater accountability following the devolution of power from the national government to the cities

(Kaplan 2014). However, the rise of urban violence and criminality remains a major risk for the region in view of the rapid expansion of cities, requiring far more attention from policy makers.

Climate Change Risks

Projections indicate that global warming will affect Africa more intensively than much of the rest of the world, with temperatures rising 3°C–4°C. The Sahel is likely to face increased desertification and dryness and consequent complexities surrounding water, irrigation projects, and dams.

The region's surface water resources, concentrated primarily in Niger, Lake Chad, Senegal, The Gambia, and the Volta River,[2] have seen their stream flows decrease since the 1970s.[3] Along with climatic issues, wider population distribution and growth are contributing to the depletion. Efforts to stem the decline through dams, irrigation, and hydroelectric projects have contributed to rising tensions over shared river basins and questions over access and ownership over resources (Maze 2014).

The extreme ecological diversity of West Africa means that the effects of climate change will vary across the region. Growing desertification will be accompanied by increased rainfall along the Sahelian-humid zone lines, which will make more agricultural space available. By 2080, the continent as a whole stands to experience a significant expansion of potential agricultural land area, much of it in the Sahel (Bossard 2009). Although this development will increase food security, it means further encroachments of agricultural settlements onto pastoral land, as well as the broader infiltration of livestock diseases such as tsetse and new areas of insect pest distribution.

Given their long history of coping with drylands and droughts, pastoralists will be less affected by reduced rainfall and more affected by factors that constrain their mobility, such as land scarcity, tenure insecurity, agricultural and agri-business encroachment, and environmental degradation. Climate change poses a particular threat to marginalized groups in West Africa, including women, because of their inability to adapt to extreme change and their gender roles (Alaga 2011). It represents a significant threat to the social, cultural, economic, and physical well-being of women who retain their economic and social standing in society by dint of their participation in the agricultural sector (Jallah-Scott 2013). Although women constitute an estimated 70 percent of the agricultural labor force in West Africa, traditional biases are expected to continue to favor men in the ownership of fertile land as climate change escalates the degradation of land, increasing the social and economic vulnerability of women.

Environmental changes are likely to reinforce tensions across the region. Population growth and pressure on natural resources will continue to intensify competition between migrants and indigenes over access to arable land, water resources, and pasture. Meanwhile, nomadic pastoralists are likely to continue to search out resources farther south, which will put pressure on coastal regions, as the advance of desertification in some areas of West Africa boosts the incentive for migration as a coping mechanism (Aning and Atta-Asamoah 2011).

Recommendations on Migration

Migration is a critical issue across the subregion because it can both create stress and facilitate resilience, particularly for youth. Despite the importance of the issue, it has received less attention in West Africa than it has in other parts of the world.

Development actors can play a role by assisting governments as they design policies on migration and citizenship with a view to unleashing the potential of migration for economic growth. More research and investigation are needed into migration in West Africa and how to develop policies that can integrate migrants.

Recommendations to address this driver of conflict and fragility include the following:

- Donors and development agencies need to scale up advice and technical support to countries as they seek to clarify citizenship issues, lending archival support, computerizing documentation, and helping ensure the security of archives, for example. There is an urgent need to improve registration and issuance of birth certificates across all countries in the region.

- Help improve countries' ability to issue legal documents to citizens, especially in remote subregions. Countries also need to clarify the legal status of migrants who do not possess identity documentation.

- Support the integration of land and migration issues into climate change adaption. Doing so calls for regional vulnerability screenings, mitigation schemes, and support for the resettlement of populations affected by climate change.

- Support the return of populations displaced by conflicts once it is safe for them to return. Many forcibly displaced populations are still living in camps or with hosts within communities because of past conflicts and displacement during the Mali and Nigeria conflicts. In addition to causing human suffering, protracted displacement is a source of further instability and conflict.

Notes

1. Major wars and civil strife in West Africa include Liberia (1989–96 and 1999–2003); Guinea-Bissau (1998); Sierra Leone (1991–2002); Côte d'Ivoire (2002 and 2010); and, to a lesser extent, Togo (2008).

2. The major valleys of the Senegal and Niger rivers are still underutilized as irrigated farmland (Bossard 2009).

3. According to the OECD, "The Niger River's (Onitsha) stream flow fell by 30 percent between 1971 and 1989; those of the Senegal and Gambia Rivers fell by almost 60 percent" (Bossard 2009, 258).

References

Abdoul, M. 2011. "Policy Frameworks for Cross-Border Transhumance." Concordis Briefing 5, Concordis International, Cambridge, United Kingdom.

Addy, D. N. 2005. "Labour Migration and Regional Integration in West Africa." Paper presented at ECOWAS Conference of Labour Ministers, Abuja, September 19–21.

Adepoju, A. 2005. "Migration in West Africa." Paper prepared for the Policy Analysis Research Programme of the Global Commission on International Migration, Human Resources Development Centre, Lagos.

———. 2006. "The Challenge of Labour Migration between West Africa and the Maghreb." International Migration Papers 84E, International Labour Organization, Geneva.

Adepoju, A., A. Boulton, and M. Levin. n.d. *Promoting Integration through Mobility: Free Movement under ECOWAS.* Geneva: United Nations High Commissioner for Refugees.

Adoho, F., S. Chakravarty, D. T. Korkoyah, M. Lundberg, and A. Tasneem. 2014. "The Impact of an Adolescent Girls Employment Program: The EPAG Project in Liberia." Policy Research Working Paper 6832, World Bank, Washington, DC. http://www-wds .worldbank.org/external/default/WDSContentServer/IW3P/IB/2014/04/03/0001583 49_20140403112059/Rendered/PDF/WPS6832.pdf.

African Union. 2013. "Policy Framework for Pastoralism in Africa: Security, Protecting and Improving the Lives, Livelihoods and Rights of Pastoralist Communities." Department of Rural Economy and Agriculture, Addis Ababa.

Alaga, E. 2011. "Gender and Security Policy in West Africa." Working Paper, Friedrich -Ebert-Stiftung, Wuse II, Nigeria. http://library.fes.de/pdf-files/bueros/nigeria/08162.pdf.

Amnesty International. 1998. "Guinea-Bissau: Human Rights under Fire." Amnesty International, New York. http://www.amnesty.org/en/library/asset/AFR30/004/1998 /en/ab9d8246-d9e4-11dd-af2b-b1f6023af0c5/afr300041998en.pdf.

———. 1999. "Guinea-Bissau: Protecting Human Rights: A New Era?" Amnesty International, New York. http://www.amnesty.org/en/library/asset/AFR30/004/1999 /fr/58dbacbe-e1d8-11dd-a03a-6b5b1e49bce3/afr300041999en.pdf.

Aning, K., and A. Atta-Asamoah. 2011. "Demography, Environment and Conflict in West Africa." KAIPTC Occasional Paper 34, Kofi Annan International Peacekeeping Training Centre, Accra.

Batmanglich, S., and L. Enria. 2014. *Real Jobs in Fragile Contexts: Reframing Youth Employment Programming in Liberia and Sierra Leone.* London: International Alert.

Beall, J., and L.-H. Piron. 2005. *DFID Social Exclusion Review.* London: Department for International Development. http://www.odi.org.uk/sites/odi.org.uk/files/odi-assets /publications-opinion-files/2301.pdf.

Bello Tukur, M. 2005. "Conflicts between Transhumant Pastoralist and Farmers in Nigeria: The Way Out." *Mohammedbello.* http://pastoralist2.wordpress.com/2013/06/11/conflic ts-between-transhumant-pastoralist-and-farmers-in-nigeria-the-way-out.

Ben-Ari, N., and E. Harsch. 2005. "Sexual Violence: An Invisible War Crime." Africa Renewal 18 (4): 1. http://www.un.org/africarenewal/magazine/january-2005/sexual -violence-invisible-war-crime.

Bigombe, B., and G. M. Khadiagala. 2003. "Major Trends Affecting Families in Sub-Saharan Africa." Department of Economic and Social Affairs. http://undesadspd.org /LinkClick.aspx?fileticket=3VvV_mL8oMw%3D&tabid=282.

Bossard, L., ed. 2009. *Regional Atlas on West Africa.* Paris: Organisation for Economic Co-operation and Development–Sahel and West Africa Club.

Brown, A., and M. Lyons. 2010. "Seen But Not Heard: Urban Voice and Citizenship for Street Traders." In *Africa's Informal Workers: Collective Agency, Alliances and Transnational Organizing in Urban Africa,* ed. I. Lindell, 33–45. London: Zed.

Campbell, H. 2014. "Boko Haram: 'Economic Fundamentalism' and Impoverishment Send Unemployed Youths into Religious Militias." *Global Research,* June 4. www .globalresearch.ca/boko-haram-economic-fundamentalism-and-impoverishment-send -unemployed-youths-into-religious-militias/5385934.

Charmes, J. 2012. "The Informal Economy Worldwide: Trends and Characteristics." *Margin: The Journal of Applied Economic Research* 6 (2): 103–22.

Clapham, C. 2003. "Sierra Leone: The Political Economy of Internal Conflict." Working Paper 20, Netherlands Institute of International Relations (Clingendael), The Hague. http://www.clingendael.org/publications/2003/20030700_cru_working_paper_20.pdf.

Commins, S. 2011. "Urban Fragility and Security in Africa." Africa Security Brief 12, Africa Center for Strategic Studies, Washington, DC. http://africacenter.org/wp -content/uploads/2011/04/ASB-12_Final-for-Web.pdf.

Cotula, L., and C. Toulmin. 2004. "Till to Tiller: Linkages between International Remittances and Access to Land in West Africa." LSP Working Paper 14, International Institute for Environment and Development and the Food and Agricultural Organization Livelihood Support Programme, London and Rome.

Cotula, L., C. Toulmin, and C. Hesse. 2004. *Land Tenure and Administration in Africa: Lessons of Experience and Emerging Issues.* International Institute for the Environment and Development and the Food and Agriculture Organization, London and Rome.

Cramer, C. 2010. "Unemployment and Participation in Violence." World Bank, Washington, DC.

Croke, Kevin, and Emilie Rees Smith. 2013. "Côte d'Ivoire Gender Background Note." Learning on Gender and Conflict in Africa Program. http://www.logica-wb.org/PDFs /LOGiCA_DissemNote3.pdf.

De Haan, C., E. Dubern, B. Garancher, and C. Quintero. 2014. "Pastoralism Development in the Sahel: A Road to Stability?" Global Center on Conflict, Security and Development, World Bank, Washington, DC.

de Verdière, M. C., C. Perret, R. Weber, and J. Brito. 2009. *West African Perspectives: Resources for Development.* Paris: Organisation for Economic Co-operation and Development–Sahel and West Africa Club.

Esson, J. 2013. "A Body and a Dream at a Vital Conjuncture: Ghanaian Youth, Uncertainty and the Allure of Football." *Geoforum* 47: 84–92.

Ferguson, J. 1999. *Expectations of Modernity: Myths and Meanings of Urban Life on the Zambian Copperbelt.* Berkeley: University of California Press.

Filani, M. O. 2012. *The Changing Face of Lagos: From Vision to Reform and Transformation.* Brussels: Cities Alliance. http://www.citiesalliance.org/sites/citiesalliance.org/files /Lagos-reform-report-lowres.pdf.

Filmer, D., and L. Fox. 2014. *Youth Employment in Sub-Saharan Africa.* Washington, DC: World Bank.

Fortune, F., O. Ismail, and M. Stephen. 2014. "Rethinking Youth, Livelihoods and Fragility in West Africa: One Size Doesn't Fit All." Fragility, Conflict, and Violence Group, World Bank, Washington, DC.

Fraser, E., and L. Hilker. 2009. "Youth Exclusion, Violence, Conflict, and Fragile States." Report prepared for the Department for International Development by Social Development Direct, London.

Gavin, M. 2008. "Africa's Restless Youth." *Current History* 106 (700): 220–26.

Hervish, A., and D. Clifton. 2012. *Status Report on Adolescence and Young People in Sub-Saharan Africa: Opportunities and Challenges.* Johannesburg and Washington, DC: United Nations Population Fund and Population Reference Bureau.

Hoffman, D. 2011. *The War Machines: Young Men and Violence in Sierra Leone and Liberia.* Durham, NC: Duke University Press.

Honwana, A. M. 2012. *The Time of Youth: Work, Social Change, and Politics in Africa.* Boulder, CO: Kumarian.

ICG (International Crisis Group). 2012. "Curbing Violence in Nigeria." Africa Report 196, ICG, Washington, DC. http://www.crisisgroup.org/~/media/Files/africa/west -africa/nigeria/196-curbing-violence-in-the-jos-crisis.pdf.

———. 2014. "Côte d'Ivoire's Great West: Key to Reconciliation." Africa Report 212, ICG, Washington, DC. http://www.crisisgroup.org/en/regions/africa/west-africa/cote -divoire/212-cote-divoire-s-great-west-key-to-reconciliation.aspx.

IIED (International Institute for Environment and Development). 1999. "Land Tenure and Resource Access in West Africa: Issues and Opportunities for the Next Twenty-Five Years." Working paper, IIED, London.

———. 2001. "Land Rights under Negotiation." *Haramata: Bulletin of the Drylands: People, Policies, Programmes* 39 (May): 12–15.

Ikelegbe, A., and D. Garuba. 2011. "Youth and Conflicts in Western Africa: Regional Threats and Potential." In *ECOWAS and the Dynamics of Conflict and Peace-Building,* ed. T. Jaye, D. Garuba, and S. Amadi, 102–04. Dakar: Council for the Development of Social Science Research in Africa.

IOM (International Organization for Migration). 2014. *Regional Strategy for West and Central Africa, 2014–2016.* Dakar: IOM. http://www.iom.int/files/live/sites/iom/files/Country /docs/IOM-Regional-Strategy-West-and-Central-Africa-2014-2016-EN.pdf.

———. n.d. *West and Central Africa.* Dakar: IOM. https://www.iom.int/cms/west-africa.

IRIN. n.d. "Mali: Culture of Migration Faces Tough New Realities." http://www.irinnews
.org/report/61471/mali-culture-of-migration-faces-tough-new-realities.

Jallah-Scott, P. 2013. "Climate Change in West Africa: The Gender Cultural
Perspective of the Threat to Agriculture and Food Security." In *Perspectives on
West Africa's Future*, Humanitarian Futures Programme, King's College, 12–14.
London: King's College. http://www.humanitarianfutures.org/wp-content/uploads
/2013/06/Perspectives-on-West-Africas-Future.pdf.

Jeffrey, C. 2010. "Geographies of Children and Youth I: Eroding Maps of Life." *Progress
in Human Geography* 34 (4): 496–505.

Jütting, J., and J. R. de Laiglesia. 2009. *Is Informal Normal? Towards More and Better Jobs
in Developing Countries*. Paris: Development Centre of the Organisation for Economic
Co-operation and Development.

Kaplan, S. D. 2014. "What Makes Lagos a Model City." *New York Times*, January 7. http://
www.nytimes.com/2014/01/08/opinion/what-makes-lagos-a-model-city.html.

Keen, D. 2002. "'Since I Am a Dog, Beware My Fangs': Beyond a 'Rational Violence'
Framework in the Sierra Leonean War." Crisis States Program Working Paper 14,
London School of Economics, Development Studies Institute, London.

———. 2005. *Conflict and Collusion in Sierra Leone*. Basingstoke, U.K.: Palgrave
Macmillan.

Keili, F. L. 2008. "Small Arms and Light Weapons Transfer in West Africa: A Stock-
Taking." *Complex Dynamics of Small Arms in West Africa* 4: 5–12. http://www
.ssrnetwork.net/uploaded_files/4508.pdf.

Konseiga, A. 2005. "New Patterns in the Human Migration in West Africa." In *Regional
Integration Beyond the Traditional Trade Benefits: Labor Mobility Contribution*, ed.
P. Lang. *Development Economics and Policy Series* 46, Frankfurt.

Langevang, T. 2008. "'We Are Managing!' Uncertain Paths to Respectable Adulthoods in
Accra, Ghana." *Geoforum* 39 (6): 2039–47. doi:10.1016/j.geoforum.2008.09.003.

Maze, K. 2014. "Land Conflict, Migration, and Citizenship in West Africa: Complex
Diversity and Recurring Challenges: A Desk Study." Fragility, Conflict, and Violence
Group, World Bank, Washington, DC.

McGovern, M. 2011. *Making War in Côte d'Ivoire*. Chicago: University of Chicago
Press.

NRC (Norwegian Refugee Council). 2012. *Land Conflict and Food Security in the
Liberian-Ivorian Border Region*. Oslo: NRC. http://www.ivorycoast.nrc.no/data/doc
_res/NRC_report_e_LR.pdf.pdf.

OECD-SWAC (Organisation for Economic Co-operation and Development–Sahel and
West Africa Club). 2006. *Ecologically Vulnerable Zone of Sahelian Countries, Atlas on
Regional Integration in West Africa*. Environment Series. Paris: OECD-SWAC.

———. 2007. "Strengthening the Role of Actors and Livestock Professionals: A Necessity
to Stimulate Regional Trade." Livestock in the Sahel and West Africa Policy Note 4,
OECD-SWAC, Paris.

Olonisakin, F. 2008. "Conflict Dynamics in West Africa: Background Analysis for the UK
Government's Africa Conflict Prevention Programme." CSDG Paper, Conflict,
Security and Development Group, King's College, London.

Oxfam. 2013. "Mali's Conflict Refugees: Responding to a Growing Crisis." Oxfam Briefing Paper 167, Oxfam, Oxford. http://www.oxfam.org/sites/www.oxfam.org/files /bp167-malis-conflict-refugees-220113-en.pdf.

Philipps, J. 2013. *Ambivalent Rage: Youth Gangs and Urban Protests in Conakry, Guinea.* Paris: Harmattan.

Philipps, J., and T. Grovogui. 2010. "Urban Youth and Political Violence in Conakry." Baseline paper, Search for Common Ground, Washington, DC. https://www.sfcg.org /programmes/ilt/evaluations/GUI_BL_Apr10_Baseline%20Paper%20Urban%20 Youth%20and%20Political%20Violence.pdf.

Refugees International. 2004. *Liberia: Major Effort Needed to Address Gender-Based Violence.* Washington, DC: Refugees International. http://reliefweb.int/report/liberia /liberia-major-effort-needed-address-gender-based-violence.

Reno, William. 2011. *Warfare in Independent Africa (New Approaches to African History).* Cambridge: Cambridge University Press.

Richards, Paul. 1996. *Fighting for the Rain Forest: War, Youth and Resources in Sierra Leone.* London: Heinemann.

Rincon, J. M. 2010. "Ex-combatants, Returnees, Land and Conflict in Liberia." DIIS Working Paper, Danish Institute for International Studies, Copenhagen.

———. 2013. "Liberia: Local Politics, State Building and Reintegration of Populations." *Forced Migration Review* 43: 12–14.

Robert, N. 2004. "The Social Dimension of Regional Integration in ECOWAS." Working Paper 49, International Labour Organization, Geneva.

Shimeles, A. 2010. "Migration Patterns, Trends and Policy Issues in Africa." Working Paper 119, African Development Bank Group, Tunis.

Sommers, M. 2007. *West Africa's Youth Employment Challenge: The Case of Guinea, Liberia, Sierra Leone and Côte d'Ivoire.* Vienna: United Nations Industrial Development Organization.

UNECA (United Nations Economic Commission for Africa). 2011. "Addressing the Youth Education and Employment Nexus in the Global Economy." Africa Youth Report, UNECA, Addis Ababa. http://www.uneca.org/sites/default/files/publications /african_youth_report_2011_final.pdf.

Van der Geest, K. 2010. "Rural Youth Employment in Developing Countries: A Global View." Overview/Synthesis 1, Food and Agriculture Organization, Rome. http:// dare.uva.nl/document/333951.

Van Gyampo, R. E., and F. Obeng-Odoom. 2013. "Youth Participation in Local and National Development in Ghana: 1620–2013." *Journal of Pan African Studies* 5 (9): 129–49.

Vigh, H. 2006. *Navigating Terrains of War: Youth and Soldiering in Guinea-Bissau.* Oxford: Berghahn.

Walton, O. 2010. "Youth, Armed Violence, and Job Creation Programs." GSDRC Research Paper, Norwegian Peacebuilding Centre, Oslo.

World Bank. 2013. *Promoting State Legitimacy, Stability and Cohesion in Areas of Low Population Density: The Case of Mali.* Washington, DC: World Bank.

Zongo, M. 2010. "Land Tenure and Migration in West Africa." Briefing Paper, Agence Française de Développement, Land Tenure and Development Technical Committee, Paris.

Chapter 4

Redressing Regional Imbalances and Distributing Mineral Resource Revenues More Equitably

Inequalities between regions and the exclusion of parts of the population are recurring drivers of conflict in West Africa. Both phenomena reflect deep-rooted factors. Awareness of these imbalances and deliberate policies to mitigate their negative effects are the most effective ways to decrease their salience as drivers of conflict.

The unequal distribution of revenues from mineral resources also contributes to fragility across the subregion. Greater awareness of the perceptions or reality of inequitable distribution and efforts to offset the problem and enhance transparency and governance are critical to managing the risk of instability.

The Time Bomb of Regional Imbalances

Wide inequalities between regions and the exclusion and marginalization of segments of the population have triggered both large-scale and low-level violence and conflict in West Africa in recent decades. Perceptions of inequality have increased the tendency to rebel against the central government, as witnessed in the 2012 Tuareg-led rebellion against the seat of power in Bamako in Mali, the 2007 rebellion in Niger, the much less violent Casamance uprising in Senegal that has been ongoing since 1982, and land clashes between the Nanumbas and the Konkombas in northern Ghana. The rise of violent ethnonationalism in Côte d'Ivoire also reflected perceptions of inequality and exclusion (Olonisakin 2008).

Horizontal Inequalities and the Risk of Conflict

The existence of severe inequalities between culturally formed groups are known as *horizontal inequalities*. Where cultural differences coincide and align with economic and political differences between groups and are not addressed or counterbalanced by political accommodation, they can significantly raise the risk of conflict (Stewart 2010).

Patterns of marginalization and exclusion have been a key cause of conflict and violence in West Africa and a source of perceived injustice (Stewart 2008; Cederman, Weidmann, and Gleditsch 2011; Cederman, Gleditsch, and Buhaug 2013), not least because the countries of the subregion are ethnically, religiously, culturally, and regionally heterogeneous. The overlap between regional and sociocultural characteristics in many groups in West Africa has led to significant geographical schisms within countries. In Côte d'Ivoire, The Gambia, Guinea, Liberia, Nigeria, and Sierra Leone, these schisms have been between the coastal regions and inland/northern areas. In Burkina Faso, Mali, and Niger, they have been between the north and the south. Horizontal inequalities also underscored the civil war in Liberia, where a major source of tension was the cultural differences and inequality between indigenous groups and the Krio (emancipated slaves and their descendants). Economic and political marginalization also contributed to ethnic violence in Guinea and Togo and worsened stratification in Mauritania.

Although there is strong overlap between region, ethnicity, and at times religion across West Africa, regional inequalities are not necessarily more relevant to political events, including conflict, than ethnic inequalities. Indeed, it is argued that group mobilization occurs primarily along ethnic lines or based on a coalition of identities. In some countries (such as Côte d'Ivoire and Nigeria), religious differences reinforce ethno-regional differences (Langer and Stewart 2014).

Identities are shifting and mutable. They depend on historical experience, group leadership, and context, with the salience of particular identities with regard to conflict often changing over time (Langer and Stewart 2014). In Nigeria's Middle Belt region, for instance, settlers and indigenes have fought over land, citizenship, identity, and political exclusion since 2001 (ICG 2012). These tensions interlock with religious and ethnic dimensions, giving the conflict a mutating aspect (Higazi 2009; Ehrhardt 2012).

Although horizontal inequalities and regional imbalances raise the risk of conflict, they are not automatic triggers. Other factors must be present for violent conflict to erupt. The manner in which inequalities are managed can decrease their salience as drivers of violence and conflict.

Despite the significant potential for regional disparities to trigger conflict and contribute to political mobilization and violence, few West African governments have addressed this source of injustice and grievance. In fact, several governments have deliberately excluded sections of the population, exacerbating intergroup tensions. A notable exception is Ghana, which has moderated the destabilizing effect of the developmental and ethno-regional divide between north and south by implementing a range of politically inclusive measures and policies. It has made "substantial progress" since 2000 in improving the socioeconomic situation in the north as well as in the south, even though the divide is still sizable (Langer and Stewart 2014). Niger has also made great progress of late in bridging its internal schisms, having taken important steps to address the marginalization of its Tuareg population (Langer and Stewart 2014).

The Origins of Regional Disparities

Within the countries of West Africa, significant socioeconomic disparities are evident between north and south and between coastal and inland areas (table 4.1). The coastal regions are generally more fertile than the hinterland, as they benefit from abundant and evenly spread rainfall throughout the year. Under colonial rule, they were the locus of the cash crops industry; the drier savannah country of the interior was relegated largely to subsistence farming. Policies adopted under colonial rule capitalized on these natural advantages, reinforcing the coastal-interior imbalance, as the French in Côte d'Ivoire and the British in Ghana and Nigeria built their capitals in the south. The regional imbalance in Côte d'Ivoire, which has experienced severe conflict between north and south, was negligible until the 1950s, when the French introduced cash crops in the south and southeast (Hinderink and Tempelman 1979). In Ghana, the socioeconomic divide between north and south was already present at independence (Langer and Stewart 2014). In Nigeria, the sharp socioeconomic north-south divide that developed from the early 1900s persisted and even deteriorated throughout the postindependence period.

The policies adopted in the postcolonial period perpetuated these imbalances, with many countries maintaining the development bias against the interior. Leaders and elites capitalized on the superior infrastructure, educational levels, and markets along the coast, as they built independent states on the systems and structures they had inherited. Schools and academic institutions were also concentrated in the south or along the coast—a further legacy of colonialism—which benefited ethnic groups from those regions, such as the

Table 4.1 Access to Electricity and Education in the North and South of Côte d'Ivoire, Ghana, Mali, and Nigeria
(percent of population)

Country	Access to electricity			No formal education		
	North	South	North-South ratio	North	South	North-South ratio
Côte d'Ivoire	43	65	0.7	69	41	1.7
Ghana	31	66	0.5	58	14	4.3
Mali	12	20	0.6	81	78	1.0
Nigeria	34	66	0.5	62	9	7.2

Sources: Langer and Stewart 2014, based on data from MSLS 2013 (Côte d'Ivoire 2012); Ghana Statistical Service 2009 (Ghana 2008); Samaké and others 2007 (Mali 2006); and National Population Commission 2008 (Nigeria 2008).

Ewe in the west of Ghana and the Igbo in Nigeria. At independence, Ghana had only one secondary school in the north (Roe and others 1992); Nigeria had 1,305 secondary schools in the south and just 18 in the north (Mustapha 2006).

The underpopulated Saharan north of the Sahelien countries, such as Mali and Niger, also tended to be neglected. This southern bias helped ignite the first postindependence conflict in West Africa, the Biafran War (1967–70). Amidst fears of political exclusion and the loss of their monopoly over bureaucratic offices, the southeastern-based Igbo ethnic group pushed for secession from the rest of the country. It also hoped to secure control over some of the oilfields and the agricultural base in the south.

In Nigeria, the risk of conflict prompted the government to redesign the constitution and make power more diffuse as a bulwark against significant political inequalities; it also relocated the capital from Lagos to Abuja, in the center of the country (Mustapha 2007). The move improved the balance between north and south, although regional disparities are still very severe, despite efforts to redistribute oil revenues across the country (table 4.2). In Togo, the political domination of northerners has counterbalanced economic inequalities between north and south (Langer and Stewart 2014).

The Durability of Horizontal Inequalities

To address horizontal inequalities and redress regional imbalances, it is sometimes necessary not just to level the playing field but to give more than proportionate resources and opportunities to deprived groups. Parental circumstances and the diminished social and cultural capital of deprived groups often perpetuate inequalities across generations. This durability of horizontal inequalities makes it important to focus on the economic as well as the social and cultural dimensions of inequality.

Insufficient recognition of and allowance by the government of the distinct cultural identity of the Tuareg people in Mali has compounded socioeconomic

Table 4.2 Access to Electricity and Education in Nigeria, by Ethnicity and Religion, 2008
(percent of population)

Ethnicity/religion	Access to electricity	No formal education
Ethnicity		
Yoruba	75	10
Igbo	70	5
Hausa-Fulani	35	80
Religion		
Christian	58	10
Muslim	41	66

Source: Langer and Stewart 2014, based on data from National Population Commission 2008.

and political grievances, which have found expression in violent uprisings against the government since independence. The flawed implementation of decentralization as a means of addressing grievances has contributed to tensions (World Bank 2013). The recurrence of conflict has widened development gaps and destroyed infrastructure. Although the deprivation of northern groups, including the Tuareg, is "not much greater" than that of some groups in the south in terms of objective measures, the Tuareg people "perceive themselves as being discriminated against in many spheres" (Langer and Stewart 2014, 55).

The multidimensional nature of horizontal inequalities means that grievances can occur along a number of dimensions, including political power at various levels, socioeconomic status, and cultural status. The greatest potential for conflict comes where political inequalities, or exclusion, intersect with socioeconomic inequalities, because this confluence heightens the risk of group mobilization (Langer 2005; Cederman, Weidmann, and Gleditsch 2011). In Côte d'Ivoire, for example, the founding president, Félix Houphouët-Boigny, ran an inclusive government and promoted national cohesion for decades through patronage mechanisms, despite the existence of severe socioeconomic inequalities between the north and the south (table 4.3) (Stewart 2010). His death, in December 1993, combined with an economic crisis and a ferocious succession struggle, helped stoke interethnic and regional tensions. It also marked the abandonment of ethno-regional balancing, which contributed substantially to the civil war a decade later.

Like Côte d'Ivoire, Ghana is marked by major ethnic, social, and economic cleavages between its northern and southern regions. Unlike Côte d'Ivoire, however, these differences have not manifested themselves in a sense of "Northernness" as the basis of political cohesion, nor has there been a "north versus south patterning of political alignments" (Brown 1982, 42).

Table 4.3 Access to Electricity and Education in Côte d'Ivoire, by Ethnicity and Religion, 2013
(percent of population)

Ethnicity/religion	Access to electricity	No formal education
Ethnicity		
Northern Mandé	78	70
Krou	70	23
Akan	55	41
Voltaic	54	64
Southern Mandé	54	43
Religion		
Christians	36	33
Muslims	27	66

Source: Langer and Stewart 2014, based on data from MSLS and others 2013.

Confronted by major ethno-regional tensions and mobilization at independence, Ghana's first president, Kwame Nkrumah, moved to promote national integration and build a regionally and ethnically inclusive cabinet. Some of his efforts were institutionalized, both formally and informally, with the president usually hailing from the south or the east and the vice president from the north.

Significant socioeconomic inequalities between the north and south of Ghana, and correspondingly, between northern and southern ethnic groups and between Muslims and Christians, have persisted since independence (table 4.4). The north-south socioeconomic divide has not escalated into a national-level conflict in recent decades largely because of attempts to promote political accommodation throughout much of the postcolonial period. Measures such as economic redistribution to the deprived northern regions and the inclusion of northern elites in key political institutions, as introduced by successive Ghanaian regimes, helped reduce the destabilizing potential of the north-south cleavage (Langer and Stewart 2014). The example of Ghana underscores the importance of recognition and acknowledgment of these inequalities, as well as of political accommodation, in building national cohesion.

Recommendations for Addressing Regional Imbalances

Many West African countries are grappling with the challenge of regional imbalances. Development actors must better balance the imperatives of growth pole strategies with strategies that address the fact that some regions have historically been marginalized, both economically and in terms of service provision. More research and investigation needs to be conducted on the impact of regional imbalances at all levels and ways in which to address the issues faced by lagging regions.

Table 4.4 Access to Electricity and Education in Ghana, by Ethnicity and Religion, 2009
(percent of population)

Ethnicity/religion	Access to electricity	No formal education
Ethnicity		
Akan	71	8
Ewe	51	16
Ga-Dangme	64	13
Mole-Dagbani	39	52
Religion		
Christians	64	14
Muslims	55	43

Source: Langer and Stewart 2014, based on data from Ghana Statistical Service 2009.

Recommendations to address this driver of conflict and fragility include the following:

- Provide policy and programmatic support to governments to address regional inequalities at the national level as part of a broader agenda of inclusive growth and equity. More investment by donors and development agencies is needed to support lagging regions, particularly at the periphery. These regions' development priorities need to be better integrated into national development plans. When lagging regions are close to or overlap with border areas, significant effort is needed to support cross-border trade and border management. In particular, a balance needs to be struck between growth pole strategies that focus on the regions most endowed with natural and human resources and strategies that support lagging regions.

- Provide support to improve the local governance of lagging regions. Most lagging regions experience governance problems. In some cases, the problem is one of capacity, but frequently it reflects dysfunctions in the modalities of governance in remote regions. Models of local governance (decentralization, deconcentration, federalism) are not always adapted as they should be. Lagging regions also experience particular challenges in service delivery, in particular in ensuring security and justice. Improving local governance and the delivery of basic services should therefore be a priority in lagging regions.

- Support governments in their efforts to systematically monitor and measure regional inequalities. Where appropriate, donors and development partners should offer technical expertise to monitor group-based inequalities and help identify policy implications. Growing subregional inequalities across all of Africa is a major source of concern; improved monitoring is essential to inform policies.

- Support a systematic stock-taking of subregional inequalities in West Africa, in collaboration with regional organizations, such as the Economic Community of West African States (ECOWAS). Encourage the cross-country exchange of lessons regarding the management of subregional imbalances.

Avoiding the "Resource Curse" by Recognizing and Addressing Social Grievances

Competition over natural resources, and tensions fueled by resource revenues, have been a critical component of much of the political violence and large-scale conflict experienced across West Africa over the past two decades. The subregion has repeatedly fallen prey to the "resource curse" (of which the propensity for conflict is one manifestation). Illicit trade in diamonds and timber funded and perpetuated the civil wars in Côte d'Ivoire, Liberia, and Sierra Leone; uprisings and violence have plagued Nigeria's oil-rich Niger Delta; and discoveries of uranium and gold have stoked tensions in Mali and Niger. In various conflicts, warring factions have been able to access "lootable" resources through artisanal extraction, which has arguably helped fuel and prolong "grievance-based" insurgencies.[1] With the waning of conventional civil wars in West Africa, the extractive industries may be stirring political violence and tensions among local communities and producing subregions. The capture of resources from the lucrative extractives economy may also support the illegitimate enrichment of political elites, which in turn generates significant political tension and violence.

Among the 11 countries covered in this chapter, the International Monetary Fund (IMF) considers 7 to be resource rich (IMF 2012b) (table 4.5). Over the past two decades, West Africa experienced a boom in extractive industry investment, on the back of soaring commodity prices and heightened resource demands from the world's emerging economies. This boom was fueled by vast new discoveries of valuable and increasingly accessible resources, such as oil and iron ore, across the region. In response, governments adopted new or revised existing mining codes to stimulate foreign direct investment in mineral extraction (Bridge 2004; Otto and others 2006).

Unprecedented levels of foreign investment in the extractive industries have presented significant economic opportunities for the region. In Ghana, the production value of mining—predominantly gold—grew by 290 percent between 2000 and 2012 (ICMM 2012, cited in Standing and Hilson 2013). Ghana's experience in ensuring transparency provides important lessons to other countries (box 4.1). In Guinea, which possesses an estimated 30 percent of global bauxite reserves, mining accounted for about a quarter of GDP and 85 percent of export earnings in 2012 (MGI 2013). Based on projected iron ore prices and production growth, the "tier-one" Simandou project is expected to generate revenues of more than 130 percent of Guinea's GDP (MGI 2013). The commencement of iron ore production has also boosted real GDP growth in Sierra Leone (World Bank 2013). Mali has become Africa's third-largest gold producer, with 71 percent of its 2012 export earnings coming from mining (Smith 2012). Iron ore production in Mauritania is expected to rise from 12 million tons in 2012 to 18 million tons in 2015 (EITI n.d.). The industry accounts for a quarter of its $4 billion economy and half of its exports (Manson and Blas 2014). Nigeria received 91 percent of its export revenues from oil and gas in 2014 (OPEC n.d.).

Resource-Related Challenges at the Regional Level

Experience demonstrates that mismanaging the benefits of extraction can lead to tension and conflict. Surges in investment have frequently been accompanied by increases in social mobilization and tensions (Maconachie, Srinivasan,

Table 4.5 Gross Domestic Product and Significance of Extractive Industry Investment in West Africa, by Country, 2005 and 2012

Country	GDP (billions of 2005 dollars)[a]		GDP per capita (billions of 2005 dollars)[a]		Real GDP growth rate (percent)[a]	Extractive industry contribution to GDP (percent)[b]			Percent export income from extractives revenues[b]			Percent of tax revenue from extractives revenues 2006–10[c]	EITI membership status, 2013[d]	Key natural resources[e]	IMF classification 2012[f]
	2005	2012	2005	2012	2005–12	2005[g]	2012[h]	2005–12[i]	2005[g]	2012[h]	2005–12				
Burkina Faso	5.5	8.1	407	493	6	0	18	6	1	78	37	—	Compliant	Gold	Resource poor
Côte d'Ivoire	16.4	19.0	941	958	2	13	18	16	28	35	32	—	Compliant	Oil, gas	Resource rich
Ghana	10.7	18.4	502	724	8	9	19	13	34	63	53	—	Compliant	Gold, oil	Resource poor
Guinea[j]	2.9	3.5	307	308	3	23	25	24	78	85	78	23	Candidate	Mining products	Resource rich
Liberia	0.5	1.2	166	276	11	—	—	—	—	—	—	16	Compliant	Gold, diamonds, iron ore	Resource rich
Mali	5.3	7.1	444	480	5	14	15	17	65	71	75	13	Compliant	Gold	Resource rich
Niger	3.4	5.0	258	290	5	7	17	11	47	76	59	—	Compliant	Uranium	Resource rich
Nigeria	112.2	177.6	804	1052	6	40	21	30	98	84	91	76	Compliant	Oil, gas	Resource rich
Senegal	8.7	10.9	773	797	4	4	6	5	24	32	28	—	Candidate	Mining products	Resource poor
Sierra Leone	1.6	2.6	318	435	7	—	—	—	—	—	—	—	Compliant	Diamond	Resource poor

Note: A country is characterized as resource rich if it has natural resource revenues that represented at least 20 percent of its total fiscal revenue or natural resource exports that represented at least 20 percent of its total exports between 2006 and 2010. Mauritania is not included. EITI = Extractive Industry Transparency Initiative; IMF = International Monetary Fund.

a. World Development Indicators.
b. Maconachie, Srinivasan, and Menzies 2014, based on data from World Integrated Trade Solutions (WITS) database and World Development Indicators. Extractive export revenue comprises the commodities in SITC sections 27 (crude fertilizer, minerals); 28 (metalliferous ores, scrap); 68 (nonferrous metals); 3 (mineral fuels); and 97 (gold nonmonetary excluding ores).
c. IMF 2012a.
d. EITI n.d.
e. EITI n.d.; IMF 2012a.
f. IMF 2012a. Countries are characterized as resource rich if they have either resource revenue or exported at least 20 percent of total fiscal revenue and exports over 2006–10 (average).
g. 2006 for Nigeria.
h. 2011 for Burkina Faso and 2008 for Guinea.
i. Last available trade data are from 2008.

BOX 4.1

Lessons from Ghana on Transparency in Extractives

Even before 2003, when it joined the Extractive Industry Transparency Initiative (EITI), Ghana was on a path toward greater transparency in the sector, as part of the democratization process and the emergence of a free media, which took place against the backdrop of strong civil society engagement in public affairs (Wilson and Van Alstine 2014). Ghana has been a pioneer in the implementation of EITI at both the national and subnational levels. It was certified as EITI compliant in 2010.

Civil society organizations in Ghana are playing a greater role in advocating for the interests of the public and contributing to the deliberations of parliamentary committees charged with oversight in the sector. In recent years, several civil society actors have developed frameworks for collective engagement with the extractives sector. Publish What You Pay—Ghana was launched in 2006, and the Platform on Oil and Gas (CSPOG) was established in 2010. Both groups bring together civil society actors and academic institutions.

The international watchdog Revenue Watch Institute ranked Ghana 15th of 58 countries on resource governance in 2013. Ghana also scored high on the institutional and legal setting components and quality control. Revenue Watch Institute also praised the transparent manner in which Ghana has managed its oil revenue fund, in particular its efforts to provide citizens with access to information on inflows and outflows of finances into the fund (Ghana News Agency 2014).

and Menzies 2014). Resource dependency may also expose the subregion to the dangers inherent in boom-and-bust commodity cycles, which can put pressure on the public finances of resource-dependent countries and deepen and extend inequalities, potentially exacerbating horizontal divisions (OECD 2013).

When the unequal distribution of resource rents intersects with ethnic or religious cleavages, the risk of ethnic rebellion or secession can escalate and spread (Stewart 2002; Østby 2008). In Niger, the primary source of resentment of the Tuareg rebel group Mouvement des Nigeriens pour la Justice (MNJ) stems from the recent expansion of uranium mining in the Aïr-Talak-Tamesna region of the country; the movement has demanded a more equitable share of mining revenues (Keenan 2008). Though the Tuareg rebellion in Mali is not directly associated with conflict over extractives, there are major concerns that events there might reignite tensions in Niger with the French mining company Areva (Elischer 2013).

Porous borders across the region have historically enabled conflict by acting as conduits through which armed struggles spill over into neighboring countries. Smuggling and the illicit trade of lootable resources, specifically diamonds, exacerbated the 1991–2002 civil war in Sierra Leone, through the cross-border exchange of diamonds for weapons with Charles Taylor of Liberia, which fueled and prolonged the conflict. Rebel groups in Côte d'Ivoire illegally exploited and exported diamonds, gold, and cocoa to finance the conflict between 2002 and 2012 (UN 2012).

The illicit transborder flow of resources such as diamonds, timber, and gold is very difficult to regulate or contain, even with sanctions or embargoes, because powerful private interests often control it. Moreover, such measures can deprive the government of potential revenue that could be used to promote development. The harmonization of the 3 percent tax on diamond exports in Guinea, Liberia, and Sierra Leone marks an attempt to reduce the extent to which rough diamonds can disappear into clandestine trade networks. Where there is even a small difference in diamond export taxes between neighboring states, smuggling will likely occur into the country where the tax rates are lowest (D4D 2006).

The discovery in West Africa of some of the richest mineral lodes on the continent presents fresh challenges for investors and governments across the region. Geological exploration revealed a multiplicity of economically exploitable low-value, high-bulk "mineral clusters" (of iron ore and bauxite, for example), which attracted the attention of foreign investors (World Bank 2010). Many of these deposits are located near national borders, underlining the need to address transborder social and environmental impacts, particularly in light of the region's porous boundary zones and history of conflict.[2] An integrated transboundary approach will be required to manage and monitor the impacts and limit the risk of interstate conflict.

Another issue is the risk of tensions over the development of shared infrastructure for the export of bulk minerals. Governments must balance the challenges of infrastructure development with security imperatives and the desire to retain control of the benefits of resource extraction and associated positive externalities (Maconachie, Srinivasan, and Menzies 2014).

The stretch of coastline from Gabon to Sierra Leone—an oil-rich area of strategic importance—has been identified as a site of potential conflict. The Bakassi Peninsula, between Nigeria and Cameroon, has experienced extreme tension in the past; the discovery of new offshore hydrocarbon deposits in other areas of the Gulf of Guinea threatens to foment tension between neighbors. Seventy percent of Africa's oil production comes from the Gulf of Guinea, which has been hit by a spate of attacks by maritime pirates, and production is likely to continue to rise in light of increasing geostrategic interest in the region (UNODC 2013).

Regional governance bodies have a critical role to play in addressing interstate tensions related to the extractives boom. Both ECOWAS and the West African Economic and Monetary Union (WAEMU) have assumed more proactive roles in mining policy and governance in the region. Initiatives include efforts to harmonize regional mining policy and legal frameworks, such as the ECOWAS Directive and the WAEMU Common Mining Code. These policies signal an interest in developing and implementing a unified mining code for West Africa, which could help mitigate instability across the region.

Intrastate Contests over the Distribution of Resource Revenues

The historical tendency of ruling elites to capture resource revenues to fuel patronage politics underpins contests over resource revenue distribution between national and subnational governments in West Africa. The redistribution of resource wealth to subnational levels in resource-rich countries such as Ghana and Nigeria remains a challenge, given the intensity of contestations between opposing groups over natural resource wealth (Maconachie, Srinivasan, and Menzies 2014). Traditional authorities, district councils, and elites have all sought greater control over mineral wealth, as affected communities have endeavored to minimize adverse impacts; assert claims to identity and land; and maximize returns from mining, as in the disputes over uranium mining in the Aïr-Talak-Tamesna region of Niger and the dispute between AngloGold Ashanti and small-scale miners in Ghana's Obuasi region (Okoh 2013). The dynamic is complicated by the extractive companies, which frequently align with power holders in their efforts to secure a stable operating environment. Part of this dynamic includes entering into opaque deals over access to resources. The inherent complexity of these developments and agreements undermines attempts at accountability and produces institutional arrangements that are likely to prioritize the demands of extractives companies over local development (Bebbington and others 2008).

The decentralization of natural resource revenues and decision making has attracted much attention as a measure to counter grievance-driven resource conflict at the local level. However, decentralization of revenues can be problematic where resource endowments are unevenly distributed geographically or societies are divided along ethnic, religious, or linguistic lines. Distribution that privileges producing regions can exacerbate tensions and motivate ethnic- or identity-based conflict—particularly given the fact that communities often bear much of the cost of extraction but do not see revenues translate into local development (Maconachie, Srinivasan, and Menzies 2014). In Nigeria, for example, 95 percent of export earnings and 65 percent of government revenues in 2010 came from the oil and gas sector, but only 9 out of 36 states produced oil (Aguilar, Caspary, and Seiler 2011). It has grappled with the question of how to divide its oil wealth across states. The northern states have supported the principle of land mass and population as criteria for resource distribution, while the oil-producing states have argued in favor of a derivative principle in which the producing regions receive larger allocations. Since 1999, 13 percent of oil proceeds have been distributed among the 25 percent of states that produce oil (Eze 2013).

Corruption remains a longstanding issue. Central governments may resist devolving revenues to the local level or supporting tax schemes that benefit catchment communities. In Sierra Leone, for example, the reluctance of the central government to devolve resources and decision making to local governments undermines local development and strengthens the relationship between paramount chiefs and central government elites (Prichard 2013).

If carried out in a transparent and participatory fashion, decentralized management of natural resources can be an effective way of channeling benefits to local communities; it can also reduce horizontal inequalities between groups (Brosio 2003; Ross, Lujala, and Rustad 2012; Brosio and Singh 2013). The three broad mechanisms to decentralize revenues are local taxes levied directly on the resource industry, direct transfers from the central government (such as the derivation principle employed by Nigeria), and indirect transfers from the central government.

The devolution of revenues to subnational actors can also trigger conflict. Ghana's Mineral Development Fund (MDF) offers an example of the development benefits of local-level revenue sharing, but it also demonstrates how such mechanisms can introduce new forms of inequality and insecurity through the ineffective use of funds, poor transparency and accountability (it funnels 45 percent of total mineral revenues through traditional authorities without effective accountability and transparency mechanisms),[3] and weak citizen participation in decision making (Standing and Hilson 2013). These concerns, often underscored by a high degree of elite capture and patronage, can unravel community cohesion and exacerbate tension and conflict. Concerns about collusion between traditional authorities and mining companies also risk marginalizing community interests and damaging cohesion.

Intracommunity Conflict Related to Natural Resources

Resource extraction has generated significant social, economic, and political stress at the community level around labor and employment, loss of land and livelihoods, environmental degradation, and insufficient consultation and compensation. Tensions around extraction can serve as triggers for violence, tapping into deep-seated structural drivers of conflict.

One source of tension comes from the high, and frequently unmet, expectations that extractive and mining companies will create significant employment opportunities. Mining has long represented a valuable source of employment and income to communities across West Africa, with artisanal and small-scale mining in particular appealing to young, single, unemployed, and unskilled laborers. However, many large companies create resource enclaves that are disconnected from the wider society (Ferguson 2006; Ackah-Baidoo 2012) and benefit largely elite groups (Ferguson 2006). Because of the capital-intensive nature of large-scale operations, the number of jobs created is usually small in comparison to the revenue generated. In Mali, for example, the Sadiola gold mine created one mining job for every $700,000 invested; the Randgold mine directly created 127 jobs, or one job for every $1.23 million invested (Pegg 2006). Some of the most vocal community opposition to the expansion of extractive industries in West Africa has been linked to companies' poor record of job creation (and by perceptions that working conditions are poor and labor exploited). Meanwhile, the migration of labor to catchment communities upends the social balance, affects resource availability, and places further pressure on the land through activities such as farming and hunting (Hilson 2002).

The appropriation of land and other livelihood resources for the expansion of extractive industries can hinder local development and lead to severe community dislocation. Conflict may occur over the control of space, the governance of territory, access to land and water, human rights, and revenue distribution. The loss of livelihood resources associated with large-scale open-pit mining is particularly damaging to communities. Mine development is often integrated with the construction of dams, roads, railways, ports, and other infrastructure, which risks intensifying competition over land, water, and energy (Bebbington and others 2008). In a 2000 report, civil society actors in Ghana described human rights violations in the country's gold mines as a "well-established pattern common to all mining communities" (Van Criekinge 2008). It revealed that gold mining operations had displaced more than 30,000 people in the Tarkwa District. In Guinea, Rio Tinto and China's Chalco admitted that "the number of displaced people [by the Simandou iron mine] is larger than many were expecting," numbering more than 10,000 (Els 2013).

Land use conflicts between communities, companies, and governments can become particularly intense when tenure is unclear—when different tenure systems overlap, ownership of surface versus subsoil is disputed, or conflicting claims over valuable minerals or hydrocarbons are at stake (Maconachie, Srinivasan, and Menzies 2014). Land acquisition associated with extractive industry investments can create and heighten existing conflicts over land, particularly when tenure is obscure or contested (Cotula 2014). In Liberia, the government issued concessions on more than half the country's land area, much of which had long been used by rural populations, opening the floodgates for disputes and tensions (EWER 2012; Land Commission of Liberia 2012). Even when companies agree to relocate communities or compensate them for land they appropriate, it is often difficult to adequately compensate for losses, particularly where land is linked to social, cultural, and spiritual identity. The fact that oil extraction in the Niger Delta occurs on indigenous lands and that companies and communities place very different values on the land may partially explain the protracted nature of the insurgency.

Resource extraction also risks undermining traditional forms of income generation, marginalizing peasant agriculture and leading to the deagrarianization of communities (Fisher 2007; Jønsson and Bryceson 2009). Artisanal and small-scale miners have been supplanted in Ghana, where central ministries granted concessions to companies in areas that were already occupied. The move strained relations between small and large-scale operators. The granting of concessions to large mining companies has usually resulted in the eviction of small-scale miners, although it has occasionally led to the demarcation of land for artisanal mining alongside large-scale operations. Tensions with the community regarding overlapping mining concessions in southeast Liberia were addressed by allowing small-scale miners to mine in selected areas and sell their gold independently (Small 2012).

Large-scale natural resource investments can impose significant environmental costs on the host country, through water pollution, deforestation, loss of biodiversity, and soil degradation. The environmental devastation wrought by extractive industries on the livelihoods of local populations is evident in the Niger Delta in Nigeria, where flaring, spillage, and waste have impinged on the livelihoods of local fishermen and farmers. Although the government has accepted environmental degradation as a legitimate cost of doing business (Pegg and Zabbey 2013), this negative externality has been a key driver of oil-related conflicts in the Niger Delta over the past two decades (Watts and Ibaba 2011).

Where companies and political elites reap the benefits of oil and producing communities are not adequately compensated for the social and environmental costs of extraction, the potential grounds for grievance and conflict increase. To prevent conflict, some companies are taking a more proactive role in incorporating environmental considerations into their business strategies (Maconachie, Srinivasan, and Menzies 2014).

The absence of community consultation and the tendency to privilege relations with elites or traditional elders can also lead to tensions, especially where their interests diverge from the interests of the rest of the community. Community consultation and participation over Sierra Leone's iron ore investments has been weak (Fanthorpe and Gabelle 2013). It remains unclear whether community engagement in the Niger Delta has had a positive impact (Pegg and Zabbey 2013).

Most West African countries require environmental and social impact assessments (ESIAs) of mining and petroleum investment, but the requirements do not necessarily facilitate environmentally sound forms of development (Maconachie, Srinivasan, and Menzies 2014). Challenges include insufficient company expertise, a lack of institutional government capacity in the scrutiny of ESIAs, failure to monitor compliance, and the weak negotiating powers of environmental agencies (Cotula 2014). Regulatory instruments also risk being coopted and rendered toothless by political elites who overstate the benefits of investment and understate its adverse impacts.

Recommendations for Distributing Mineral Resource Revenues More Equitably

The conversion of resource rents into sustainable development—with meaningful citizen engagement—remains an ongoing challenge in West Africa. If managed effectively, resource endowments can generate significant revenue flows, which could greatly improve the quality of life across the region.

To overcome the historical challenges of weak governance and elite capture of resources, and increase the community's social and economic benefits, West African countries, along with development partners, need to both broaden and deepen their focus on governance reform. Efforts should look beyond building the capacity of national institutions involved with extractives to include developing regional mechanisms, engaging subnational authorities, and understanding the influence of developed country regulation on outcomes in West Africa. Particular attention needs to be paid to raising awareness of conflict triggers that arise in host communities and developing more effective citizen engagement frameworks. A key priority is to broaden governance initiatives through stringent monitoring of corporate governance and regulatory regimes from developing countries and subnational state and quasi-state authorities. More research and investigation are needed to deepen understanding of how extractives and mining companies relate to and interact with communities at the local level.

Recommendations to address this driver of conflict and fragility include the following:

- Gain a deeper, multilayered understanding of the political economy of extraction in different country contexts, at both the macro and micro levels in order to influence design of investments in the sector.

- Broaden the understanding of governance as it relates to extractives, encourage the recognition of the role played by natural resource revenues in political bargaining at the local level, examine dynamics at the subnational level between different actors as a means to inform dialogue between stakeholders, and encourage the acknowledgment of transboundary resource management issues.

- Encourage transparency that goes beyond revenue reporting to encompass the social, environmental, and livelihood costs of investment in extractives, as part of the focus on governance.

- Increase investment in mechanisms to reduce community-based conflicts and community grievances around extractive industry projects.

Notes

1. A wide range of scholars has explored the links between lootable resources and civil violence, drawing different conclusions from compiled datasets on wars and intermittent conflicts (see Collier and Hoeffler 2004; Berdal 2005; Korf 2005; Regan and Norton 2005). Humphreys (2005) notes that diamonds tend to shorten civil wars by facilitating military victories, not negotiated settlements. In contrast, Ross (2004a, 2004b) observes that lootable resources could make conflict so profitable that one or more combatants lose their incentive to reach a peace settlement. Le Billon (2001, 2006) reinforces this view.
2. The Nimba region of Côte d'Ivoire, Guinea, and Sierra Leone and the Mano River watershed, spanning the border between Liberia and Sierra Leone, are two transborder mining areas of regional sensitivity (World Bank 2010).
3. It is currently unclear how decisions about the use of funds are made. Consequently, the government has discussed plans to implement a Minerals Development Fund Bill, which would provide the legal framework that management of the fund now lacks, helping enhance accountability (personal communication with Prof. Gavin Hilson, University of Sussex, April 22, 2014).

References

Ackah-Baidoo, A. 2012. "Enclave Development and 'Offshore Corporate Social Responsibility': Implications for Oil-Rich Sub-Saharan Africa." *Resources Policy* 37 (2): 152–59.

Aguilar, J., G. Caspary, and V. Seiler. 2011. "Implementing EITI at the Subnational Level." Extractive Industries for Development Series 23, World Bank, Washington, DC.

Bebbington, A., D. Bebbington, J. Bury, J. Lingan, J. Muñoz, and M. Scurrah. 2008. "Mining and Social Movements: Struggles over Livelihood and Rural Territorial Development in the Andes." *World Development* 36 (12): 2888–905.

Berdal, M. 2005. "Beyond Greed and Grievance—and Not Too Soon." *Review of International Studies* 31 (4): 687–98.

Bridge, G. 2004. "Mapping the Bonanza: Geographies of Mining Investment in an Era of Neoliberal Reform." *Professional Geographer* 56 (3): 406–21.

Brosio, J. 2003. "Oil Revenue and Fiscal Federalism." In *Fiscal Policy Formulation and Implementation in Oil-Producing Countries*, ed. J. Davis, R. Ossowski, and A. Fedelino, 243–69. Washington, DC: International Monetary Fund.

Brosio J., and R. J. Singh. 2013. "Revenue Sharing of Natural Resources: International Practices and Possible Options for Africa." Draft Paper, World Bank, Washington, DC.

Brown, D. 1982. "Who Are the Tribalists? Social Pluralism and Political Ideology in Ghana." *African Affairs* 81: 37–69.

Cederman, L.-E., K. S. Gleditsch, and H. Buhaug. 2013. *Inequality, Grievances, and Civil War*. New York: Cambridge University Press.

Cederman, L.-E., N. B. Weidmann, and K. S. Gleditsch. 2011. "Horizontal Inequalities and Ethnonationalist Civil War: A Global Comparison." *American Political Science Review* 105 (3): 478–95.

Collier P., and A. Hoeffler. 2004. "Aid, Policy and Growth in Post-Conflict Societies." *European Economic Review* 48 (5): 1125–45.

Cotula, L. 2014. *Foreign Investment, Law and Sustainable Development: A Handbook on Agriculture and Extractive Industries.* London: International Institute for Environment and Development. http://pubs.iied.org/pdfs/17513IIED.pdf.

D4D (Diamonds for Development). 2006. "The Current State of Diamond Mining in the Mano River Basin and the Use of Diamonds as a Tool for Peace Building and Development." Background paper, Diamonds for Development Subregional Conference, Monrovia, Liberia, June.

Ehrhardt, D. 2012. "Struggling to Belong: Nativism, Identities, and Urban Social Relations in Kano and Amsterdam." Ph.D. dissertation, University of Oxford.

EITI (Extractive Industries Transparency Initiative). n.d. "Mauritania." EITI, Oslo. http://eiti.org/Mauritania.

Elischer, S. 2013. "After Mali Comes Niger: West Africa's Problems Migrate East." *Foreign Affairs* February 12. http://www.foreignaffairs.com/articles/138931/sebastian-elischer /after-mali-comes-niger.

Els, F. 2013. "Simandou Railway Will Uproot 10,000 People." *Mining.com*, October 17. http://www.mining.com/simandou-railway-will-uproot-10000-people-52462.

EWER (Early Warning Response Working Group). 2012. "Agricultural Land Concessions and Conflict in Liberia." Policy Analysis Brief, Monrovia, Liberia. http://www.lern .ushahidi.com/media/uploads/page/3/EWERPolicyBriefLiberia.

Eze, C. 2013. "Nigeria: New Revenue Formula—Niger Delta Demands 50 Percent Derivation." *Daily Trust*, October 11. http://allafrica.com/stories/201310110635.html.

Fanthorpe, R., and C. Gabelle. 2013. *Political Economy of Extractives: Governance in Sierra Leone.* Washington, DC: World Bank.

Ferguson, J. 2006. *Global Shadows: Africa in the Neoliberal World Order.* Durham, NC: Duke University Press.

Fisher, E. 2007. "Occupying the Margins: Labour Integration and Social Exclusion in Artisanal Mining in Africa." *Development and Change* 38 (4): 735–60.

Ghana News Agency. 2014. "Ghana's Natural Resource Funds Well-Governed." April 25. http://www.ghananewsagency.org/economics/-ghana-s-natural-resource-funds-well -governed-rwi--74058.

Ghana Statistical Service. 2009. *Ghana: Demographic and Health Survey, 2008.* Calverton, MD: ICF International. http://dhsprogram.com/pubs/pdf/FR221/FR221[13Aug2012] .pdf.

Higazi, A. 2009. "Interpreting Religious Conflict in Nigeria." M.Phil. thesis, Department of International Development, CRISE, University of Oxford.

Hilson, G. 2002. "An Overview of Land Use Conflict in Mining Communities." *Land Use Policy* 19: 65–73.

Hinderink, J., and G. J. Tempelman. 1979. *Development Policy and Development Practice in Ivory Coast: A Miracle or a Mirage?* The Netherlands: Geografisch Instituut, Rijksuniversiteit Utrecht.

Humphreys, M. 2005. "Natural Resources, Conflict, and Conflict Resolution: Uncovering the Mechanisms." *Journal of Conflict Resolution* 49 (4): 508–37.

ICMM (International Council on Mining and Metals). 2012. *The Role of Mining in National Economies*. ICMM: London.

IMF (International Monetary Fund). 2012a. "IMF, World Bank Back $4 Billion Côte d'Ivoire Debt Relief." *IMF Survey Magazine*, June 26. https://www.imf.org/external /pubs/ft/survey/so/2012/car062612a.htm.

————. 2012b. "Macroeconomic Policy Frameworks for Resource-Rich Developing Countries." IMF Policy Paper, Washington, DC.

ICG (International Crisis Group). 2012. "Curbing Violence in Nigeria." Africa Report 196, ICG, Washington, DC. http://www.crisisgroup.org/~/media/Files/africa/west -africa/nigeria/196-curbing-violence-in-nigeria-i-the-jos-crisis.pdf.

Jønsson, J. B., and D. F. Bryceson. 2009. "Rushing for Gold: Mobility and Small-Scale Mining in East Africa." *Development and Change* 40 (2): 249–79.

Keenan, J. 2008. "Uranium Goes Critical in Niger: Tuareg Rebellions Threaten Sahelian Conflagration." *Review of African Political Economy* 117: 449–66.

Korf, B. 2005. "Rethinking the Greed-Grievance Nexus: Property Rights and the Political Economy of War in Sri Lanka." *Journal of Peace Research* 42 (2): 201–17.

Land Commission of Liberia. 2012. *Land Rights, Private Use Permits and Forest Communities*, by Paul De Wit. Consultant report, Monrovia. http://eeas.europa.eu /delegations/liberia/documents/press_corner/20130916_01.pdf.

Langer, A. 2005. "Horizontal Inequalities and Violent Group Mobilisation in Côte d'Ivoire." *Oxford Development Studies* 33 (1): 25–45.

Langer, A., and F. Stewart. 2014. "Regional Imbalances, Horizontal Inequalities and Violent Conflicts: Insights from Four West African Countries." Fragility, Conflict, and Violence Group, World Bank, Washington, DC.

le Billon, P. 2001. "The Political Ecology of War: Natural Resources and Armed Conflicts." *Political Geography* 20 (5): 561–84.

————. 2006. "Securing Transparency: Armed Conflicts and the Management of Natural Resource Revenues." *International Journal* 62 (1): 93–107.

Maconachie, R., R, Srinivasan, and N. Menzies. 2014. "Responding to the Challenge of Fragility and Security in West Africa: Natural Resources, Extractive Industry Investment, and Social Conflict." Fragility, Conflict, and Violence Group, World Bank, Washington, DC.

Manson, K., and J. Blas. 2014. "Glencore Closer to Iron Ore Ambition." *Financial Times*, March 30. http://www.ft.com/cms/s/0/0768684e-b7f1-11e3-92f9-00144feabdc0 .html#axzz34pVJSzbp.

MGI (McKinsey Global Institute). 2013. *Reverse the Curse: Maximizing the Potential of Resource-Driven Economies*. New York: MGI.

MSLS (Ministère de la Santé et de la Lutte contre le Sida), and others. 2013. *Côte d'Ivoire: Demographic and Health Survey, 2011–2012*. Calverton, MD: ICF International. http:// dhsprogram.com/publications/publication-FR272-DHS-Final-Reports.cfm.

Mustapha, A. R. 2006. "Ethnic Structure, Inequality and Governance of the Public Sector in Nigeria." In *Ethnic Inequalities and Public Sector Governance*, ed. Y. Bangura. Basingstoke, United Kingdom: Palgrave Macmillan.

———. 2007. "Institutionalising Ethnic Representation: How Effective Is the Federal Character Commission in Nigeria?" CRISE Working Paper 43, Centre for Research on Inequality, Human Security and Ethnicity, University of Oxford.

National Population Commission. 2008. "Nigeria: Demographic and Health Survey, 2008." Abuja, Nigeria. http://dhsprogram.com/pubs/pdf/FR222/FR222.pdf.

OECD (Organisation for Economic Co-operation and Development). 2013. *Fragile States 2013: Resource Flows and Trends in a Shifting World*. Paris: OECD-DAC International Network on Conflict and Fragility.

Okoh, G. A. 2013. "Grievance and Conflict in Ghana's Gold Mining Industry: The Case of Obuasi." *Futures*, September 30. http://www.sciencedirect.com/science/article/pii /S0016328713001201.

Olonisakin, F. 2008. "Conflict Dynamics in West Africa: Background Analysis for the UK Government's Africa Conflict Prevention Programme." CSDG Paper, Conflict, Security and Development Group, King's College, London.

OPEC (Organization of the Petroleum Exporting Countries). n.d. "Nigeria Facts and Figures." http://www.opec.org/opec_web/en/about_us/167.htm.

Østby, G. 2008. "Polarization, Horizontal Inequalities and Violent Conflict." *Journal of Peace Research* 45 (2): 143–62.

Otto, J., C. Andrews, F. Cawood, M. Doggett, P. Guj, F. Stermole, J. Stermole, and J. Tilton. 2006. *Mining Royalties: A Global Study of Their Impact on Investors, Government, and Civil Society*. Washington, DC: World Bank.

Pegg, S. 2006. "Mining and Poverty Reduction: Transforming Rhetoric into Reality." *Journal of Cleaner Production* 14: 376–87.

Pegg, S., and N. Zabbey. 2013. "Oil and Water: The Bodo Spills and the Destruction of Traditional Livelihood Structures in the Niger Delta." *Community Development Journal* 48 (3): 391–405.

Prichard, W. 2013. "Building a Fair, Transparent and Inclusive Tax System in Sierra Leone." Tax Justice Network Africa/BAN/NACE, Nairobi. http://www.nacesl.org /SaloneReport_Final%20print%20out.pdf.

Regan, P. M., and D. Norton. 2005. "Greed, Grievance, and Mobilization in Civil Wars." *Journal of Conflict Resolution* 49 (3): 319–36.

Revenue Watch Institute. 2013. *The 2013 Resource Governance Index: A Measure of Transparency and Accountability in the Oil, Gas, and Mining Sector*. New York: Revenue Watch Institute. http://www.resourcegovernance.org/sites/default/files/rgi_2013_Eng.pdf.

Roe, A., H. Schneider, G. Pyatt, and Development Centre of the Organisation for Economic Co-operation and Development. 1992. *Adjustment and Equity in Ghana*. Paris: Development Centre of the Organisation for Economic Co-operation and Development.

Ross, M. L. 2004a. "How Do Natural Resources Influence Civil War? Evidence from Thirteen Cases." *International Organization* 58 (1): 35–67.

———. 2004b. "What Do We Know about Natural Resources and Civil War?" *Journal of Peace Research* 41 (3): 337–56.

Ross, M. L., P. Lujala, and S. A. Rustad. 2012. "Horizontal Inequality: Decentralizing the Distribution of Natural Resource Revenues, and Peace." In *High-Value Natural Resources and Post-Conflict Peacebuilding*, ed. P. Lujala and S. A. Rustad, 251–59. New York: Routledge.

Samaké, S., and others. 2007. *Mali: Demographic and Health Survey, 2006*. Calverton, MD: ICF International. http://dhsprogram.com/publications/publication-FR199 -DHS-Final-Reports.cfm.

Small, R. 2012. "Artisanal and Small-Scale Mining in and Around Protected Areas and Critical Ecosystems Project: Liberia Case Study Report." Final report, Estelle Levin Limited and WWF. http://www.estellelevin.com/wp-content/uploads/2013/12/ASM -Liberia-Final.pdf.

Smith, M. 2012. "The Impact of Mali's Political Problems on the Gold Industry." *Gold Investing News*, December 5. http://goldinvestingnews.com/30155/mali-political -problems-gold-industry-coup-great-quest-metals-mining.html.

Standing, A., and G. Hilson. 2013. *Distributing Mining Wealth to Communities in Ghana: Addressing Problems of Elite Capture and Political Corruption*. Bergen, Norway: Anti-Corruption Resource Centre.

Stewart, F. 2002. "Crisis Prevention: Tackling Horizontal Inequalities." *Oxford Development* Studies 28 (3): 245–62.

———. ed. 2008. *Horizontal Inequalities and Conflict: Understanding Group Violence in Multiethnic Societies*. Basingstoke, United Kingdom: Palgrave Macmillan.

———. 2010. "Horizontal Inequalities as a Cause of Conflict: A Review of CRISE Findings." CRISE Overview Number 1, Centre for Research on Inequality, Human Security, and Ethnicity, Oxford University Press, Oxford.

UN (United Nations). 2012. "Fragile States and Development in West Africa." Economic Commission for Africa, Sub-Regional Office for West Africa, Niamey, Niger.

UNODC (United Nations Office on Drugs and Crime). 2013. *World Drug Report 2013*. Vienna: UNODC. http://www.unodc.org/unodc/secured/wdr/wdr2013/World_Drug _Report_2013.pdf.

Van Criekinge, J. 2008. "Africa: Conflicts and Mining-Induced Displacement." *Broken Rifle* 77 (February). http://wri-irg.org/node/3582.

Watts, M., and S. I. Ibaba. 2011. "Turbulent Oil: Conflict and Insecurity in the Niger Delta." *African Security* 4 (1): 1–19.

Wilson, E., and J. Van Alstine. 2014. "Localising Transparency: Exploring EITI's Contribution to Sustainable Development." University of Leeds, International Institute for Environment and Development, United Kingdom. http://pubs.iied.org/pdfs /16555IIED.pdf.

World Bank. 2010. "West Africa Mineral Sector Strategic Assessment (WAMSSA): An Environmental and Social Strategic Assessment for the Development of the Mineral Sector in the Mano River Union." Report 53738-AFR, World Bank, Washington, DC.

———. 2013. *Promoting State Legitimacy, Stability and Cohesion in Areas of Low Population Density: The Case of Mali*. Washington, DC: World Bank.

Chapter 5

Managing the Competition for Power in Order to Reduce the Fragility of Political Institutions

Institutions play a central role in managing violence and conflict; few are more critical for this purpose than the institutions that govern political processes and systems. Since the end of the Cold War, the contest for control over the political processes that guarantee access to resources for different groups in society has been at the core of much of the conflict and instability experienced across West Africa.

The competition over resources in Africa has intensified alongside the demographic explosion. It has also been exacerbated by incremental improvements in education and the establishment of a small middle class that aspires to more accountable government. A better-educated population harbors high expectations for its ability to access resources.

Many Africans are now contesting the notion that a small group of individuals can claim exclusive control over an entire country's resources. Control by one group, family, clan, or ethnicity is becoming less tolerated, and demands for more open and representative political systems are on the rise. Faced with domestic and international pressures, countries are slowly opening up their political systems and using elections to both transfer and decentralize power to the local level. At the same time, there is immense pressure from people in power to maintain the status quo, as political power in many African countries remains key to control over and access to resources.

West Africa is in the throes of a critical transition away from authoritarianism toward a more open type of political system. This process has been accompanied by violence and large-scale confrontation (table 5.1 and annex table 5A.1). The transformation of political institutions is therefore central to moving out of fragility and reducing the risks of conflict in West Africa.

Table 5.1 Fatalities as a Result of Election-Related Violence in West Africa

Country	Description
Côte d'Ivoire	Côte d'Ivoire has seen a gradual increase in election-related violence: according to the U.S. State Department, 10 people died as a result of violence related to the 1995 elections, an estimated 500 people were killed in election-related violence in 2000, and 3,000 people died in the disputed elections of 2010.
Guinea	More than 70 people were killed during the country's first multiparty elections (in 1993), and the 2010 elections were also marred by violence. More than 50 people died in violence in the run-up to legislative elections in 2013.
Nigeria	Election-related violence increased since transition to civilian rule in 1999. Estimates put the death toll from violence during national elections at 100 in 2003, 300 in 2007, and 800 in 2011. Local elections have also been marred by violence, with an estimated 700 people killed in the aftermath of 2008 elections in the Middle Belt city of Jos.
Togo	An estimated 500 people were killed in election-related violence in 2005, following the death of President Eyadéma. Faure Gnassingbé, the son of President Eyadéma, won the election.

Sources: International Republican Institute 1994; U.S. Department of State 1995, 1996, 2001, 2006; Human Rights Watch 2004, 2011; Campbell 2010; Alemika 2011; ICG 2011; Knutsen 2013.

The Postcolonial Centralization of Power

After independence, the overwhelming majority of West African leaders centralized power. The shift toward an autocratic political system with zero tolerance for competition was built on the character of the extractive colonial state. Many postcolonial states failed to dismantle the despotic institutions that had been nurtured under colonialism. In other countries, radical regimes fashioned systems of centralized despotism under the cover of tackling the vestiges of colonial decentralized despotism (Mamdani 1996). This pattern was replicated across most of the continent in the wake of independence. Postindependence experiments with democratization were "relatively rare and short-lived" (Marshall 2005, 8). Indeed, of the 39 independence-era African states, 18 adopted autocratic regimes, 11 were anocracies (mixed or incoherent forms of government), and Zaire was entirely devoid of an effective central government; only 9 countries embraced democracy. A key feature of government during this period was the adoption of one-party systems, which leaders posited was integral to rapid economic growth (Young 2012).

Of the West African states that set a course for democratization in the wake of independence, Nigeria and Sierra Leone slipped into autocratic rule within 10 years. The Gambia lasted nearly 40 years before it succumbed to autocratic rule in 1994 (it has continued to buck the democratization trend) (Marshall 2005). Meanwhile, those countries that had adopted mixed forms of government after independence fell into autocratic rule within 15 years, and by the late 1980s, the large majority of countries in West Africa were governed as dictatorships—either civilian or military (Marshall 2005). Sierra Leone initiated a democratic transition in the 1960s, as did Benin, Burkina Faso, Ghana (twice), and Nigeria in the 1970s; however, none of these attempts lasted more than five years before these countries once again reverted to autocratic rule (Marshall 2005).

To a large degree, competition for political power and access to resources in the postcolonial state shaped the move to centralize control of the party and the state. With very few exceptions, where leaders were faced with the choice of consolidating their grip on power or taking a longer-term view and building inclusive institutions while encouraging development and economic growth, they chose the former path (Acemoglu and Robinson 2012). In Sierra Leone, Siaka Stevens, who served as prime minister from 1967 to 1971 and as president from 1971 to 1985, perpetuated the existence of extractive economic institutions, which had remained untouched since colonialism. Doing so created the conditions for extractive political institutions—institutions in which "power is valuable [because it] is unchecked and brings economic riches" (Acemoglu and Robinson 2012, 343). Their creation helped spawn a neopatrimonial system that left no resistance to leaders who abused the powers of state. Another insidious consequence of extractive institutions is that by creating "unconstrained power and great income inequality," they heighten the stakes for political power (Acemoglu and Robinson 2012, 343). To the victor go all the spoils of the "excessive" power and wealth generated by the state, thereby creating the "incentives for infighting in order to control power and its benefits" (Acemoglu and Robinson 2012, 344).

Leaders consolidated their grip on power and resources by securing control of the party through which they had come to power. An example is Kwame Nkrumah of Ghana, who spearheaded the country's drive for independence and became its first leader in 1957. He quickly banned opposition parties, dismantled the institutions of the Convention People's Party, which he had founded, and railroaded through legislation that declared him president for life (Opalo 2011). President João Bernardo Vieira of Guinea-Bissau ousted his predecessor (the independence-era leader Luís Cabral) in a coup in order to ensure that the political party answered solely to him. In some cases, leaders took the personalization of power that came about as a result of the no-holds-barred competition over resources to its logical extreme, maintaining power until their death. Others, like Nkrumah, went so far as to declare themselves president for life. West African leaders who ensconced themselves in the chief political seat as "leaders for life" include Togo's Gnassingbé Eyadéma, who held power longer than any of the region's other leaders (38 years) (Carbone 2013); Félix Houphouët-Boigny of Côte d'Ivoire, who spent 33 years in power; Dawda Jawara, who spent 32 years at the helm of The Gambia; and William Tubman of Liberia and Blaise Compaoré of Burkina Faso, both of whom ruled for 27 years (see annex tables 5A.2 and 5A.3).

Although Cold War ideologies were more influential in the Horn of Africa and Southern Africa than in West Africa, the centralizing tendency of many postcolonial West African leaders was accompanied by the adoption of a statist economy and alignment with socialist principles that further consolidated the levers of power. Some of pan-Africanism's pioneers, including Nkrumah, Sékou Touré of Guinea, and Modibo Keïta of Mali, were heavily influenced by Marxism and espoused a form of statist politics (Schmidt 2007). Nkrumah in particular embraced a statist orientation between independence in 1957 and his ouster in 1966, alternating between invoking the common citizen and moving toward participation and fearing the exercise of citizenship and repressing opponents (Cooper 2002).

The autocratic political structure that was the preferred form of governance among postcolonial leaders vested itself in one-party dictatorships. The state became the vortex of factional struggles for power, with political elites and the ruling parties of the neopatrimonial regimes relying on coercion and corruption to secure resources and rents. Lacking legitimacy and inclusiveness, the ruling apparatus applied a combination of patronage and terror to maintain its grip on power. It was in this potent mix of greed, exploitation, and misrule that the seeds of future conflict and violence in West Africa were sown.

Table 5.2 Successful Military Coups in West Africa since 1960, by Country

Country	Number of successful military coups	Years	Year of last successful coup
Benin	7	1963, 1965 (3), 1967, 1969, 1972	1972
Burkina Faso	7	1966, 1974, 1980, 1982, 1983, 1987, 2014	2014
Côte d'Ivoire	2	1999, 2002	2002
Gambia, The	1	1994	1994
Ghana	5	1966, 1972, 1978, 1979, 1981	1981
Guinea	2	1984, 2008	2008
Guinea-Bissau	4	1980, 1999, 2003, 2012	2012
Liberia	1	1980	1980
Mali	3	1968, 1991, 2012	2012
Mauritania	6	1978, 1979, 1980, 1984, 2005, 2008	2008
Niger	4	1974, 1996, 1999, 2010	2010
Nigeria	6	1966 (2), 1975, 1983, 1985, 1993	1993
Sierra Leone	5	1967, 1968, 1992, 1996, 1997	1997
Togo	2	1963, 1967	1967

Source: Shillington 2004; Barka and Ncube 2012; media sources.

Military Coups

Military coups continuously challenged the stranglehold that dictators and "Big Man" presidents kept on the state in the decades following independence. West Africa experienced more than twice as many attempts (successful and unsuccessful) at unconstitutional changes of government (including military coups) in the decades after 1960 as any other subregion on the continent (Barka and Ncube 2012).

The region's first coup took place in Togo in 1963, with the ouster and murder of the country's first president, Sylvanus Olympio, who had adopted an autocratic single-party system that largely marginalized the north. After the coup, the military handed over power to a consortium of opposition groups, as it was too weak to consolidate power and the ousted regime had significant backing in the capital city (Young 2012).

Between 1960 and 2010, West Africa experienced 106 failed and successful coups—many times more than in East Africa (48), Central Africa (35), or Southern Africa (16) (see annex table 5A.4). The level of coup activity varied considerably within West Africa. Senegal, often held up as an example of political stability in West Africa, and Cabo Verde have never experienced a successful coup. Benin and Burkina Faso have each had seven, Mauritania has had six, Ghana and Sierra Leone have each had five, and Guinea-Bissau and Niger have each had four (table 5.2).

Military coups have come about as the result of a number of factors; their origins and forms have varied. They represent another manifestation of the competition for political power, as excluded and marginalized elites in single-party states resorted to military coups to wrest power from incumbents. Indeed, a major cause of coups in West Africa has been ethnic antagonisms "stemming from cultural plurality and political competition," as well as the existence of strong militaries with a "factionalized officer corps" (Kposowa and Jenkins 1993, 126). Competition among elites inside the military and the civilian government has largely driven coups in the subregion. By the mid-1960s, military coups had become the method of choice to displace regimes; they remained as such until the wave of democratization in 1990 opened up West Africa's political arena (Young 2012).

Coups were also the result of external intervention in the state, either by neighboring states or states farther away. Nkrumah was accused of complicity in the region's first coup, in Togo, with some observers claiming that he wanted to annex Togo (the claim was never substantiated) (Willoughby 2013). Another factor was the role of economic downturns: tightened budgets often meant a reduction in the size of the army or unpaid salaries, both of which could trigger coups (O'Kane 1993).

Military coups did not inevitably lead to the replacement of a civilian dicta-torship by a military one. In Benin, Burkina Faso, Ghana, Nigeria, and Sierra Leone, for example, the military voluntarily withdrew in favor of electoral democracy and allowed the restoration of civilian regimes (Young 2012). In the early days of Benin's independence, the military intervened because of frustra-tion with the sclerosis induced by political competition. An attempt to institute multiparty politics resulted in a "three-player ethno-regional game"; efforts to impose single-party rule resulted in a military coup in 1963 (Young 2012). The intrusion proved temporary, with elections organized for the following year. These interventions to alter the political landscape were often brief, however, or, as in Sierra Leone, civilian governments soon collapsed back into autocracies (Young 2012).

In the past two decades, some military coups were triggered by attempts to amend or fiddle with constitutions to prolong a leader's tenure in power, signal-ing growing intolerance of the phenomenon of "president for life." The February 2010 coup in Niger was directly linked to the attempt by President Mamadou Tandja to manipulate the country's constitutional arrangements and retain his hold on power (Souaré 2010). Invoking the constitution, Nigeria's Senate rejected President Olusegun Obasanjo's May 2006 attempt to pass a bill to extend his stay in power by a third term. The move marked a key moment in the country's political development, particularly as military coups had been respon-sible for the overthrow of Nigeria's First and Second Republics (Posner and Young 2007).

Almost half (50) of the 106 successful and unsuccessful coups in West Africa took place between 1970 and 1989; 19 were recorded between 1960 and 1969 (see annex table 5A.4). The period between 1990 and 2010 saw 37 coups.

The largest drop-off in coup activity came in the first decade of the 21st century, as regularized multiparty elections became the accepted means of power transfer. Three main factors have been credited for the decline. The first was the move by several governments toward inclusive politics and increased political competition, which took place amidst calls for democratization from both citizens and the international community. The second factor was the role of regional bodies, such as the Economic Community of West African States (ECOWAS) and the African Union, and policy instruments, including the Lomé Declaration; the African Charter on Democracy, Elections, and Governance; and the Protocol on Democracy and Good Governance of ECOWAS. These measures strengthened norms that helped socialize elites and the military and discourage military coups. The third factor in deterring plotters and prospec-tive putschists has been the role played by security sector reform programs (see chapter 6).

Notwithstanding progress made in recent years in stabilizing the form of power transfers, West Africa continues to experience coups. The March 2012 coup in Mali caught many by surprise, as it came just weeks ahead of planned elections and the outgoing president had made clear his intentions to hand power over to a democratically elected leader (Ogude 2012). The same year a coup in Guinea-Bissau halted the second round of an election that former prime minister Carlos Gomes Júnior was expected to win. ECOWAS has played a critical role in both Guinea-Bissau and Mali, but its interventions have come under scrutiny, amidst allegations of inconsistency and double standards in its response (Hounkpe 2012).

Disillusioned with civilian politicians, some groups have strongly supported military rule in recent years (Coulibaly and Bratton 2013). Afrobarometer surveys reveal support for military rule in Mali both before and after the 2012 coup. Although challenges remain, significant progress has been made, as demonstrated in Ghana and Nigeria, the regional trendsetters in terms of coups. Both countries have transitioned to civilian rule as a result of domestic factors, with Ghana heralded as a model for successful democratic transition following several peaceful handovers of power.

The Lost Decade: The Unexpected Impact on Democratization

The global economic crisis of the 1970s dealt a blow to the already weakened economies of West Africa by sending the prices of international commodities crashing. As part of the legacy of colonialism, the economies of several West African countries depended on commodities, such as coffee, copper, and cocoa. The shocks generated by the fall in prices sent these economies into a tailspin, with far-reaching social consequences (Obi n.d.). Per capita income declined across the region. Benin, Burkina Faso, and Mali, which were buffered by relatively high resource flows, saw contractions of less than 1 percent a year, but other countries, including Liberia, Niger, and Nigeria, registered annual declines of more than 3 percent (Ghai and Hewitt de Alcántara 1990). Average annual growth of gross domestic product (GDP) in West Africa dropped from 2.2 percent between 1975 and 1980 to about 0.5 percent by 1985 (Aning and Atta-Asamoah 2011).

West African countries experienced a deterioration in their terms of trade, an increase in real interest rates on external debt, and reduced inflows of resources. Indebtedness grew, and state revenues dwindled. The state, already largely unresponsive to its citizenry, proved incapable of delivering even the most basic services amidst mismanagement, corruption, unemployment, crumbling infrastructure, a drop in food production, and deficient social services (Darnton 1994). The adoption of structural adjustment programs to restore macroeconomic imbalances further depressed the economy in the short term

(Barka and Ncube 2012), with retrenchment of workers in civil services, reduction of subsidies, and cuts in investment programs.

The economic crisis called into question the state's legitimacy and critically exposed its weaknesses. In many countries, the state buckled under the weight of compound pressures, which triggered military coups in Liberia and Sierra Leone and led to unrest in Benin, Burkina Faso, The Gambia, Ghana, Mali, Nigeria, and Senegal (Obi n.d). The crisis precipitated calls for democratization and access to resources, amidst challenges to political stability and state hegemony (Obi n.d.). The fragile foundations of political stability began to come apart in countries such as Côte d'Ivoire, which had been lauded for its economic prosperity and interethnic harmony. As funds dried up and the country's dependence on cocoa exacerbated the pain of the economic crisis, politicians used ethnicity as a crude instrument with which to justify the exclusion and marginalization of migrants from the north, including people with origins in neighboring Burkina Faso and Mali, who had worked the land in the south for decades (North 2011).

The crisis of the state actually fueled the drive toward democratization. Hard hit by economic decline, unemployment, and poverty, and with blocked mobility and aspirations (Ikelegbe and Garuba 2011), youth became the agents of change. As GDP plummeted, average annual population growth in West Africa increased from 2.6 percent in 1975 to about 2.8 percent in 1980, while also changing in composition (Aning and Atta-Asamoah 2011). The youth population increased markedly during this time, in part because of lower life expectancy and higher birth rates, accompanied by rapid increases in the size of the urban population (see chapter 3). Young people witnessed the rapid deterioration of their living conditions on the back of the cumulative effects of the failure of the nation-building project and the structural adjustment program (OECD-SWAC 2005). In Benin, Burkina Faso, Ghana, Mali, Nigeria, and Senegal, youth—particularly students—played a decisive role in fostering political changes. The crisis threatened the employment prospects of students who had gained a toehold into the university system, regarded as the critical entry point to a world of greater opportunity.

The first protests kicked off on university campuses in Benin in 1989; within the year, they had incorporated other segments of society, spreading across the region. In Mali, protests in 1990 were sparked not by university students but by young unemployed graduates, who mobilized against the one-party state. A year later, the movement helped bring an end to the 23-year rule of Moussa Traoré. The capacity of students to question the worldview that governments presented to them "helped shape their political agency" (Zeilig and Dawson 2008, 21). Their simultaneous interaction with the wave of democratization sweeping the region and agitation against authoritarian rule became the conduit through which they transmitted their anger and frustration (Ikelegbe and Garuba 2011).

The End of the Cold War and the Collapse of the State in Côte d'Ivoire, Guinea-Bissau, Liberia, and Sierra Leone

The deep-seated crisis of state legitimacy gave rise to many conflicts, exacerbated by failures of governance, exclusionary policies, corruption, lack of avenues for dissent (N'Diaye 2011), and associated severe economic dislocations (Luckham and others 2001). By the 1990s, authoritarian regimes' grip over patronage and violence began to slip, in part because of the patrimonialism of the state itself but also as a consequence of the tightening of donor purse strings, calls for democratization, and the focus on economic reform. Decades of atrophy and the collapse of institutions meant that the state was unable to fend off challenges to its authority. The pressure on budgets curtailed the elite's recourse to patronage and state assets, forcing leaders to bow to demands for democratization. The end of the Cold War signaled the shift to a more passive stance toward Africa by the United States and the former colonial powers, stripping away the layer of protection and the near invincible status that authoritarian rulers had enjoyed.

In Sierra Leone, President Siaka Stevens capitalized so effectively on the extractive institutions established by the colonial rule and so undermined the foundations of the state that by the time the Revolutionary United Front under Foday Sankoh launched its attack in 1991, there was no line of defense. The extractive institutions concentrated power and wealth in the hands of the elites, impoverished the population, blocked development, neglected investment in public services, and decimated the state (Acemoglu and Robinson 2012). Driven by fear of overthrow, Stevens "emasculated" the military, making it easy for the rebel force to overrun the country. The bloody civil war lasted 10 years (until 2002), but the weakness of the state was such that by the first year of the war it had collapsed.

Although many West African neopatrimonial regimes faced similar stresses and challenges, not all of them followed a trajectory that culminated in civil war and the incapacitation of the central state. The multiplicity of courses charted by countries across the region ranged from civil war (Côte d'Ivoire, Guinea-Bissau, Liberia, Sierra Leone) to political violence and insurgency short of civil war (Mali, Niger) and peaceful political transitions (Benin, Burkina Faso, The Gambia, Senegal). In Benin, democracy came about as the result of a broad process in which elites came together. Senegal transitioned to multiparty democracy in the 1970s, and both Ghana and Nigeria moved from military to civilian rule in the 1990s.

In the absence of institutional legitimacy, a key determinant of a country's ability and capacity to withstand political violence and civil war was the nature of the elite bargains established by the ruling parties of neopatrimonial regimes

(Lindemann 2008). Inclusive elite bargains (Williams 2011) were essential to accommodate the "high social fragmentation" of ethnic or regional cleavages that were a legacy of the past (Lindemann 2008, 17). Patterns of marginalization, political exclusion, and the persecution of rival groups underscored the civil wars in Côte d'Ivoire and Liberia; the violence in Guinea, Nigeria's Niger Delta, and Togo; and the long-running Casamance insurgency in Senegal.

The consequences of weak political and economic institutions and the failure to forge inclusive elite bargains is evident in Côte d'Ivoire. For several decades, President Houphouët-Boigny ran an inclusive government and kept the peace, despite the existence of severe socioeconomic inequalities between the north and south. His death in December 1993 brought to the surface several issues that contributed to civil war, including the political and economic exclusion of northerners and their resentment toward the "insufficient state recognition" of the Muslim faith (Stewart 2010). Despite a lack of institutional legitimacy, President Houphouët-Boigny was able to maintain political stability by forming an inclusive elite bargain that included elites from various ethnic groups. The danger of elite pacts is that however inclusive they may be, they are short lived and do not provide the sustained ability to cope with stresses, unless they translate into deep economic and institutional reforms that foster broader-based development (World Bank 2011).

Difficult Steps toward Democratization

Multiparty elections conducted through the ballot box have increasingly become the standard of legitimacy for leaders in West Africa: since 2009, all sitting presidents have either been elected via multiparty elections or confirmed in the same way (Musah 2009). Power has gradually become institutionalized as political transitions take place through elections rather than violent coups and assassinations. However, new forms of violence and disorder emerged following the dismantling of authoritarian structures, as the partially reformed state proved to be substantially weakened (Young 2004).

The democratization project has posed significant challenges, not the least of which is the risk of violence around elections, precipitated by the high stakes involved in the process, often exacerbated by the nature of the electoral system in place (see table 5A.1). The winner-takes-all system has been described as "an obstacle to democracy in Africa's highly ethnicized politics" (Mesfin 2008, 3) that does not adequately express the will of the voter. The Political Instability Task Force, a U.S. government–sponsored research project, which examined 141 episodes of instability worldwide between 1955 and 2003, concluded that partial democracies with factionalism resulted in the creation of regimes that were exceptionally unstable and at the highest risk of severe instability. Additionally, both the majority system and the plurality system exaggerate the parliamentary representation of the largest political party (Mesfin 2008; Williams 2011). In some cases, elections have spawned the ethnicization of politics and the hardening of ethnic identities. In Guinea, for example, challengers and incumbents alike are accused of having played up interethnic divisions to manipulate ethnicity as a mobilizing factor.

The retreat into identity politics reflects the challenge of institutionalizing democracy in ethnically diverse societies or very centralized political systems in which institutions that moderate conflict are weak. Democratic mechanisms risk being manipulated or politicized, which fuels dissent among more marginalized groups. In addition, elites compete for supporters when they find their political power dwindling, even resorting to violence. Where elections are perceived as zero-sum games and elites rely on ethnicity to rally supporters, election outcomes can consolidate power within a single ethnic group and its elites, to the exclusion of other groups (Bekoe 2008).

The threat of democratic regression looms large in West Africa because of the growing phenomenon of unconstitutional changes of government (Omotola 2011), which go against both the will of the people and regional norms (see annex table 5A.5). Incumbents in Guinea, Nigeria, and Togo turned to institutional channels in an attempt to extend their time in office beyond constitutionally mandated limits. President Obasanjo of Nigeria did not succeed in his attempt, but Lansana Conté of Guinea and Gnassingbé Eyadéma of Togo did. Senegal came close to a constitutional crisis in the run-up to its February 2012 elections, when the incumbent Abdoulaye Wade's run for a constitutionally questionable third term sparked deadly clashes between protestors and police (Freedom House 2013). Strong public opposition and street protests in Burkina Faso in 2014 against attempts by President Blaise Compaoré (in power since 1987) to amend the constitution to allow him to run for another term ended with his ouster. In Togo, citizens took to the streets to demand the reintroduction of term limits, which would bar the current president from throwing his hat into the ring in 2015. The same debate has been raging in Benin, giving rise to concerns that such actions can undermine elite pacts and cooperation and trigger military coups and unconstitutional changes of power.

The challenges of consolidating democracy in West Africa also include the refusal of incumbents (such as Laurent Gbagbo in Côte d'Ivoire) to concede power to winners in an election and the recurrence of military coups (in Guinea and Mauritania in 2008, Niger in 2009 and 2010, Guinea-Bissau in 2009 and 2012, Mali in 2012, and Burkina Faso in 2014). The countries that have recorded the most successful transitions from an autocratic political system to a democratic one include countries that experienced limited cases of armed conflict since 1945, such as Benin, Ghana, and Senegal (Marshall 2005). Mali had been cited as a West African success story until the 2012 coup, which was triggered by the military's dissatisfaction with how the government handled the insurgency in the north.

Other challenges include the high cost of political campaigns and electoral administration, which lock out potential contenders, as well as the lack of internal organization and management of political parties, in particular opposition parties, which hinders their ability to mount successful challenges (Musah 2009). Media and civil society have played a key role in West African countries (notably in Ghana, Liberia, and Nigeria) in mediating between citizens and the people vested with political power while also pushing for reform and greater civil liberties. Civil society has played a prominent role in diffusing tensions where incumbents have tried to cling to political power (in Nigeria, for example). Regional bodies such as ECOWAS, supported by the African Union and international actors, have helped manage elections and peacefully resolve disputes by establishing norms and developing policy instruments such as the Praia Declaration on Elections and Stability in West Africa.

Citizen Engagement: A Call to Action

Civil society and advocacy groups have been a key plank of citizen engagement and participation in West Africa since independence—and at the forefront of the push toward democratization across the subregion. They have benefited greatly from the expansion of the political space.

The authoritarian system of governance, the militarized state, and its extractive institutions meant that many groups suffered from oppression and restrictions. The effect was to galvanize professional bodies—from lawyers, doctors, and intellectuals to women's groups, journalists, labor unions, and students—which agitated and contributed to the expansion of political freedoms (Ibrahim 2003).

Ghana stands out in West Africa as a country in which civil society and citizen engagement has acted as a force for social and political change. The Ghana Bar Association, and elites in Ghana, were integral to the rejection of a union government in 1977, demanding instead a multiparty liberal democratic model. The country's long history of teacher activism helped strengthen civil society overall. Despite its narrow base, civil society in Ghana has fostered a liberal culture of resistance to state interference. Over the years, this culture has been a "constant ally" in the push for greater political and other freedoms (Ibrahim 2003).

Nigeria also has a vibrant civil society, which includes a vocal media corps and dynamic trade, professional, and student unions. It has retained considerable autonomy and capacity for resistance in the face of state repression and arbitrary violence (Ibrahim 2003).

Civil society is an important player in increasing state accountability for development across Sub-Saharan Africa, in particular through the political relations between citizens, civil society, and state leadership (Devarajan, Khemani, and Walton 2011). Through awareness campaigns, advocacy, and policy and programmatic interventions, civil society has taken advantage of the openings created by democratic governance in the subregion and brought issues onto global and regional agendas (Olonisakin 2010). However, civil society actors, and the media, have not always spoken with one voice; it was not until the conflicts of the late 1980s and 1990s began to devastate the region that a "people-conscious civil society emerged to challenge the elite monopolization of civil society" (Olonisakin 2010).

Religious institutions—from churches and mosques in Liberia and Sierra Leone to the Christian Association of Nigeria (CAN)—have historically played an important role in resolving conflict. But at times they have also fueled conflict, by inciting followers (Olonisakin 2010). The emergence of nongovernmental organizations (NGOs) designed to galvanize civil society, as well as foreign sponsorship of such organizations and other expressions of mass participation, have helped this movement grow (Olonisakin 2010).

The opportunities and openings created by democratization have enabled citizens and civil society to participate directly in holding state and public officials to account. They have been supported in this endeavor by local actors such as the media and the private sector as well as by donors and development agencies. Efforts to increase transparency as a means of triggering social accountability through participation have taken root, and various community-driven development initiatives and mechanisms to maximize beneficiary feedback have been adopted as a way to foster political inclusion (World Bank 2014). Decentralization is also increasingly being used to restructure and reform governance structures in a bid to reduce the distance between local authorities and local populations and encourage grassroots participation in local development activities (Boko and McNeil 2010). In fragile states, improved transparency, citizen participation, and social accountability can help strengthen the social contract between the state and citizens and shore up the state's legitimacy (World Bank 2014) (box 5.1). Social accountability can also increase political inclusion, thereby reducing perceptions of injustice, particularly when it is linked to the distribution of resources across various groups (World Bank 2014). With the discovery of substantial oil and gas reserves in Ghana in 2007, the government called on donor partners for assistance in managing the emerging sector; developing a

---

BOX 5.1
_____

Citizen Participation as a Lever of Good Governance

Citizen engagement is a cornerstone of social accountability. It helps build a state's legitimacy and credibility, foster political inclusion, and enhance development effectiveness.

Across West Africa, the push for greater openness and transparency, bolstered by the advent of new technologies that facilitate communication and the free flow of information, has given citizens the means and tools by which to hold officials and the state accountable. Social media, e-governance, and mobile phone technology improve the flow of information between citizens and public officials and increase transparency in electoral processes. In addition, some governments have opened dialogue on contentious subjects (Smyth and Best 2013).

Nigeria has published its federal, state, and local budgets since 2004, in an effort to improve governance outcomes and foster debate (World Bank 2008). The initiative garnered much public support and has enabled civil society and the media to play a more active and informed role in public debate, which contributes to setting national priorities. The initiative was received less enthusiastically by elements of the political elite, who found their rents and vested interests threatened by the drive for transparency and openness. However, the decision to invite public scrutiny as part of a broader reform program has the potential to affect the way in which citizens hold governments and public officials accountable and to help ensure that development resources serve public interests (World Bank 2008).

_____

strong civil society and legal framework; and helping avoid governance risks, such as elite capture and revenue misuse (World Bank 2012).

Efforts by donors to advance democracy and governance objectives through civil society and citizen engagement mechanisms have had mixed results. In Ghana, the character of the civil society organization and its relationship to the state have had more bearing on results than the levels of donor funding (Gaventa and Barrett 2010). In interventions that attempt to increase citizen participation in project design or the efficacy and credibility of projects, the outcome has been as dependent on project design as the level of social cohesion in the community or the initial conditions of inequality (Devarajan, Khemani, and Walton 2011). Foreign funding has at times skewed the composition of civil society to favor a highly select group of organizations that typically represents the urban middle class and focuses on issues such as good governance, sometimes alienating grassroots organizations (Gaventa and Barrett 2010). In some self-help organizations with mainly female members, the injection of donor funds resulted in a shift in membership and leadership toward younger and better-educated women (Devarajan, Khemani, and Walton 2011).

On the whole, external support by donors and development partners has helped strengthen women's involvement in democratization by highlighting gender equality and women's empowerment (Belanger 2012). Indeed, the precarious socioeconomic situation of women in Sub-Saharan Africa, combined with pressure from patriarchal cultures, can potentially facilitate women's empowerment (Belanger 2012). Although women have played a prominent role in peacebuilding efforts in the region, the status and leadership with which it endowed them has failed to translate into meaningful postconflict gains in terms of political participation or greater leverage in the decision-making process (Alaga 2010).

An additional benefit of democratization is that it facilitates the emergence of a "plurality of information" (OECD-SWAC 2005). Private publications and newspapers proliferated, breaking the monopoly over the control of information; private radio and television followed. As with civil society and religious organizations, the media played a key role in the democratization process; it was the first institution to strike "a ringing blow" at the dictatorships in power (OECD-SWAC 2005). The role of the media has not been without controversy, however: in Côte d'Ivoire, Reporters without Borders accused media outlets of exacerbating latent tensions and disseminating false rumors (OECD-SWAC 2005).

The information and communications technology revolution, a key facilitator of the uprisings during the Arab Spring, has offered a range of new technologies for economic development since the 1990s. The emergence of a "networked public sphere" (Smyth and Best 2013) provides an alternative to traditional media, whose chief deficiency today is neither vibrancy nor standing but the scarcity of resources, which results in inadequate coverage of events. Social networks and the Internet have proven to be powerful tools for transparency and accountability in West Africa, as well as forces for change. In Liberia and Nigeria, the use of social media during the 2011 elections helped increase transparency and reduce tensions by providing information during the electoral process. Nigeria's Enough Is Enough—a coalition of individuals and youth organizations aligned to promote good governance and public accountability— has had considerable impact through social networks. As corruption continues to dog many West African nations, and concerns surrounding transparency and accountability remain preeminent, social media have increasingly played the role of watchdog, helping monitor and guard against election-related fraud in Nigeria, for example (Smyth and Best 2013).

Citizenship and the Ethnicization of Politics

The exclusion of segments of the population from political power and economic resources on the basis of geography, race, ethnicity, or religion has inflamed

BOX 5.2

The Politicization of Ethnicities in Guinea

The politicization of ethnicities in Guinea is a relatively recent phenomenon. The 2010 elections were characterized by voting along ethnic lines and high levels of ethnic tensions; they marked the first time the country had seen such a pronounced hardening of political identities. The 1984 death of the country's first president, Sékou Touré, led to a military coup by Lansana Conté, who seized power and ruled for nine years. Conté's death, in 2008, provided a second chance for genuine democratization.

Although the 2010 elections oversaw the peaceful transition to civilian rule, they brought ethnicity to the fore as a political idea (ICG 2011). The presidential elections were marred by delays in organizing crucial parliamentary elections, corruption, mistrust, and rising ethnic tensions (Human Rights Watch 2013). Politics has been defined as a "strategic issue in itself" in Guinea (ICG 2011); in earlier elections, it manifested itself as intercommunal violence. Guinea is crudely understood as made up of four ethno-geographic blocs: the Soussou, on the coastal plains; the Peul, in the mountains; the Malinke, in the eastern savannah; and the Forestiers, in the forests. Communities and associations of these groups have increasingly become political battlegrounds, with the outcomes of elections and the political process seen as a win for the entire ethnic group (ICG 2011).

---

tensions in West Africa since colonial days. One form of exclusion is the ethnicization of politics. To ensure their continued tenure in power, elites have historically resorted to rallying supporters along ethnic lines (box 5.2).

Political elites have also excluded and marginalized individuals, not just groups, on the basis of citizenship, as a means of discrediting and delegitimizing political opponents. In Côte d'Ivoire, various attempts were made to exclude Alassane Ouattara, a northern opposition figure and now president of the country, from competing in elections on the basis of his "foreignness." In line with the concept of *Ivoirité*, Ouattara was prevented from running in the 1995 presidential elections on the grounds that one of his parents was from Burkina Faso. Subsequent leaders perpetuated this form of exclusion (Whitaker 2005). The political exclusion of Ouattara was the trigger for rebellion by soldiers from the north. They tapped into simmering discontent among the country's northern Muslims (World Bank 2011), who faced daily harassment and saw Ouattara's exclusion as symbolic of their own exclusion, as well as of their religion.

Exclusion based on citizenship and geography of location or origin has also been witnessed in Liberia and Nigeria. In Liberia, the Mandingo people are considered outsiders, and their claims to land and citizenship are contested. Members of other Liberian tribes often claim that the Mandingo have abused the hospitality of Liberians by registering land and claiming citizenship; perceptions of injustice stemming from these divergent interpretations risk triggering violence (Marc and others 2013).

In 1980, political rivals of Alhaji Shugaba, the majority leader of a state assembly in Nigeria, declared him an alien and had him deported on the grounds that his father was not born in Nigeria (Whitaker 2005). In the Middle Belt region, in Plateau State, during the transition to civilian rule in 1999, politicians from communities that regarded themselves as indigenous began to politicize the process of handing out indigene certificates. The result was to marginalize residents from other communities and deny them access to employment and power.

Proving citizenship, and availing oneself of the benefits conferred by this confirmation of identity, has been complicated by the fact that most West African populations, in particular rural people, do not have access to documentation such as identity cards or national passports, because of illiteracy, poverty, and corruption (Adepoju, Boulton, and Levin n.d.). The cost of obtaining an identity card or even a birth certificate, the distance to urban centers, and the limited institutional presence in rural areas further impede securing formal documentation. The lack of documentation remains a source of fragility across the continent, exacerbated by a sense that people migrating from the north to the richer southern coast are seizing the benefits of the natural wealth from local populations.

Some countries, such as Senegal, seem to have avoided the ethnicization of politics; its elites have been careful not to play up ethnic differences politically. Some political scientists have suggested that its success in this regard stems from the fact that its highly respected founding father, Léopold Senghor, was himself from a minority group and a Catholic in a Muslim country.

Recommendations for Reducing the Fragility of Political Institutions

The increase in political openness in West Africa has contributed to stability, although the transition to democracy has, in some cases, triggered a surge in political violence. Support to strengthen political institutions is therefore a crucial dimension of stability in the region. Most development organizations lack a mandate to intervene in a country's internal politics. They can, however, make important contributions to improving the functioning of political institutions.

Recommendations to address this driver of conflict and fragility include the following:

- So that political debates are well informed, governments should provide relevant technical and economic information to the public, through NGOs, and the press. Development partners should support these processes by disseminating lessons from international experiences and support government communications strategies.

- Donors should improve and increase their support to strengthen political institutions, such as parliaments and other deliberating bodies. There is scope for improving West Africa's political systems. Assistance can come in the form of support to electoral systems and mechanisms for disseminating information to the public and from organizations in charge of overseeing the rights of citizens (such as ombudsmen and others). Exchanges between deliberative bodies and bodies in charge of citizens' rights across West Africa should be encouraged to share innovations. ECOWAS has an important role to play in this regard. Experiences of institutional transformation from other regions, such as Latin America, that have transitioned from autocracy to democracy could be useful.

- Governments should scale up mechanisms for social accountability and transparency in order to ensure that citizens have a greater voice in their own development. Many countries and development partners already include mechanisms for participation and transparency. Such mechanisms need to remain a priority to ensure that development continues to hold political systems accountable.

- Governments should support inclusive national dialogue and peace discussions when tensions appear, before conflict risks turn violent. Donor agencies can play an important role in supporting these dialogues.

Annex 5.A: Political Leadership in West Africa

Table 5A.1 Election-Related Violence in West Africa, 1990–2013

Country	Election years	Frequency of high electoral violence
Benin	1991, 1995, 1996, 1999, 2001, 2003, 2006, 2007, 2011	Never
Burkina Faso	1991, 1992, 1997, 1998, 2002, 2005, 2007, 2010	Never
Cabo Verde	1991, 1995, 1996, 2001, 2006, 2011	Never
Côte d'Ivoire	1990, 1995, 2000, 2010, 2011	Usually
Gambia, The	1992, 1996, 1997, 2001, 2002, 2006, 2007, 2011, 2012	Never
Ghana	1992, 1996, 2000, 2004, 2008, 2012	Never
Guinea	1993, 1995, 1998, 2002, 2003, 2010, 2013	Occasionally
Guinea-Bissau	1994, 1999, 2004, 2005, 2008, 2009, 2012, 2014	Never
Liberia	1997, 2005, 2011	Never
Mali	1992, 1997, 2002, 2007, 2013	Never
Mauritania	1992, 1996, 1997, 2001, 2003, 2006, 2007, 2009	Occasionally
Niger	1993, 1995, 1996, 1999, 2004, 2009, 2011	Occasionally
Nigeria	1992, 1993, 1998, 1999, 2003, 2004, 2007, 2011	Usually
Senegal	1993, 1998, 2000, 2001, 2007, 2012	Occasionally
Sierra Leone	1996, 2002, 2007, 2012	Never
Togo	1993, 1994, 1998, 1999, 2002, 2003, 2005, 2007, 2010	Usually

Sources: Africa Elections Database 2012; Strauss and Taylor 2012.
Note: Elections include general elections and legislative elections. The most violent elections occurred in Côte d'Ivoire in 2010, Guinea in 2013, Nigeria in 2011, and Togo in 2005. The description of the nature of election violence is from Strauss and Taylor (2012).

Table 5A.2 Manner in Which Longest-Serving Leaders in West Africa Left Office

Leader (background)[a]	Country	Years in office[b]	How leader left office
Gnassingbé Eyadéma (military)	Togo	38	Died in office (2005)
Félix Houphouët-Boigny (civilian)	Côte d'Ivoire	33	Died in office (1993)
Dawda Jawara (civilian)	Gambia, The	32	Overthrown in coup (1994)
Blaise Compaoré (military)	Burkina Faso	27	Forced out of power (2014)
William Tubman (civilian)	Liberia	27	Died in office (1971)
Ahmed Sékou Touré (civilian)	Guinea	26	Died in office (1984)
Lansana Conté (military)	Guinea	24	Died in office (2008)
Moussa Traoré (military)	Mali	23	Overthrown in coup (1991)
Maaouya Ould Sid'Ahmed Taya (military)	Mauritania	21	Overthrown in coup (2005)
Jerry Rawlings (military)	Ghana	20	Left office after serving his two constitutional terms (2001)
Léopold Sédar Senghor (civilian)	Senegal	20	Resigned (1981)

a. The designation of "military" in the leader's background is based on whether the leader served in the armed forces of his country before becoming president. It does not apply to leaders who fought for colonial armed powers during World War II, such as Léopold Senghor.
b. Years in office refers to unbroken period, excluding previous stints in power. President Rawlings' period in office after a 1979 coup before handing power to a civilian administration is therefore not included.

Table 5A.3 Years in Office of West African Leaders as of 2014

Country	Current leader (background)	Years in office	Years in office of immediate predecessor
Benin	Thomas Yayi Boni (civilian)	8	10
Burkina Faso	Michel Kafando (civilian)	Appointed transitional president in November 2014	27
Cabo Verde	Jorge Carlos Fonseca (civilian)	3	10
Côte d'Ivoire	Alassane Ouattara (civilian)	4	11
Gambia, The	Yahya Jammeh (military)	20	32
Ghana	John Dramani Mahama (civilian)	2	3
Guinea	Alpha Condé (civilian)	4	1
Guinea-Bissau	José Mário Vaz (civilian)	Elected in June 2014	2
Liberia	Ellen Johnson Sirleaf (civilian)	8	3
Mali	Ibrahim Boubacar Keïta (civilian)	1	1
Mauritania	Mohamed Ould Abdel Aziz (military)	5	5 months
Niger	Mahamadou Issoufou (civilian)	3	1
Nigeria	Goodluck Jonathan (civilian)	4	3
Senegal	Macky Sall (civilian)	2	12
Sierra Leone	Ernest Bai Koroma (civilian)	7	9
Togo	Faure Gnassingbé (civilian)	9	38

Note: Figures for predecessors show the unbroken period in power by the leader who preceded the incumbent, including leaders who held office during political transitions. They do not include earlier years in office by the leader.

Table 5A.4 Number of Military Coups in Africa, by Subregion, 1960–2010

Subregion	1960–69	1970–89	1990–2010	Total
West Africa	19	50	37	106
Eastern Africa	10	26	12	48
Central Africa	8	14	13	35
Southern Africa	0	10	6	16
Total	37	100	68	205

Sources: Shillington 2004; Barka and Ncube 2012.
Note: Figures include both failed and succesful coups.

Table 5A.5 Presidential Term Limits in West Africa, by Country

Country	Existence of presidential term limits	Attempts at circumventing
Benin	Yes: Article 42 of the constitution sets term limits of two five-year terms.	The opposition has accused President Yayi Boni of campaigning for a constitution reform bill that would scrap presidential term limits. The president has denied these claims.
Burkina Faso	Yes: Article 37 of the constitution sets term limits of two five-year terms.	An attempt to amend the constitution in October 2014 to enable the incumbent president to run for another term triggered street protests and riots, including the storming of the Parliament and the occupation of the television station. The protests culminated in President Compaoré's removal from power.

(continued next page)

Table 5A.5 (continued)

Country	Existence of presidential term limits	Attempts at circumventing
Cabo Verde	Yes: Article 146 of the 1992 constitution provides for presidential term limits. Pedro de Verona Rodrigues Pires, the former president of Cabo Verde, rejected suggestions for a constitutional amendment that would have enabled him to run for a third term. This decision, along with his stewardship of the economy, led to his award of the Ibrahim Prize for Achievement in African Leadership in 2011.	None
Côte d'Ivoire	Yes: Article 35 of the constitution provides that the president is elected for a five-year term and is reelected only once.	None
Gambia, The	No: The opposition has begun demanding term limits.	None
Ghana	Yes: Article 66 provides for term limits of two four-year terms. Presidential term limits are entrenched in the Ghanaian constitution and can be changed only through a referendum, not legislation or presidential decree.	The National Democratic Congress (NDC) party suggested removing term limits in 1997, while in power. The proposal was abandoned following strong protests by civil society groups and opposition parties.
Guinea	Yes: Article 27 of the constitution sets term limits of two five-year terms.	In 2001, term limits were removed following a constitutional referendum. The 2010 constitution restored term limits.
Guinea-Bissau	No	None
Liberia	Yes: 1986 constitution sets term limits of two six-year terms.	None
Mali	Yes: Article 30 of the constitution of 1992 sets term limits of two five-year terms.	None
Mauritania	Yes: Article 99 of the constitution, passed in a referendum in 2006, sets term limits of two five-year terms. A new president must also take an oath not to try to alter the term limits.	None
Niger	Yes: Term limits were removed by a controversial constitutional referendum in 2009. However, President Mamadou Tandja, who wanted to run for a third term, was overthrown in a coup. In 2010, Niger reinstated the two-term limit through adoption of a new constitution in a referendum. The president is restricted to two terms of five years each.	None
Nigeria	Yes: Two four-year terms. Nigeria- Article 137 provides that a person shall not be qualified to run for the office if they have already been elected in the same position for two consecutive terms. The duration of a term in office is four years.	In 2006, the Nigerian Senate defeated an attempt to amend the constitution to allow President Obasanjo to run for a third term.
Senegal	Yes: The 2001 constitution sets term limits of two seven-year terms but stipulates that limits can be removed by referendum or constitutional amendment. In March 2015, President Macky Sall announced that a referendum would be held in 2016 on the issue of reducing the term in office of the president from seven to five years as an example for Africa.	In 2012, President Abdoulaye Wade ran for a third term, arguing that the provision on term limits did not apply to him because it came into effect after he had been elected. The constitutional court ruled in the president's favor and allowed him to run.

(continued next page)

Table 5A.5 (continued)

Country	Existence of presidential term limits	Attempts at circumventing
Sierra Leone	Yes: Article 46(1) of the constitution sets term limits of two five-year terms. Term limits can be amended by either a two-thirds vote in Parliament or a simple majority in a referendum.	No amendments have taken place to date, but there is a debate in Sierra Leone about alleged plans to amend the constitution to allow the president to run for a third term.
Togo	No: In 2014, Parliament considered a bill that would have reestablished term limits, which were eliminated in 2002 by an act of Parliament. Although legislators from the ruling party defeated the bill, it triggered large street protests in November 2014, with citizens demanding the reinstatement of term limits.	Parliament removed presidential term limits in 2002.

Sources: Vencovsky 2007; Omotola 2011; Africa Report 2014; Freedom House (https://freedomhouse.org).

References

Acemoglu, D., and J. Robinson. 2012. *Why Nations Fail: The Origin of Power, Prosperity, and Poverty.* New York: Crown.

ACLED (Armed Conflict Location and Event Data Project). n.d. "ACLED Version 4 (1997–2013)." http://www.acleddata.com/data/version-4-data-1997-2013.

Adepoju, A., A. Boulton, and M. Levin. n.d. *Promoting Integration through Mobility: Free Movement under ECOWAS.* Geneva: United Nations High Commissioner for Refugees.

Africa Elections Database. 2012. http://africanelections.tripod.com, accessed June 22, 2014.

Africa Report. 2014. "Africa in 2014." Africa Report, Paris. http://www.theafricareport.com/Africa-in-2014.html.

Alaga, E. 2010. "Challenges for Women in Peacebuilding in West Africa." Policy Brief 18, Africa Institute of South Africa, Pretoria. http://www.ai.org.za/wp-content/uploads/downloads/2011/11/No-18.-Challenges-for-Women-in-Peacebuilding-in-West-Africa.pdf.

Alemika, E. 2011. "Post-Election Violence in Nigeria: Emerging Trend and Lessons." Cleen Foundation, Lagos. http://cleenfoundation.blogspot.com/2011/07/post-election-violence-in-nigeria.html.

Aning, K., and A. Atta-Asamoah. 2011. "Demography, Environment and Conflict in West Africa." KAIPTC Occasional Paper 34, Kofi Annan International Peacekeeping Training Centre, Accra.

Barka, H. B., and M. Ncube. 2012. "Political Fragility in Africa: Are Military Coups d'Etat a Never-Ending Phenomenon?" Economic Brief, African Development Bank, Tunis.

Bekoe, D. A. 2008. "Democracy and African Conflicts: Inciting, Mitigating, or Reducing Violence." In *Democratization in Africa: What Progress toward Institutionalisation?* 29–39. Washington, DC: National Intelligence Council.

Belanger, C. 2012. "Women and Democratization in West Africa: The Case of Cercle d'Autopromotion pour le Développement Durable." *Journal of Pan African Studies* 4 (10): 289–304.

Boko, S., and M. McNeil. 2010. "Monitoring Resource Flows in Decentralising African States." In *Social Accountability in Africa: Practitioners' Experiences and Lessons*, ed. V. Ayer, M. Claasen, and C. Alpin-Lardies. Johannesburg: South African Institute of International Affairs.

Campbell, J. 2010. "Electoral Violence in Nigeria." Contingency Planning Memorandum 9, Council on Foreign Relations, New York. http://www.cfr.org/nigeria/electoral -violence-nigeria/p22930.

Carbone, G. 2013. *Leadership Turnovers in Sub-Saharan Africa: From Violence and Coups to Peaceful Elections?* Analysis 192, Italian Institute for International Political Studies, Milan.

Cooper, F. 2002. *Africa since 1940: The Past of the Present.* Cambridge: Cambridge University Press.

Coulibaly, M., and M. Bratton. 2013. "Crisis in Mali: Ambivalent Popular Attitudes on the Way Forward." *Stability: International Journal of Security and Development* 2 (2): 1–10.

Darnton, J. 1994. "'Lost Decade' Drains Africa's Vitality." *New York Times*, June 19. http:// www.nytimes.com/1994/06/19/world/lost-decade-drains-africa-s-vitality. html?src=pm&pagewanted=1.

Devarajan, S., S. Khemani, and M. Walton. 2011. "Civil Society, Public Action, and Accountability in Africa." Policy Research Working Paper 5733, World Bank, Washington, DC. http://elibrary.worldbank.org/doi/pdf/10.1596/1813-9450-5733.

Freedom House. 2013. "Senegal." Freedom House, Washington, DC. http://www .freedomhouse.org/report/freedom-world/2013/senegal#.U3B-8K2SxdI.

Gaventa, J., and G. Barrett. 2010. "So What Difference Does It Make? Mapping the Outcomes of Citizen Engagement." Working Paper, Institute of Development Studies, Brighton, United Kingdom. http://www.ids.ac.uk/files/dmfile/Wp347.pdf.

Ghai, D., and C. Hewitt de Alcántara. 1990. "The Crisis of the 1980s in Sub-Saharan Africa, Latin America, and the Caribbean: Economic Impact, Social Change, and Political Implications." *Development and Change* 21 (3): 389–426.

Hounkpe, M. 2012. "ECOWAS in the Face of Crises in Mali and Guinea Bissau: A Double Standard Dilemma?" IPRIS Viewpoints 108, Portuguese Institute of International Relations and Security, Open Society Initiative for West Africa.

Human Rights Watch. 2004. "Nigeria's 2003 Elections: The Unacknowledged Violence." Human Rights Watch, New York. http://www.hrw.org/reports/2004/nigeria0604 /nigeria0604.pdf.

———. 2011. "Nigeria: Post-Election Violence Killed 800." Human Rights Watch, New York. http://www.hrw.org/news/2011/05/16/nigeria-post-election-violence-killed-800.

———. 2013. *World Report 2013: Guinea.* New York: Human Rights Watch. http://www .hrw.org/world-report/2013/country-chapters/guinea.

Ibrahim, J. 2003. *Democratic Transition in Anglophone West Africa.* Monograph Series. Dakar: Council for the Development of Social Science Research in Africa (CODESRIA). http://www.codesria.org/IMG/pdf/Ibrahim.pdf.

ICG (International Crisis Group). 2011. "Guinea: Putting the Transition Back on Track." Africa Report 178, ICG, Brussels. http://www.crisisgroup.org/en/regions/africa /west-africa/guinea/178-guinea-putting-the-transition-back-on-track.aspx.

Ikelegbe, A., and D. Garuba. 2011. "Youth and Conflicts in Western Africa: Regional Threats and Potential." In *ECOWAS and the Dynamics of Conflict and Peace-Building*, ed. T. Jaye, D. Garuba, and S. Amadi, 102–04. Dakar: Council for the Development of Social Science Research in Africa (CODESRIA).

International Republican Institute. 1994. "Guinea Presidential Election Report, 19 December 1993." International Republican Institute, Washington, DC. http://www .iri.org/sites/default/files/Guinea's%201993%20Presidential%20Election.pdf.

Knutsen, E. 2013. "Deaths of Protesters Herald Guinea's Election." *Al Jazeera*, May 31. http://www.aljazeera.com/indepth/features/2013/05/2013531131553623253.html.

Kposowa, A. J., and J. C. Jenkins. 1993. "The Structural Sources of Military Coups in Postcolonial Africa, 1957–1984." *American Journal of Sociology* 99 (1): 126–63.

Lindemann, S. 2008. "Do Inclusive Elite Bargains Matter? A Research Framework for Understanding the Causes of Civil War in Sub-Saharan Africa." Discussion Paper 15, Development Studies Institute, London School of Economics.

Luckham, R., I. Ahmed, R. Muggah, and S. White. 2001. "Conflict and Poverty in Sub-Saharan Africa: An Assessment of the Issues and Evidence." IDS Working Paper 128, Institute of Development Studies, Brighton, United Kingdom.

Mamdani, M. 1996. *Citizen and Subject: Contemporary Africa and the Legacy of Late Colonialism*. Princeton, NJ: Princeton University.

Marc, A., A. Willman, G. Aslam, and M. Rebosio, with K. Balasuriya. 2013. "Societal Dynamics and Fragility: Engaging Societies in Responding to Fragile Situations." Background paper, World Bank, Washington, DC.

Marshall, M. G. 2005. "Conflict Trends in Africa, 1946–2004: A Macro-Comparative Perspective." Report prepared for the Africa Conflict Prevention Pool, Government of the United Kingdom, London.

Mesfin, B. 2008. "Democracy, Elections and Political Parties: A Conceptual Overview with Special Emphasis on Africa." ISS Paper 166, Institute for Security Studies, Pretoria.

Musah, A. 2009. "West Africa: Governance and Security in a Changing Region." Africa Program Working Paper, International Peace Institute, New York.

N'Diaye, B. 2011. "Conflicts and Crises: Internal and International Dimensions." In *ECOWAS and the Dynamics of Conflict and Peacebuilding*, ed. T. Jaye and S. Amadi. Dakar: CDD West Africa, Consortium for Development Partnerships, Council for the Development of Social Science Research in Africa (CODESRIA). http://www.codesria .org/spip.php?article1533.

North, J. 2011. "The Roots of the Côte d'Ivoire Crisis." *Nation*, April 25. http://www .thenation.com/article/159707/roots-cote-divoire-crisis.

Obi, Cyril. n.d. "Conflict and Peace in West Africa." Nordic Africa Institute, Uppsala, Sweden. http://www.nai.uu.se/publications/news/archives/051obi/index.xml?Language=sv.

OECD-SWAC (Organisation for Economic Co-operation and Development–Sahel and West Africa Club). 2005. *Building Peace and Democracy in West Africa*.

Cotonou, Benin: Forum of Political Parties, the Media, and Civil Society in West Africa. http://www.oecd.org/swac/publications/38521154.pdf.

Ogude, Helen. 2012. *Coups in West Africa: A Reflection of Deficiencies in Africa's Electoral Democracies?* Consultancy Africa Intelligence, Johannesburg. http://www .consultancyafrica.com/index.php?option=com_content&view=article&id=1032:co ups-in-west-africa-a-reflection-of-deficiencies-in-africas-electoral-democracies-&catid =42:election-reflection&Itemid=270.

O'Kane, R. 1993. "Coups d'État in Africa: A Political Economy Approach." *Journal of Peace Research* 3 (3): 251–70.

Olonisakin, F. 2010. "Regional Security from Below: The Case of ECOWAS." Occasional Paper for Institute for Strategic and Development Studies (ISDS), Philippines.

Omotola, J. S. 2011. "Unconstitutional Changes of Government in Africa: What Implications for Democratic Consolidation?" NAI Discussion Paper 20, Nordic Africa Institute, Uppsala, Sweden. http://www.isn.ethz.ch/Digital-Library/Publications/Detail/?id=142832.

Opalo, K. 2011. *Ethnicity and Elite Coalitions: The Origins of "Big Man" Presidentialism in Africa*. Palo Alto, CA: Stanford University Press.

Posner, D., and D. Young. 2007. "The Institutionalisation of Political Power in Africa." *Journal of Democracy* 18 (3): 125–37.

Schmidt, E. 2007. "Black Liberation and the Spirit of '57: The Ghana-Guinea Legacy." Paper presented at the "Conference on Black Liberation and the Spirit of '57," Binghamton University, New York, November 2–3. http://www2.binghamton.edu/fbc /archive/schmidt.pdf.

Shillington, K. 2004. *Encyclopedia of African History*, vols. 1–3. New York: Routledge.

Smyth, T. M., and M. L. Best. 2013. "Tweet to Trust: Social Media and Elections in West Africa." In *Proceedings of the Sixth International Conference on Information and Communication Technologies and Development: Full Papers*, vol. 1, 133–41. http://dl.acm.org/citation .cfm?id=2516617&dl=ACM&coll=DL&CFID=489551003&CFTOKEN=83240886.

Souaré, I. K. 2010. *A Critical Assessment of Security Challenges in West Africa*. Situation Report, Institute of Security Studies, Paris.

Stewart, F. 2010. "Horizontal Inequalities as a Cause of Conflict: A Review of CRISE Findings." CRISE Overview 1, Centre for Research on Inequality, Human Security, and Ethnicity, Oxford.

Strauss, S., and C. Taylor. 2012. "Democratization and Electoral Violence in Sub-Saharan Africa, 1990–2008." In *Voting in Fear: Electoral Violence in Sub-Saharan Africa*, ed. D. A. Bekoe, 15–38. Washington, DC: U.S. Institute of Peace Press.

U.S. Department of State. 1995. "Guinea Human Rights Practices, 1994." Country Report, U.S. Department of State, Washington, DC. http://dosfan.lib.uic.edu/ERC /democracy/1994_hrp_report/94hrp_report_africa/Guinea.html.

———. 1996. "Côte d'Ivoire Human Rights Practices, 1995." Country Report, Washington, DC. http://dosfan.lib.uic.edu/ERC/democracy/1995_hrp_report/95hrp _report_africa/CotedIvoire.html.

———. 2001. "Côte d'Ivoire: Country Reports on Human Rights Practices." Country Report, U.S. Department of State, Washington, DC. http://www.state.gov/j/drl/rls /hrrpt/2000/af/773.htm.

———. 2006. "Togo." Country Report, U.S. Department of State, Washington, DC. http://www.state.gov/j/drl/rls/hrrpt/2005/61597.htm.

Vencovsky, D. 2007. "Presidential Term Limits in Africa." *Conflict Trends* 2: 15–21. http://www.isn.ethz.ch/Digital-Library/Publications/Detail/?ots591=0c54e3b3-1e9c-be1e-2c24-a6a8c7060233&lng=en&id=102020.

Whitaker, B. 2005. "Citizens and Foreigners: Democratisation and the Politics of Exclusion in Africa." *African Studies Review* 48 (1): 109–26.

Williams, P. D. 2011. *War and Conflict in Africa*. Cambridge: Polity Press.

Willoughby, S. 2013. "Remembering Sub-Saharan's First Military Coup d'État Fifty Years On." London School of Economics and Political Science. http://blogs.lse.ac.uk/africaatlse/2013/08/19/remembering-sub-saharan-africas-first-military-coup-detat-fifty-years-on.

World Bank. 2008. "Nigeria's Experience Publishing Budget Allocations: A Practical Tool to Promote Demand for Better Governance." Social Development Note, World Bank, Washington, DC. https://openknowledge.worldbank.org/bitstream/handle/10986/11138/469250NWP0Box31UBLIC10SDN1DFGG1Note.pdf?sequence=1.

———. 2011. *World Development Report 2011: Conflict, Security and Development*. Washington, DC: World Bank.

———. 2012. *Supporting Good Governance for Growth: Lessons from World Bank Engagement in Ghana's Emerging Oil and Gas Sector*. Washington, DC: World Bank.

———. 2014. "Opening the Black Box: Contextual Drivers of Social Accountability Effectiveness." Draft Report, Social Development Department, World Bank Washington, DC.

Young, C. 2004. "The End of the Post-colonial State in Africa? Reflections on Changing African Political Dynamics." *African Affairs* 103 (410): 23–49.

———. 2012. *The Post-Colonial State in Africa: Fifty Years of Independence, 1960–2010*. Madison: University of Wisconsin Press.

Zeilig, L., and M. Dawson. 2008. "Introduction: Student Activism, Structural Adjustment, and the Democratic Transition in Africa." *Journal of Higher Education in Africa* 6 (2&3): 6–21.

Chapter 6

Reforming the Security Sector

The inability of security forces to deflect and counter threats to the state and citizens has posed one of the primary challenges for countries in West Africa since independence. In many cases, the armed forces themselves have threatened citizen well-being, often intervening and commandeering power.

In the more than two decades since the end of the Cold War, some West African countries have undergone a process of democratization. Ghana and Nigeria, for example, have made strides in transforming their civil-military relations and improving the quality of their security sectors. In contrast, other countries—The Gambia, Guinea-Bissau, Mauritania, Niger, Togo, and, recently, Mali—have grappled with the imbalance (Houngnikpo 2012). In some countries, the fragility of democratic institutions enables military leaders to remain extremely influential in politics, undermining institutions and weakening the mechanisms of governance that underpin state-society relations. The dominance of the military closes off space for political participation and impedes political processes, with undesirable consequences for development, economic growth, and social cohesion. It also increases the risk of power contestations becoming violent.

Reforms have improved civil-military relations, but the security forces need to adapt further to confront new challenges—such as trafficking, piracy, and religious extremism—that have the potential to destabilize tracts of the subregion (see chapter 2). Keeping the armed forces out of politics and ensuring that adequate checks and balances are put in place will help protect citizens at a time when new security threats are emerging.

Certain security threats to the subregion have been more pronounced within a specific conflict system, wherein cross-border connections based on shared ethnic, linguistic, cultural, and religious ties can facilitate the spread of conflict among neighbors, as in the case of the countries of the Mano River Basin (see chapter 1 for an explanation of West Africa's conflict systems). The tendency of conflicts to cluster around a specific system strengthens the case for a regional rather than a country-by-country approach to combating security threats. Such an approach may involve designing interventions that mitigate drivers of conflict, particularly as they relate to border communities, or even imposing sanctions on warmongers and perpetrators from neighboring states.

Authoritarianism, Ethnicization, and the Degradation of the Security Forces since Independence

Poor leadership and the weak capacity of the postcolonial state contributed to the creation of dysfunctional security institutions and impeded the management of security threats. Colonial-era practices, such as the policy of favoring specific communities or regions in recruiting people to the armed forces, helped weaken security institutions. At independence, the armed forces of many states were perceived as dominated by and loyal to a particular ethnic group or region rather than to the nascent state itself (Fawole and Ukeje 2005). The north-south divide was particularly pronounced in Benin, Ghana, Nigeria, Sierra Leone, and Togo (Kandeh 2004b). Francophone countries also faced the economic and logistical challenge of integrating citizens who had been recruited by France from across West Africa to fight in its various military campaigns—in particular in Europe and Indochina—into their new national armies. In Togo, pressure to integrate returnee soldiers into the armed forces contributed to the subregion's first military coup in 1963, after the president refused to sanction such a move (Kandeh 2004b).

The neopatrimonial style of leadership that several heads of state adopted contributed to the degradation and dysfunction of the security forces. The purging of security elites and the stacking of the forces with a hierarchy loyal to the leadership undermined security institutions and militarized politics (Snyder 1992). Failure to build security institutions that were inclusive, professional, effective, and ethnically and regionally representative helped create some security threats. The 1968 military coup in Benin, for example, which was carried out by members of the armed forces from the north, reflected the rejection of an institution viewed as dominated by southerners (Kandeh 2004b). Where leaders failed to fully control the security forces, they opted to weaken these institutions so that they would no longer pose a threat to their authority.

Countries with authoritarian forms of governance that upheld the security of the regime over the security of the state—Liberia under William Tubman and William Tolbert, for example—saw institutions transformed into personal fiefdoms (Fayemi 2004). In Côte d'Ivoire, Liberia, Mali, and Sierra Leone, political elites undermined the capacity and morale of the armed forces in a bid to avert military coups and challenges to their authority and rule. In Sierra Leone, President Siaka Stevens "deliberately embarked on a state security-weakening project" (Fayemi 2004, 4) in order to consolidate his personalized rule. The systematic deinstitutionalization of the state and its appendages left little or no capacity to confront the violent uprisings and civil wars of the early 1990s.

One strategy leaders used to control the armed forces was to fragment the security apparatus by creating and elevating an elite presidential guard that was accountable only to the president. In Ghana, this approach contributed to unrest in the ranks of the armed forces that culminated in the 1966 coup (Barany 2013). In Sierra Leone, President Stevens questioned the loyalty of the professional military. He therefore established alternative power centers in the Internal Security Unit (ISU) and the Special Security Division (SSD) (Fayemi 2004). The result was security forces that were not adequately structured, financed, or controlled to fend off threats (Ero 2000; Mehler 2012).

The strategy of divide and control contributed to the ethnicization of the military. In Guinea and Guinea-Bissau, members of a particular ethnic group dominated sections of the military corps, which risked delegitimizing them (Mehler 2012). The practice split the forces both along ethnic and regional lines as well as between the different ranks of the officer corps. Co-opting the senior leadership of the security forces while ignoring the rank and file undermined the integrity of the institutions and resulted in a breakdown in hierarchy. It also precipitated a number of subaltern military coups. Such coups took place in Burkina Faso, Ghana, Liberia, and Mali (Kandeh 1996, 2004a); Sierra Leone experienced three of them (in 1968, 1992, and 1997) (for a discussion of and statistics on coups, see chapter 5).

The economic crises of the 1980s, together with the unmasking of state decay brought about by decades of neopatrimonialism and corruption, had a direct impact on the security sector in Liberia and Sierra Leone. Salaries to soldiers were delayed, and their uniforms and equipment began to deteriorate; amidst a breakdown of discipline, soldiers engaged in looting (Herbst 2004; Bates 2008). The capacities of national security systems were put to the test when civil wars broke out in both countries, as it became clear that the security institutions were incapable of fending off the well-organized and well-funded rebel groups that emerged in the late 1980s and early 1990s. Government forces were so weak that when confronted by well-trained rebels and armed groups, they collapsed or splintered into groups of "sobels" (soldiers by day and rebels by night). The deviation from the republican ethos and professionalism of the armed forces was complete with the disintegration of the military apparatus into mercenary organizations (Mehler 2012), ethnic armed factions such as the Kamajors (traditional hunters from the Mende ethnic group in Sierra Leone) (Fayemi 2004), and a support base for warlords such as Charles Taylor. After 1997, no single body of the security forces in Liberia was at the service of the population (Mehler 2012); with the end of the Cold War and the "removal of the imperial security umbrellas" (Olonisakin 2008), the increasing availability and circulation of small arms helped fuel conflicts. Reliance on private military companies such as Executive Outcomes, Sandline, and the Gurkha Security Services to fill the void left by the decimated armed forces "further deepened the de-institutionalization of the mainstream forces" (Fayemi 2004, 4) and added to the chaotic mosaic of nonstate security actors on the ground.

Several countries in West Africa struggled to establish a monopoly over violence in their territories. Their failure to do so opened the door for nonstate actors, including the Arakan Boys in Ghana; the Area Boys, the Bakassi Boys, and the Civilian Joint Task Force in the northeast regions of Nigeria; and vigilante groups and militias in Liberia, Mali, and Sierra Leone (Small Arms Survey 2006). In some situations, these outfits provided security to citizens. However, their unchecked power has posed a threat, as vigilantes and militias are prone to politicization by the elites or risk becoming excessive and arbitrary (Olonisakin 2008). Nigeria's Bakassi Boys, for example, which spread into multiple states with the blessings of their governors, spiraled out of control as the group's leadership dissipated and engaged in extrajudicial killings and arbitrary arrests (Small Arms Survey 2006).

The end of the Cold War saw the capability of the armed forces weakened across Africa, as many of the generous military assistance programs from the superpowers ended. This weakness was witnessed as recently as 2012 in Mali, following the Tuareg-led uprising that triggered a military coup by disaffected soldiers. Former president Amadou Toumani Touré, who had been a general, weakened the military, in part out of fear of a coup. He gave preferential treatment to the Red Berets (the presidential guard and parachute regiment) (ICG 2014) and left the ill-equipped Green Berets to deal with the Tuareg uprisings. Tensions were rooted in the fact that Touré had been in charge of the Red Berets when he overthrew the regime of Moussa Traoré in 1991. Corruption during the Touré regime undermined the military and had ramifications for the north, where all but a few soldiers deserted. Some observers accused the state of complicity with criminal networks in the north (Onuoha and Thurston 2013).

Human Rights Violations, Abuse of Power by the State, and the Weak Rule of Law

Many authoritarian political systems in the subregion have resorted to oppression and human rights abuses to tackle violent protest against injustice (perceived and real) (World Bank 2011). The people charged by the state with providing security, especially the police, have perpetrated abuses and used excessive force against civilians. The human rights and fundamental freedoms of citizens have been violated with impunity, through detentions, arbitrary arrests, even murder. Security services have engaged in sexual violence (in the 2009 rape and murder of opposition supporters by the military in Guinea, for instance) (Human Rights Watch 2009; Alaga 2011). The highly masculine institutional culture of the military forces facilitates the sexual harassment of both civilians and female military personnel (Alaga 2011). A 2010 assessment by the Women Peace and Security Network Africa found that no security sector institution in West Africa had attained its 20 percent target recruitment of women and that women held no more than 8 percent of senior ranking positions in the sector (WIPSEN-Africa 2010).

The sense of injustice is compounded by the failure of the state to hold law enforcement officials and military personnel accountable when they violate citizens' rights. The sense of prejudice that arises from such situations is exacerbated and reinforced by official complacency of misdemeanors, which perpetuates the resulting social exclusion (Olonisakin 2008). In most cases, justice systems have remained largely dysfunctional and the rule of law weak. Few citizens have confidence in the impartiality and independence of the administration of justice. The neglect of due process "robbed institutions of their legitimacy and credibility" (N'yong'o 1992, 100), while the proliferation of regulatory rules and administration created new opportunities for corruption and further weakened state-society linkages.

The atrophy of legal institutions and frameworks has had far-reaching consequences for the legitimacy of many countries' security sectors. The severe dysfunction of Liberia's judicial system, for instance, was one of the causes of the civil war there, as governing elites co-opted the justice system as a political tool through which to exercise and legitimize their power, creating a crisis of confidence in the system and stripping it of its credibility (ICG 2006). The absence of enforcement mechanisms in Liberia allowed the illegal expropriation of resources, including timber, which was laundered through a legal supply chain by Charles Taylor (World Bank 2011).

Defense Budgets in West Africa

Defense budgets across West Africa are on the rise. Sub-Saharan Africa as a whole is a lucrative market for defense equipment, with total annual expenditure between 2010 and 2013 averaging $23 billion (SIPRI Database).

The sector receives 0.6–1.8 percent of gross domestic product (GDP) in Guinea-Bissau and 4 percent in Mauritania. Ghana more than doubled its military spending in 2013, to $306 million, up from $109 million in 2012. Donor funding provided another $47 million in 2013 (Perlo-Freeman and Solmirano 2014).

Despite the relatively small size of their security forces, security expenditures in many West African countries consume a disproportionate share of their budgets, particularly when faced with security threats. Mali hired 15,000 personnel in 2012 (World Bank 2013a)—an increase of 50 percent—and raised wages in the army 37 percent. Military expenditure rocketed 50 percent in Mali (despite a one-third drop in revenue). Niger increased its military spending by 80 percent in 2012, forcing significant resource allocation (Zounmenou 2014). Its wage bill for security forces amounted to about a third of the country's total wage bill in 2012. Wages for the security forces increased 65 percent between 2010 and 2012, following the recruitment of 5,000 personnel and an 85 percent increase in wages for police officers (World Bank 2013b).

Nigeria's military capacity remains the most developed in West Africa, with an annual budget of $2.2 billion (Adebajo 2002) and 95,000–100,000 troops. As the regional hegemon, Nigeria has been instrumental to the ability and capacity of the Economic Community of West African States (ECOWAS) to intervene in regional conflicts (Alli 2012). It has 363 tanks, more than 1,400 armored vehicles, 294 aircraft, and 84 helicopters, and it recently beefed up its maritime capability in a bid to counter piracy. The naval budget represents 20 percent of the defense budget. With its 20,000-strong naval force and warships, Nigeria is among the few West African nations with the capacity to monitor its maritime territory.

Weak state capacity—and the limited ability to defend maritime waters—has contributed to a surge in maritime piracy (Bridger 2013). In response, the International Maritime Organization (IMO) has established a West and Central Africa Maritime Security Trust Fund, to which a number of donors (including China, Japan, and the United Kingdom) have made pledges. Nigeria also provides a large number of UN peacekeeping troops (2,961 as of 2015), almost as many as Ghana (3,012) and Senegal (3,079) (UN n.d.) (box 6.1). It is a primary contributor to ECOWAS missions as well (Sule 2013).

BOX 6.1

Centers of Excellence for International Peacekeeping in West Africa

Seamlessly integrating and operationalizing peacekeeping troops from different nations into a coherent force is a challenge, given the different forms and levels of rigor in the training of troops. A number of centers of excellence have been established across West Africa to address the problem (Aning 2010). They include the Kofi Annan International Peacekeeping Training Centre (KAIPTC); the National Defence College in Abuja, Nigeria; and the Peacekeeping School of Bamako, Mali. The three institutions have developed and operationalized a common peacekeeping course for training personnel from the subregion who are deployed to peacekeeping operations around the world.

The centers have played an important role in training troops and promoting dialogue on civil-military relations at both the national and subregional levels. KAIPTC in particular is the subregional focal point for the Finnish-funded Africa Civil-Military Coordination (ACMC) program, which is hosted by the African Centre for the Constructive Resolution of Disputes (ACCORD).

(continued next page)

Box 6.1 (continued)

Donors have played an important role in establishing, expanding, and ensuring the viability of some of these centers. KAIPTC was established in part with funding from Germany and the United Kingdom; other donors contributed to its expansion and funded training programs (Aning 2010). The Peacekeeping School in Bamako has also benefited from donor funding, which supported the establishment and expansion of the center and its relocation to Bamako.

Challenges of Reform

Military and security forces across the region have benefited from the opportunities for political reform offered by democratization, restoration of the rule of law, reform of the justice administration, and reinforcement of the capacities of the armed forces through security sector reform projects. The donor community has played a major role in efforts to reform and restructure the security forces in West Africa since the mid-1990s. Military coups, and the civil wars in Côte d'Ivoire, Guinea-Bissau, Liberia, and Sierra Leone, prompted a reappraisal of the hands-off approach to security sectors, as the security-development nexus became a key element of donor policy in conflict-affected countries.

Although regional frameworks and collective security mechanisms to address security threats in West Africa had been in place since the late 1970s and early 1980s, they took effect only in the 1990s, during the region's civil wars. The interventions by ECOWAS in Liberia and Sierra Leone, under the auspices of a Nigerian-led and -funded force, filled the void left by the weakness of national armies and accelerated the transformation of the regional peace and security architecture. A comprehensive institutional and normative framework has been created to respond to conflicts and instability, but the existing regional peace and security architecture cannot effectively deal with the emerging threats of terrorism, maritime security, and drug trafficking, each of which requires specific strategies. Reforms are needed to increase the security forces' ability to deal with conventional threats and to allow them to deal with emerging challenges.

The challenges to security sector reform in West Africa have proved daunting, and the results have been mixed. Côte d'Ivoire has made some progress, adopting a new security sector reform strategy, conducting a census of the country's security forces, and establishing (in 2012) an authority in charge of disarmament, demobilization, and reintegration. Progress beyond this point has been limited, however, and experts argue that more improvement has been made on paper than on the ground (World Politics Review 2013). Ahead of elections in 2015, the United Nations warned that reforms to the security sector are needed to safeguard peace.

The breakdown of security has been a key source of fragility in Guinea-Bissau. Reforming that country's security sector is therefore critical to restoring state credibility and citizen security. The authorities and the international community have set three goals: restoring the state's legitimate control and accountability over the use of force, addressing the fiscal burden of an oversized security sector, and responding to the demands of armed personnel for improved living conditions. A roadmap for reform has been designed, and in 2009–11 the government in power laid the foundation for a potentially meaningful reform process. ECOWAS is financing the reform, including a pension fund, a critical ingredient for peacefully retiring security personnel (box 6.2).

Liberia's security system has improved markedly, with significant gains in the training or retraining of officers across security institutions. Sierra Leone has implemented a comprehensive reform program (box 6.3).

Many efforts elsewhere have been largely ad hoc, the accidental byproducts of a broader reform agenda, or achieved incrementally (Fayemi 2004). They have therefore had limited success in shifting power relations or entrenching institutional transformation (Fayemi 2004). The issue of ownership of reform of the security sector has not been accorded sufficient centrality in the process, which could threaten its long-term viability.

BOX 6.2

A New Chapter for Guinea-Bissau

Guinea-Bissau has wrestled with a series of challenges since independence, including poverty, a highly politicized military, weak institutions, and, recently, drug trafficking. But peaceful presidential and parliamentary elections in April 2014 may be ushering in a new chapter for the beleaguered coastal state. The elections led to the restoration of constitutional order and the formation of an inclusive government. In a second positive development, in September 2014, the chief of the armed forces, who had led a coup in 2012, was dismissed.

Central to change has been progress in security sector reform. Through ECOMIB (the ECOWAS mission in Bissau), ECOWAS addressed the reform of army pensions, which was needed to shrink the size of the armed forces. In July 2013, it was announced that 17,000 military personnel had expressed willingness to retire (Uzoechina 2014). The ECOMIB mission was also credited with creating an environment conducive to peaceful elections in 2014.

Progress has renewed donor interest in reengaging in the country. In November 2014, the International Contact Group on Guinea-Bissau (ICG-GB) met for the first time in two years, and discussions were held about hosting an international donor conference for Guinea-Bissau (UN Security Council 2014).

BOX 6.3

Sustained Reform of the Security Sector in Sierra Leone

Sierra Leone's experience of security sector reform has attracted much scholarly interest, both because of its comprehensiveness and the long-term nature of donor engagement. That involvement marked a shift in development thinking in the late 1990s on the need to frame security as integral to development. The United Kingdom signed a 10-year memorandum of understanding with Sierra Leone in 2002, with the International Military Advisory and Training Team (IMATT), the British Army's team in Sierra Leone, greatly benefiting from this long-term commitment (Godwin and Haenlein 2013).

Sierra Leone's reform program was comprehensive and holistic, involving the army, the intelligence services, the police, the justice sector, and related institutions. It benefited from strong interministry coordination and cooperation with the United Kingdom (the lead donor) and other donors (Bendix and Stanley 2008). A key element of the program was reform of the police force, based on a model of "local needs policing," in which members of the force collaborate with communities in order to provide security (Albrecht 2010).

Today, Sierra Leone's army is regarded as a capable and effective force, and public perceptions of it are positive (Godwin and Haenlein 2013). It has contributed forces to two important peace operations (in Darfur and in Somalia). In a remarkable turnaround, in 2013 Sierra Leone provided more troops to peace operations per capita than Nigeria (Godwin and Haenlein 2013).

To be effective, security sector reform requires strong political commitments and an overhaul of governance, which can come about only through internal processes, as demonstrated by Ghana, Nigeria, and Senegal (box 6.4). Improvements in accountability, the rule of law, and the security sector need to be coordinated. Once political commitment is in place, technical support and financing can play a critical role—but there is no substitute for political commitment. In this sense, peer pressure and the framework provided by regional mechanisms are critical for the future stability of West Africa.

Areas in Need of Reform

Domestic, regional, and international attempts have sought to reform and reposition the security services. Despite these efforts, the security institutions in many countries have been unable to fend off emerging threats, such as maritime piracy, drug trafficking, and violent attacks by extremist groups, and they remain heavily influential in politics.

BOX 6.4

Senegal: A Model for Civil-Military Relations

Senegal stands out as a rare success story in a subregion that has struggled with its civil-military relations since independence. A large part of its success in avoiding the pitfalls that contributed to political instability in many of its neighbors can be traced back to the deal struck between President Léopold Sédar Senghor and General Jean Alfred Diallo in 1962, in the heady years after independence. At the outset, the president and the chief of staff of the army laid down a foundation for future civil-military relations in which the armed forces would play an important role in Senegal's development while serving under civilian leadership.

A second key factor is the concept of the *Armée-Nation*, Senegal's own version of military-civilian collaboration, through which the armed forces fostered development in sectors such as infrastructure, health, education, and environmental protections. The contribution of the armed forces to improving service provision, training, and research in the health sector in particular has garnered praise both locally and internationally. The model has also helped establish a climate of trust between political and military elites and between the public and the armed forces.

A third contributing factor has been the high quality of leadership at both the civilian and military levels, which has strengthened political stability and upheld civil-military relations. It has been supported by a culture of professionalization within the armed forces, including a clear chain of command, mechanisms for civilian control over the armed forces, and a competitive recruitment process.

Sources: Partners for Democratic Change 2010; Diop 2013.

Its strong military capability notwithstanding, Nigeria is struggling to counter and neutralize the threat posed by radical groups such as Boko Haram, which is threatening to extend its reach into Cameroon, Chad, and Niger. Nigeria had to call on the military assistance of foreign partners, including the United States, following the kidnappings of schoolgirls in the northeast in 2014. Nigeria has struggled in the past to put an end to violence by armed groups such as the Movement for the Emancipation of Niger Delta (MEND). Rooted in long-running socioeconomic and political grievances and discontents, these security threats are not easily quelled through conventional warfare, which troops and security forces are trained in.

A report by the Presidential Committee on Security Challenges in the Northeast Zone found that security agencies suffer from a variety of problems. It cites operational lapses, rivalry, underfunding, lack of adequate equipment, and lack of collaboration (Federal Government of Nigeria 2011). The military has also come under fire for its role in alleged human rights abuses, torture, and other forms of mistreatment of the civilian population (Human Rights Watch 2013; Amnesty International 2014), charges the Nigerian authorities have dismissed as unfounded.

Failure to adapt the armed forces to new threats in part reflects their unchanged mission statements, which remain geared toward addressing conventional warfare threats. The focus remains firmly on external security, despite the fact that greater threats lie elsewhere. Security forces need to redefine their mission statements (Kandeh 2004a; Ouédraogo 2014). Doing so would have implications for training, staffing, size, and formation.

The reintegration of armed groups and nonprofessional soldiers has been an issue in many countries that have exited from conflict. Liberia and Sierra Leone have succeeded in this endeavor; Côte d'Ivoire is still struggling with demobilizing and reintegrating former militias into civilian life. This process has taken much more time and effort than expected. In view of the size of its armed forces, Guinea-Bissau needs to retire many of its officers (see box 6.2). With the peace talks nearing completion in Mali, the issue of disarmament, demobilization, and reintegration is becoming central to achieving sustainable peace. In 2009, Nigeria offered amnesty to militias in the Niger Delta involved in crimes including attacking oil infrastructure and kidnapping oil workers. In return for handing in their weapons, they received pardons, were offered vocational and nonviolence training, and were paid $410 per month until they found work. More than 26,000 young people took the package, contributing to a decrease in violence and an increase in oil revenues. Some militants reportedly returned to fighting, however, or transferred their efforts to offshore piracy (IRIN 2011).

Many military forces in West Africa need to become more professional by demobilizing troops that lack the requisite skills and ability of modern security forces, as well various militias and paramilitary groups. Côte d'Ivoire, Liberia, and Sierra Leone have disarmed, demobilized, and reintegrated former soldiers and provided them with skills training. Some 103,019 combatants were disarmed and demobilized in Liberia, including 8,523 boys and 2,440 girls (Zounmenou 2008). In Sierra Leone, 72,490 combatants were demobilized, including 6,854 child soldiers (UN Office of the Special Representative for Africa 2007). Major efforts in this regard are still needed in many West African countries.

Wages in many of West Africa's security forces are inadequate and irregularly paid. The average monthly salary of soldiers in West Africa ranges from $75 in Togo to $305 in Nigeria (Touchard 2014). Low salaries and lack of adequate equipment reduce morale. The police and gendarmerie are also poorly paid, leaving them vulnerable to corruption. Meanwhile, rivalry between the police, gendarmerie, presidential guards, and special forces threatens to compromise law and order.

Except in The Gambia and Nigeria, police forces are understaffed. Globally, there are 350 policemen for every 100,000 people; the United Nations recommends a minimum of 222 policemen for every 100,000 people (Harrendorf, Heiskanen, and Malby 2010). Mali and Niger have only about 50 policemen per 100,000 people; Côte d'Ivoire, Ghana, and Guinea have fewer than 100; and Sierra Leone has nearly 200. Nigeria recruited 370,000 police officers between 2000 and 2008, raising its ratio to 205 police per 100,000 people (Fayemi 2005).

A further challenge has been the lack of funding for and insufficient attention to gender equality. Incorporation of a gender element into security sector reform programs in West Africa came about only as a result of donor support and consultations with citizens during the reform process. In Liberia and Sierra Leone, for example, consultations with women's groups—in some cases accompanied by donor conditionality that gender be incorporated in the terms of reference—led to gender-related security sector reforms (Alaga 2011).

Reform of the armed forces is critical, but it needs to be conducted hand in hand with development of governance structures and oversight capacities of the civilian authorities. A significant challenge has been ensuring the parallel development of an "effective and overarching governance framework" (Fayemi 2004, 7) in order to pair security sector reform with a more comprehensive restructuring agenda.

Recommendations for Reforming the Security Sector

The manifold challenges of security in West Africa affect stability, national cohesion, development, and economic growth. Because of their limited mandates, most development actors are not well placed to intervene in the security sector. A possible point of intervention is to leverage key competencies, particularly regarding governance and fiscal aspects of the security sector.

Recommendations to address this driver of conflict and fragility include the following:

- Extend reforms for governance and accountability to the security sector (most countrywide governance reforms exclude security ministries). Oversight mechanisms play an essential role in protecting the population from the excesses of the security services, reducing corruption and nepotism risks, increasing the cost-effectiveness of the security sector, and helping governments maintain the momentum of security sector reform across the region. The same type of mechanisms recommended for other ministries and public agencies should be adopted in the security sector.

- Promote the fiscal sustainability of the sector through interventions that relate to budgeting, expenditure, wages, and costing while introducing strong financial control mechanisms. Development partners can engage in this area as part of overall public expenditure reviews and improvement of countries' public financial management.

- Improve justice and conflict resolution systems, and strengthen the rule of law. Development support has been insufficient in these areas, particularly in light of their importance for stability and conflict prevention. Support can be channeled through formal justice systems, including the connection between formal and traditional justice, as well as mechanisms for mediating conflict and addressing local grievances outside of formal justice systems. Mechanisms for conflict resolution can also be integrated into sectoral projects pertaining to land, pastoral activities, health, and education. Improving justice and strengthening the rule of law necessitate broader approaches than focusing on the Ministry of Justice alone.

- Evaluate the success of security sector reform programs in the region, especially through impact assessments. Increasing understanding of what works is essential if reforms are to be scaled up.

- Establish partnerships with regional organizations, such as ECOWAS, to strengthen security and justice, with a focus on the emerging regional security architecture, and support the developmental aspects of these policies (for example, demobilization programs, pension programs for the military, and improved management and follow-up of public expenditures). Working through regional organizations reduces the danger of political risks for development organizations and donors and ensures dissemination of region-wide experiences.

References

Adebajo, A. 2002. *Liberia's Civil War: Nigeria, ECOMOG and Regional Security in West Africa.* Boulder, CO: Lynne Rienner.

Alaga, E. 2011. "Gender and Security Policy in West Africa." Working Paper, Friedrich-Ebert-Stiftung, Wuse II, Nigeria. http://library.fes.de/pdf-files/bueros/nigeria/08162.pdf.

Albrecht, P. A. 2010. "Transforming Internal Security in Sierra Leone: Sierra Leone Police and Broader Justice Sector Reform." Report 7, Danish Institute for International Studies, Copenhagen. http://www.dcism.dk/graphics/Publications/Reports2010/RP2010-07_transforming_Sierra_Leone_web.pdf.

Alli, W. O. 2012. "The Role of Nigeria in Regional Security Policy." Friedrich-Ebert-Stiftung, Abuja, Nigeria. http://library.fes.de/pdf-files/bueros/nigeria/09372.pdf.

Amnesty International. 2014. *Welcome to Hell Fire: Torture and Other Ill-Treatment in Nigeria.* New York: Amnesty International. http://www.amnesty.org/en/library/asset/AFR44/011/2014/en/2ef7e489-a66d-4213-af3d-a08e1e4ca017/afr440112014en.pdf.

Aning, K. 2010. "Landmarks in Peacekeeping Training in West Africa and the Role of the Kofi Annan International Peacekeeping Training Centre." AISA Policy Brief 32, Africa Institute of South Africa, Pretoria. http://www.ai.org.za/wp-content/uploads /downloads/2011/11/No-32.-Landmarks-in-peacekeeping-training-in-West-Africa -and-the-role-of-the-Kofi-Annan-International-peacekeeping-training-centre.pdf.

Barany, Z. 2013. "Explaining Military Responses to Revolutions." Arab Center for Research and Policy Studies, Doha, Qatar. http://english.dohainstitute.org/file/get/e3e6e805-6f90 -48c8-8f31-4aa92078aa7c.pdf.

Bates, R. 2008. *When Things Fell Apart: State Failure in Late-Century Africa.* Cambridge: Cambridge University Press.

Bendix, D., and R. Stanley. 2008. "Security Sector Reform in Africa: The Promise and the Practice of a New Donor Approach." Occasional Paper, African Centre for the Constructive Resolution of Disputes, Mount Edgecombe, South Africa. http://www .gsdrc.org/go/display&type=Document&id=4977.

Bridger, J. M. 2013. "West Africa Turns Limited Resources to Addressing Piracy in Gulf of Guinea." *World Politics Review,* July 9. http://www.worldpoliticsreview.com/articles/13077 /west-africa-turns-limited-resources-to-addressing-piracy-in-gulf-of-guinea.

Diop, B. 2013. "Civil-Military Relations in Senegal." In *Military Engagement: Influencing Armed Forces Worldwide to Support Democratic Transition; A Handbook Project. Vol. 2: Regional and Country Studies.* Washington, DC: Council for a Community of Democracy. http://www.ccd21.org/military_handbook/volume _two/12_senegal.pdf.

Ero, C. 2000. "Sierra Leone's Security Complex." Working Paper, Center for Defence Studies, King's College, London. http://securityanddevelopment.org/pdf/work3.pdf.

Fawole, W. A., and C. Ukeje. 2005. "Introduction." In *The Crisis of the State and Regionalism in West Africa: Identity, Citizenship and Conflict,* ed. W. A. Fawole and C. Ukeje. Dakar: Council for the Development of Social Science Research in Africa (CODESRIA). http://www.codesria.org/spip.php?article99.

Fayemi, J. K. 2004. "Governing Insecurity in Post-Conflict States: The Case of Sierra Leone and Liberia." In *Reform and Reconstruction of the Security Sector,* ed. A. Bryden and H. Hänggi, 179–206. Munster, Ireland: LIT. http://www.apcof.org/files/5175_8 .pdf.

———. 2005. "Pursuing Security in the Postconflict Phase: Reflections on Recent African Cases and Their Implications for Current and Future Peace Operations." Paper presented at the Fourth Geneva Centre for Security Policy Workshop on Peace Operations, Geneva, June 12–13. ftp://budgie2.ethz.ch/gcsp/e-tilljune06/meetings /Research_Seminars/EU-Peace_Ops/2005/Fayemi.pdf.

Federal Government of Nigeria. 2011. *The Presidential Committee Report on Security Challenges in the North-East Zone.* Abuja: Federal Government of Nigeria.

Godwin, A., and C. Haenlein. 2013. "Security-Sector Reform in Sierra Leone: The UK Assistance Mission in Transition." *RUSI Journal* 158 (6). https://www.rusi.org /publications/journal/ref:A52B036B3C82F9/#.VCLw3_mSywc.

Harrendorf, S., M. Heiskanen, and S. Malby, eds. 2010. *International Statistics on Crime and Justice.* HEUNI Publication 64, European Institute for Crime Prevention and Control, Helsinki. http://www.unodc.org/documents/data-and-analysis /Crime-statistics/International_Statistics_on_Crime_and_Justice.pdf.

Herbst, J. 2004. "African Militaries and Rebellion: The Political Economy of Threat and Combat Effectiveness." *Journal of Peace Research* 41 (3): 357–69.

Houngnikpo, M. C. 2012. "Africa's Militaries: A Missing Link in Democratic Transitions." Africa Security Brief 17, Africa Center for Strategic Studies, Washington, DC. http://ndupress.ndu.edu/Portals/68/Documents/archives/asb/ASB-17.pdf.

Human Rights Watch. 2009. "Guinea: Stadium Massacre, Rape Likely Crimes against Humanity." December 17. http://www.hrw.org/news/2009/12/17/guinea-stadium-massacre-rape-likely-crimes-against-humanity.

———. 2013. "Nigeria: Massive Destruction, Deaths from Military Raid." May 1. http://www.hrw.org/news/2013/05/01/nigeria-massive-destruction-deaths-military-raid.

ICG (International Crisis Group). 2006. "Liberia: Resurrecting the Justice System." Africa Report 107, ICG, Brussels. http://www.crisisgroup.org/~/media/files/africa/west-africa/liberia/liberia%20resurrecting%20the%20justice%20system.pdf.

———. 2014. "Mali: Reform or Relapse." Africa Report 201, ICG, Brussels. http://www.crisisgroup.org/~/media/Files/africa/west-africa/mali/210-mali-reform-or-relapse-english.pdf.

IRIN. 2011. "Analysis: Niger Delta Still Unstable Despite Amnesty." November 25. http://www.irinnews.org/report/94306/analysis-niger-delta-still-unstable-despite-amnesty.

Kandeh, J. D. 1996. "What Does the 'Militariat' Do When It Rules? Military Regimes: The Gambia, Sierra Leone and Liberia." *Review of African Political Economy* 23 (69): 387–404.

———. 2004a. "Civil-Military Relations." In *West Africa's Security Challenges: Building Peace in a Troubled Region*, ed. A. Adebajo and I. Rashid. Boulder, CO: Lynne Rienner.

———. 2004b. *Coups from Below: Armed Subalterns and State Power in West Africa.* Basingstoke, United Kingdom: Palgrave Macmillan.

Mehler, A. 2012. "Why Security Forces Do Not Deliver Security: Evidence from Liberia and the Central African Republic." *Armed Forces and Society* 38 (1): 49–69.

N'yong'o, P. 1992. "Democratisation Processes in Africa." *Review of African Political Economy* 19 (54): 97–102.

Olonisakin, F. 2008. "Conflict Dynamics in West Africa: Background Analysis for the UK Government's Africa Conflict Prevention Programme." CSDG Paper, Conflict, Security and Development Group, King's College, London.

Onuoha, F. C., and A. Thurston. 2013. "Franco-African Intervention in Mali and Security Issues." Al Jazeera Center for Studies, Doha, Qatar. http://studies.aljazeera.net/en/reports/2013/02/201321984743627825.htm.

Ouédraogo, E. 2014. "Advancing Military Professionalism in Africa." Research Paper 6, Africa Center for Strategic Studies, Washington, DC. http://africacenter.org/wp-content/uploads/2014/07/ARP-6-EN.pdf.

Partners for Democratic Change. 2010. *Senegal's Armée-Nation: Lessons Learned from an Indigenous Model for Building Peace, Stability and Effective Civil-Military Relations in West Africa.* Washington, DC: Partners for Democratic Change. http://www.partnersglobal.org/where/africa/senegal/Senegals%20Armee%20Nation.pdf/at_download/file.

Perlo-Freeman, S., and C. Solmirano. 2014. "Trends in World Military Expenditure, 2013." SIPRI Fact Sheet, Stockholm International Peace Research Institute. http://books.sipri.org/product_info?c_product_id=476.

SIPRI (Stockholm International Peace Research Institute) Database. 2000–13. *Defense Budget in Africa.* http://www.sipri.org.

Small Arms Survey. 2006. "Small Arms Survey 2006: Unfinished Business." Small Arms Survey, Geneva. http://www.smallarmssurvey.org/publications/by-type/yearbook/small-arms-survey-2006.html.

Snyder, R. 1992. "Explaining Transitions from Neopatrimonial Dictatorships." *Comparative Politics* 24 (4): 379–99.

Sule, A. M. 2013. "Nigeria's Participation in Peacekeeping Operations." Peace Operations Training Institute, Williamsburg, VA. http://cdn.peaceopstraining.org/theses/sule.pdf.

Touchard, L. 2014. "Armées africaines: Pourquoi sont-elles si nulles?" *Jeune Afrique.* http://www.jeuneafrique.com/Article/JA2709p026_033.xml0.

UN (United Nations). n.d. "Troop and Police Contributors." UN, New York. http://www.un.org/en/peacekeeping/resources/statistics/contributors.shtml.

UN Office of the Special Representative for Africa. 2007. "Peace, Stability, and Development." Report to the Second International Conference on DDR and Stability in Africa, Kinshasa, Democratic Republic of Congo, June 12–14.

UN Security Council. 2014. "Briefing and Consultations on Guinea-Bissau." *What's in Blue,* November 17, New York. http://www.whatsinblue.org/2014/11/briefing-and-consultations-on-guinea-bissau-3.php#.

Uzoechina, O. 2014. "Security Sector Reform and Governance Processes in West Africa: From Concepts to Reality." DCAF Policy Paper 35, Geneva Centre for the Democratic Control of Armed Forces. http://www.dcaf.ch/Publications/Security-Sector-Reform-and-Governance-Processes-in-West-Africa-From-Concepts-to-Reality.

WIPSEN-Africa (Women Peace and Security Network Africa). 2010. *Gender Assessment of Security Sector Institutions in West Africa.* A WIPSEN-Africa Publication (Supported by the Urgent Action Fund).

World Bank. 2011. *World Development Report 2011: Conflict, Security and Development.* Washington, DC: World Bank.

———. 2013a. *Malian Defense and Security Forces Financial Management Assessment Report.* Washington, DC: World Bank.

———. 2013b. *Niger Security Sector Public Expenditure Review.* Washington, DC: World Bank.

World Politics Review. 2013. *Global Insider: Security Sector Reform Stalling in Côte d'Ivoire.* Washington, DC: World Bank. http://www.worldpoliticsreview.com/trend-lines/12959/global-insider-security-sector-reform-stalling-in-cote-d-ivoire.

Zounmenou, D. 2008. "Managing Post-War Liberia: An Update." ISS Situation Report, Institute for Security Studies, Pretoria. http://www.issafrica.org/publications/situation-reports/situation-report-managing-post-war-liberia-an-update-david-zounmenou.

———. 2014. "West Africa: An Overview of Security Threats and Responses." Fragility, Conflict, and Violence Group, World Bank, Washington, DC.

Chapter 7

Addressing the Challenges of Legal Pluralism and Improving the Management of Land

Land management and property rights are multifaceted and interlaced with complexities and contradictions across Africa. Challenges include legal pluralism in land governance, ineffective management of land, unequal distribution and discriminatory policies, and artificial boundaries and their consequences. All of these issues are complicated by population growth, land scarcity, the acquisition of land by large firms for mining or plantation agriculture, environmental degradation, and climate change.

Land has been at the heart of much conflict in Africa, and West Africa is no exception. In fact, almost every large-scale incident of conflict and violence has had a land dimension (Van der Auweraert 2013). In Côte d'Ivoire, the conflict between migrant workers and traditional landowners in the west of the country was one of the main components of the decade-long conflict, making western Côte d'Ivoire the region that was worst affected by the conflict (McGovern 2011). Nigeria's Middle Belt has been prone to violence between migrants from the north and local communities that has caused thousands of deaths. The conflict in Mauritania around the Senegal River is in large part linked to land and the fact that pastoral populations who lost their cattle are putting pressure on sedentary populations along the river to access the fertile lands. Many pastoralists in the Sahel are struggling to find resources for their herds, which creates major tensions. The conflicts in Liberia and Sierra Leone also featured a land dimension.

Even where land has not been a precursor to conflict, the breakdown of systems during conflict can result in the emergence or intensification of latent frustrations or inequities surrounding land and resources. Opposing forces may leverage such grievances to score political points and rally support or cement alliances. Control over land and resources is often seen as a symbolic war gain or used to fund and reward war efforts. Postconflict land disputes usually center on a clash of rights between returnees and the current occupiers of the land (Maze 2014). They can threaten or undermine peacebuilding efforts, particularly if displaced populations face significant dispossession.

Land is a key resource for most West African economies and a significant contributor to gross domestic product (GDP), employment, and export earnings (Cotula, Toulmin, and Hesse 2004; AU, AfDB, and ECA 2011). A variety of pressures have increased competition for land among multiple land users, government municipalities, urban elites, and foreign investors. Scarcity has increased the value of land, making land ownership—and clarity regarding ownership—more desirable.

The Challenge of Legal Pluralism

The complexity of West Africa's land issues derives from the coexistence of formal and informal systems of land tenure, with overlapping jurisdictions, contradictory rules, and competing authorities. Legal pluralism—which includes customary and statutory land tenure, Sharia, informal arrangements, and hybrids of all of them—takes the form of a network of interlocking and contradictory systems and institutions. In general, statutory systems govern urban areas and customary systems cover rural areas, which constitute the majority of West Africa's land area (Cotula, Toulmin, and Hesse 2004); peri-urban lands fall between the two.

Access to land and resources under customary systems is an integral part of social relationships. Historically, land ownership was determined by virtue of first clearance. Common principles hold that land belongs to a community (consisting of a family, lineage, or village) as opposed to individuals. The group charged with ownership often endows the land with spiritual or sacred dimensions. In principle, the land is inalienable, meaning it cannot be sold (Zongo 2010). Customary systems are based on diverse and sometimes incompatible localized practices and norms.[1] Largely unwritten, they are flexible, negotiable, and able to evolve to accommodate external influences, such as Sharia, economic factors, and other cultural and political interactions (Cotula, Toulmin, and Hesse 2004).[2] Land chiefs typically derived their authority from their status as descendants of community founders, conquest, or the magic/religious alliance with the *genii loci* (spirits of the place) (Delville 1998).

The family, community, or lineage retains the primary rights to the land, regardless of its usage, and the prerogative to lend those rights to "outsiders" through leasing arrangements, tenancies, share contracts, or loans (Cotula, Toulmin, and Hesse 2004). Tenants typically have secondary or derived rights (IIED 2001). The principle of lending or renting land to outsiders over long periods of time is a point of contention between different land tenure systems, as migrants often assume they have purchased land that indigenous populations consider to be inalienable and rented out to migrants on long-term loan or lease. Tensions deriving from the stranger-host relationship in western Côte d'Ivoire and ambiguities over the status of land tenure stem from disparities between indigenous peasant farmers and people they consider "strangers" who have profited from the cocoa economy. The rhetoric of reclaiming "patrimonial" land has proved popular as a strategy of populist politics among indigenous populations in the west; returning educated youth have played a key role in encouraging their elders to reclaim land sold to strangers (McGovern 2011).

Returning refugees and internally displaced persons face questions, uncertainty, and insecurity over land ownership in Côte d'Ivoire, Liberia, and Sierra Leone. Ambiguity over land tenure has led to tensions in Liberia between young excombatants who occupied land they considered "wrongfully" possessed in the past and displaced members of the Mandingo tribe, who held papers to that land (Rincon 2010).

Under statutory systems of land tenure, which came into being during colonial times, land rights are allocated and confirmed through the issuance of titles or other forms of registration of ownership (Cotula, Toulmin, and Hesse 2004). Unlike their customary counterpart, state systems are based on written laws and regulations, acts of centralized or decentralized government agencies, and judicial decisions. Colonial policy also adopted a principle known as "land to the tiller" (*mise en valeur*), whereby rights are obtained by working the land. Sharia also embraces this principle. This principle reaffirms customary claims of "first clearance" rights, but it allows the government to expropriate unused or underused customary landholdings. The practice has hurt pastoralists, in particular by infringing on pastoral corridors, as "grazing" is not considered land cultivation. In West Africa, only Mali and Niger recognize and protect pastoral grazing land (Cotula, Toulmin, and Hesse 2004).

Informal and customary practices offer local populations an alternative to the limited coverage of the statutory systems (AUC, AfDB, and ECA 2011), which is reinforced by the very limited presence of the state in rural areas and its ineffective management of resources (Cotula, Toulmin, and Hesse 2004). Customary systems remain the most common way of seeking redress in rural settings. In Liberia, the majority of citizens turn to customary law for justice and recourse; in Sierra Leone, about 85 percent of disputes are settled through informal systems (Olonisakin, Ikpe, and Badong 2009). Land tenure can also be regulated informally, through "informal formalization" (Zongo 2010), as in Benin, Burkina Faso, and Côte d'Ivoire. These arrangements often have limited legal value, particularly under formal statutory law, however, and they risk conflicting with unwritten agreements of previous landholders.

Migrants and women often believe that the formal statutory system provides better guarantees for their land rights than customary norms. A growing number of women are pushing to strengthen their land claims in the face of increasing land values and scarcity and a gender equity discourse that helps shape policy reform. Women—who have been marginalized from land ownership under customary systems and often can access land only indirectly through a male intermediary—are organizing to more effectively advocate for their land rights and pool their resources, through Women Land Access Trusts, for instance. A trend toward land donations from fathers to daughters has been observed in many West African countries (Koné 2011). This practice promotes gender equality, women's empowerment, economic development, and most likely peace.

Legal pluralism can offer recourse for people who lack the means to access formal systems of justice in a timely manner, particularly in postconflict settings. In postwar Sierra Leone, for example, "customary law officers" served as an interface between different legal systems (Unruh 2009); in postconflict Liberia, where the formal system was perceived as failing and lacking in objectivity, legal pluralism enabled resolution in a timely and appropriate manner (Isser, Lubkemann, and N'Tow 2009). However, legal pluralism can sow confusion and tension where too many competing authorities—land chiefs, village chiefs, administrative executives, regional customary authorities, religious authorities, local government bodies, judges, and various village/intervillage or communal committees—claim legitimacy in overlapping jurisdictions. It can also result in discrimination against "outsiders."

In Liberia, for example, the Constitution's recognition of two different legal systems—statutory law to govern "civilized" Americo-Liberians and missionaries, and customary laws that cover "natives," non-Christians, and indigenous Africans—has sown confusion regarding land ownership. The statutory system applies to all Liberians, but the customary system still refers to the adjudication of cases based on whether a citizen is deemed to be "native" or "civilized," according to the historical classification system. This distinction lends itself to "forum shopping," in which people with superior knowledge of competing systems and resources opt for the more advantageous forum (Delville 1998). Moreover, because losing parties can appeal to alternative systems, rulings are likely to be challenged and canceled. The challenge is thus not legal pluralism per se but the lack of standing of decisions (Delville 1998).

Options for Land Management

Land management policies across West Africa have failed to adapt to changing times or respond adequately to the population's needs. Under colonial rule, attempts by the French to convert public land to private land did not make much progress. Large tracts of land were declared under public domain, and customary systems persisted. The British sought to establish territorial control through alliances with senior customary rulers. They introduced a system of freehold tenure alongside a form of land administration based on customary law. Regardless of the system, enforcing land law has proven challenging, with decisions and resolutions governing land claims usually reflecting the power, influence, and vested interests of the various stakeholders (IIED 1999).

Colonial policies regarding land and other renewable natural resources (forests, inland and marine fisheries, pastures, and so on) were "state-centric"— and for the most part remain so to this day. The state maintained control over forests irrespective of established customary use and land rights. This practice continues to have ramifications over the use of specific forest resources.[3] Both the colonial state and the postcolonial state appropriated prime agricultural and urban lands and redistributed them. The colonial state allocated land to foreigners, their descendants, and investment companies; political elites in the postcolonial state passed substantial land parcels to other elites, their affiliates, and multinational corporations (Maze 2014).

The early 1990s saw a move toward decentralized governance structures, particularly in Francophone West Africa. In Burkina Faso, Ghana, and Senegal, smallholders began to set up farmers associations and national networks and federations (Nelen and others 2013). Senegal, for instance, called for amendments to statutory systems to provide more room for local level governance and land management (IIED 1999). Several Francophone countries made progress in devolving land management to village-level authorities using the *gestion de terroirs villageois* approach, although it has yet to receive legal recognition.

Less than 5 percent of the land in West Africa is held under formally registered titles—a testament to the formidable challenges to registration (Cotula, Toulmin, and Hesse 2004). Obstacles include high costs, multiple claims to rights, and the tendency of the process to favor the literate and the wealthy, and the social impact of severing historical and cultural connections to land. Across West Africa, land has been and continues to be unequally distributed, with the number of "land poor" in both rural and urban areas on the rise. Land grabbing has been especially rampant (IIED 1999). Unfarmed land, which may actually be fallow grazing land or a community agricultural reserve, is viewed as unoccupied and thus becomes the state's "eminent domain" (IIED 1999). This land remains uncultivated and is regarded de facto as open access, but it is likely to lead to landlessness and displacement if and when the state makes claims on it, particularly in light of the region's growing agri-business sector and urban speculations.

Although increased land scarcity is one of the most frequently cited factors in fueling land tensions, competition, and conflict, only 36 percent of the cropland in West Africa is cultivated (Bossard 2009). Climate change, environmental degradation, population growth, and agri-business, among other factors, have reduced the amount of land available and contributed to land grabbing. However, land scarcity is as much about access and distribution of land. For instance, a decreasing number of people own larger tracts of land; large segments of the population live on degraded land (UNDP 2003, 2013); land that is available cannot be purchased; and rising land values and corruption act as an impediment to land acquisition. Intensified competition for land and resources, and rising land values, can increase land tenure insecurity and landlessness.

The deterioration of land quality is likely to intensify over the next 30 years as a result of population growth, landholding fragmentation, and climate variability (UNDP 2013). Population growth and urbanization, already the leading causes of deforestation, will place additional demands on energy sources (Bossard 2009). Land conflict could ensue, as land remains among the sole livelihood opportunities for the unskilled youth who join the labor market every year.

Since 2000, West Africa has seen the emergence of foreign and domestic investors who buy, lease, or acquire by other means concessions to large tracts of land on which they grow food, produce fuel, or mine extractives (Lund 2011). Although the consequences of large-scale land acquisition in Africa have yet to be thoroughly investigated, firms have been criticized for allegedly buying up the bulk of fertile land and marginalizing small-scale farmers. Many observers see this practice as a new form of agricultural colonialism or a throwback to the failed large-scale industrial farming efforts of the 1960s–70s when land was expropriated.

Case studies from Benin, Burkina Faso, Mali, and Niger reveal a number of concerns that could spur conflicts where competing land claims are already a source of tension. They include a lack of transparency in transactions, the risk of land loss for groups with secondary rights, lack of clarity in the terms of agreements, an increase in formalized land grabbing, and displacement.[4] The magnitude of rural land under the control of agro-investors outside the community is unknown, as many transactions are not written and are made under customary systems.[5] In many instances, investors avoid formalizing the full property title, because procedures are considered lengthy and fastidious and formalizing would incur taxation. Many investors in Burkina Faso accept *procès verbal de palabra* (written accounts of a discussion held in the presence of an authority). Others obtain provisional land allocation certificates that are valid for five years.[6] As agri-business grows, investors will likely seek stronger tenure security by obtaining statutory or freehold rights, which could bring the underlying tensions of conflicting systems to the fore (Le Meur and others 2006). River basins in The Gambia and Senegal, including in the Casamance, are examples of areas that are attractive for land development, settlement, and enterprise development (IIED 1999).

Land has played a pivotal role in many of West Africa's conflicts, for a host of reasons, including issues connected to access and control over resources and political manipulation that plays upon local land tensions in an effort to build alliances (table 7.1) (Maze 2014). In Côte d'Ivoire, exclusive citizenship laws that restricted access to resources, particularly to land in the western forest regions that were the heartland of the country's cocoa economy, were one of the main triggers of war and still remain a challenge. The use of land to host opposing forces during conflict has also exacerbated tensions. Also problematic are territorial gains to symbolize military victories and the use of land by belligerents for personal enrichment or as a spoil of war. In Liberia, tensions are ongoing where the armed forces used land to reward allies and loyal combatants.

There will be no peace-building progress across the continent until the land issue is addressed. Formalizing all land ownership is neither possible nor probably effective, but greater efforts are needed to establish mechanisms for resolving land disputes and facilitating transactions and consolidation. Although this agenda is a long-term one, it requires more immediate attention.

Recommendations for Addressing the Challenges of Legal Pluralism and Improving the Management of Land

Land lies at the heart of many of the challenges facing West Africa, where it is closely linked to livelihoods and the economy. Clarifying the status of land ownership under parallel legal systems is a major challenge throughout Africa. Development organizations can play an important role in helping countries address these challenges. It is difficult to get donors and development agencies to be sufficiently engaged in land reform, which is perceived as very political, with high risks and not always in need of large-scale projects.

Land reforms are time consuming and need sustained and long-term commitment from development partners and donors. To ensure the permanence of commitments, projects should be flexible. Partners should include smaller projects, which are more manageable and easier to achieve. Development agencies should complement efforts by government. More research and investigation are needed into the impact of land grabbing, its potential to exacerbate tensions, and the ways in which it contributes to conflict and violence.

Recommendations to address this driver of conflict and fragility include the following:

- Help governments improve and modernize land administration while supporting the progressive reform of land ownership. There is need to acknowledge that land reform will take a long time and that quick fixes rarely work in this area.

Table 7.1 Land-Related Conflicts in West Africa

Conflict	Duration	Land dimension
Casamance conflict (Senegal)	1982–present	Regarded as one of the key causes of the conflict in the Casamance region, land became an issue following a clash between the beliefs and traditions of the Diola and the land policies initiated by the Senegalese authorities. The Diola maintained a system of customary land tenure in which land, particularly sacred forests, is inviolable and passed down from one generation to the next. Introduction of the National Domains Act of 1964 undermined this system by handing ownership of all land not under legal title deed to the state. The act enabled communities from outside the Casamance to acquire land, disrupting the Diola system of land ownership and contributing to the dispossession of its people (Fall 2010; Gehrold and Neu 2010).
Mauritania and Senegal War	1989–90	Contestations over land ownership in the fertile Senegal River Valley set this conflict into motion. Historically, land in the region was customarily owned and managed by sedentary communities, such as the Halpulaar and Soninké. A new land law initiated by the Mauritanian authorities in 1983 allowed the state to confiscate land and turn ownership over to communities from the country's north (Human Rights Watch 1994). Together with other examples of perceived discrimination, the move led to the formation in 1986 of the Forces de Libération Africaines de Mauritanie (FLAM) in defense of the interests of the country's black population. Tensions led to skirmishes between Mauritania and Senegal, the severing of diplomatic ties, and the deportation from Mauritania of thousands of Senegalese and black Mauritanians (Magistro 1993; Human Rights Watch 1994).
Liberian civil wars	1989–96 and 1999–2003	Land played a critical role in the Liberian civil wars as part of broader disputes over ethnicity and citizenship, especially in the rural counties of Lofa, Nimba, and Bong. Land disputes in Lofa county arose from clashes between the "indigenous" Loma, who asserted their right to control land on the basis of autochthony, and the Mandingo, who were regarded as migrants. The relationship was complicated by the Mandingo's economic power, which upended the balance of power with regard to access to land. Some members of the indigenous community viewed the civil wars as opportunities to reclaim land rights (Boas 2005; NRC 2012).
Sierra Leone civil war	1991–2002	Land disputes in the lead-up to the civil war in Sierra Leone were particularly prominent in the south and linked to abuses arising from the chieftaincy system. Chiefs played a key role in land access; they were blamed for rural marginalization and poverty, especially among youth. Tensions over land access contributed to the frustrations of youth, increasing the danger that they would be recruited to organized violence (Keen 2003; Unruh 2008).
Côte d'Ivoire civil war	2002–04 and 2011	Land disputes have been a significant source of conflict in Côte d'Ivoire, particularly in relation to citizenship. They are most pronounced in the west of the country, where they are the result of disputes between people who consider themselves native to the area, migrants from other parts of the country, and migrants from neighboring countries, especially Burkina Faso. Tensions rose in the early 1990s, stoked by competition for political power, economic challenges, and demographic pressures. They spilled over into contestations regarding control of and access to land (NRC 2012; ICG 2014).
Northern conflict (Ghana)	Intermittent since independence	Incidents of violence in Northern Ghana over the past few decades centered on chieftaincy and succession, but they also involved land administration and management. Some communities historically embraced acephalous leadership systems; others were governed under hierarchical systems. Ethnic communities with a history of acephalous systems of leadership demanded the creation of a paramount chieftaincy to represent their interests. They objected to chiefs from communities with hierarchical systems holding land in trust for all communities and claiming tribute from all land users (Assefa 2001).

- Encourage commitments to gender equity in land law and management by ensuring gender-sensitive project design and providing women with additional resources to increase tenure security, such as agricultural loans.
- Integrate conflict-resolution mechanisms into legal reforms and rural development projects, including pastoralism. There is a big gap in local-level mediation mechanisms and protection of basic rights of citizens around land. Mechanisms that mediate conflicts between pastoralists and farmers need to be scaled up.
- Encourage and support national or subregional dialogues on issues relating to land, and promote the enhancement of understanding, research, and awareness among researchers, government officials, civil society, and other stakeholders. Land issues are central to West Africa's conflict dynamics. More debate is needed within society regarding the evolution of land ownership and property rights, especially of collective land. These debates should help ensure that public policies align with the concerns of stakeholders.
- Conduct more analysis on land reform and conflict risks in West Africa that takes account of issues such as land titling, in order to understand where the bottlenecks are. Such analysis could form the basis of future roadmaps and the identification of priority areas for action in each country. Analysis should include the dynamics of land conflicts.
- Conduct much more systematic analysis of the conflict risks associated with the large-scale acquisition of land. This analysis needs to produce specific recommendations on improving the social benefits of such land purchases for local populations and reducing conflict risks.

Notes

1. Competing customary claims come from descendants of "firstcomers" and "latecomers," descendants of maternal and paternal lines, and people who worked the land at different periods, for example. Settlement of these disputes often depends on the relations of power (IIED 1999).
2. Sharia, which recognizes universal land rights for all Muslims, has influenced the customary systems in parts of The Gambia, Guinea, Guinea-Bissau, Mauritania Niger, and Nigeria. Private rights are established by 10 years of continuous occupation and land use. Landholders who do not cultivate their own land are obliged to have it worked by others, otherwise their ownership lapses. Women may own land but may not inherit it. This rule leads to conflict with some other customary principles of succession, notably among matrilineal societies.
3. "Even where laws on carbon rights may be present, they may not distinguish between rights of local communities to sequestered carbon (actually stored carbon); carbon sinks natural entities that retain the carbon, including land (above and

below ground); subsurface carbon; tree ownership when separate from land owner-ship; carbon sequestration potential; carbon credits (the right to pollute an amount equivalent to the carbon sequestered in, or emissions avoided from, a natural sink); and use rights (for example, easements, leases, profits)" (USAID 2013).

4. According to Hilhorst, Nelen, and Traoré (2011), 58 percent of agro-investors reported that they had purchased "their" land and 36 percent indicate having leased it. The parties that transferred this land may have different perceptions. In 28 percent of cases, the land was already (partly) used for farming, implying displacement of the former land users.

5. Hilhorst Nelen, and Traoré (2011) find that 45 percent of investors were based in the local government area or province, 37 percent lived in the capital, and 10 percent lived abroad.

6. Despite lack of clarity over the nature of land transfers (gifts, loans, and sales) in many villages in Burkina Faso, the children of people who cede land have the right to renegotiate transactions with new actors and to convert loans of indefinite duration into sales. The new actors insist that they have bought the land, whereas customary authorities and other members of the family may claim that the lands have only been leased. When sales are recognized, not all members of the family are informed of or associated with the transaction. The sale may be negotiated by a single person, who tends to be the one to pocket the money.

References

Assefa, H. 2001. "Coexistence and Reconciliation in the Northern Region of Ghana." In *Justice and Coexistence: Theory and Practice*, ed. M. Abu-Nimer, 165–86. Lanham, MD: Lexington.

AUC (African Union Consortium), AfDB (African Development Bank), and ECA (Economic Commission for Africa). 2010. *Framework and Guidelines on Land Policy in Africa: Land Policy in Africa: A Framework to Strengthen Land Rights, Enhance Productivity and Secure Livelihoods*. Addis Ababa: AUC.

Boas, M. 2005. "A Funeral for a Friend: Contested Citizenship in the Liberian Civil War." Fafo Institute for Applied International Studies, Oslo. http://www.open.ac.uk /socialsciences/bisa-africa/confpapers/Boas%20exeter%2008.pdf.

Bossard, L., ed. 2009. *Regional Atlas on West Africa*. Paris: OECD-SWAC (Organisation for Economic Co-operation and Development–Sahel and West Africa Club).

Cotula, L., C. Toulmin, and C. Hesse. 2004. *Land Tenure and Administration in Africa: Lessons of Experience and Emerging Issues*. London and Rome: International Institute for the Environment and Development and Food and Agriculture Organization.

Delville, P. L. 1998. "Harmonising Formal Law and Customary Land Rights in French-Speaking West Africa." Groupe de Recherches et d'Echanges Technologiques (GRET), Paris.

Fall, Aïssatou. 2010. "Understanding the Casamance Conflict: A Background." KAIPTC Monograph 7, Kofi Annan International Peacekeeping Training Centre, Accra. http:// www.kaiptc.org/publications/monographs/monographs/monograph-7-aissatou.aspx.

Gehrold, S., and I. Neu. 2010. "Caught between Two Fronts—in Search of Lasting Peace in the Casamance Region: An Analysis of the Causes, Players and Consequences." KAS International Report, Konrad-Adenauer-Stiftung e.V., Berlin. http://www.kas.de /wf/doc/kas_20669-544-2-30.pdf?100930131457.

Hilhorst, T., J. Nelen, and N. Traoré. 2011. "Agrarian Change Below the Radar Screen: Rising Farmland Acquisitions by Domestic Investors in West Africa." Results from a survey in Benin, Burkina Faso, and Niger, Royal Tropical Institute and SNV Netherlands Development Organisation, Amsterdam.

Human Rights Watch. 1994. *Mauritania's Campaign of Terror: State-Sponsored Repression of Black Africans.* New York: Human Rights Watch. http://www.hrw.org/sites/default /files/reports/MAURITAN944.PDF.

ICG (International Crisis Group). 2014. "Côte d'Ivoire's Great West: Key to Reconciliation." Africa Report 212, ICG, Brussels. http://www.crisisgroup.org/en/regions/africa/west -africa/cote-divoire/212-cote-divoire-s-great-west-key-to-reconciliation.aspx.

IIED (International Institute for Environment and Development). 1999. "Land Tenure and Resource Access in West Africa: Issues and Opportunities for the Next Twenty-Five Years." Working Paper, IIED, London.

———. 2001. "Land Rights under Negotiation." *Haramata: Bulletin of the Drylands: People, Policies, Programmes* 39 (May): 12–15.

Isser, D. H, S. C. Lubkemann, and S. N'Tow. 2009. "Looking for Justice: Liberian Experiences with and Perceptions of Local Justice Options." Peaceworks 63, U.S. Institute of Peace, Washington, DC.

Keen, D. 2003. "Greedy Elites, Dwindling Resources, Alienated Youths: The Anatomy of Protracted Violence in Sierra Leone." *International Politics and Society* 2. http://www .fes.de/ipg/IPG2_2003/ARTKEEN.HTM.

Koné, M. 2011. "Women and Land." Briefing Paper, Agence Française de Développement, Land Tenure and Development Technical Committee, Paris. http://www.agter.asso.fr /IMG/pdf/2011_ctf_fiche-pedag_kone_femmes-et-foncier_en.pdf.

Le Meur, P. Y., P. Hochet, M. Shem, and O. Touré. 2006. "Conflict over Access to Land and Water Resources within Sub-Saharan Dry Lands: Underlying Factors, Conflict Dynamics and Settlement Processes." Groupe de Recherches et d'Echanges Technologiques (GRET), Paris.

Lund, C. 2011. "Land Rights and Citizenship in Africa." Discussion Paper 65, Nordic Africa Institute, Uppsala.

Magistro, J. 1993. "Crossing Over: Ethnicity and Transboundary Conflict in the Senegal River Valley." *Cahiers d'Études Africaines* 130 (33/2): 201–32.

Maze, Kerry. 2014. "Land Conflict, Migration, and Citizenship in West Africa: Complex Diversity and Recurring Challenges." Desk Study, Fragility, Conflict, and Violence Group, World Bank, Washington, DC.

McGovern, Mike. 2011. *Making War in Côte d'Ivoire.* Chicago: University of Chicago Press.

Nelen, J., A. Idrissou, B. W. Sanou, and N. Traoré. 2013. "Responses to Rising Farmland Acquisitions in West Africa: Fostering Accountability in Land Governance at the

Local Level." SNV Netherlands Development Organisation, West-Africa, Royal Tropical Institute Amsterdam. Paper presented at the Annual World Bank Conference on Land and Poverty, Washington, DC, April 8–11.

NRC (Norwegian Refugee Council). 2012. "Land Conflict and Food Security in the Liberian-Ivorian Border Region." Norwegian Refugee Council, Oslo. http://www .ivorycoast.nrc.no/data/doc_res/NRC_report_e_LR.pdf.pdf.

Olonisakin, F., E. Ikpe, and P. Badong. 2009. "The Future of Security and Justice for the Poor: A Blue Sky Think Piece." CSDG Policy Study 21, Conflict, Security and Development Group, London.

Rincon, J. M. 2010. "Ex-combatants, Returnees, Land and Conflict in Liberia." DIIS Working Paper, Danish Institute for International Studies, Copenhagen.

UNDP (United Nations Development Programme). 2003. "Conflict-Related Development Analysis (CDA)." Bureau for Crisis Prevention and Recovery, New York.

———. 2013. *Human Development Report 2013: The Rise of the South: Human Progress in a Diverse World*. New York: UNDP.

Unruh, J. 2008. "Land Policy Reform, Customary Rule of Law and the Peace Process in Sierra Leone." *African Journal of Legal Studies* 2: 94–117.

———. 2009. "Humanitarian Approaches to Conflict and Post-Conflict Legal Pluralism in Land Tenure." In *Uncharted Territory: Land, Conflict and Humanitarian Action*, ed. S. Pantuliano. Warwickshire: Practical Action.

USAID (U.S. Agency for International Development). 2013. *Land Tenure and Property Rights Matrix: Trees and Forests Overlay*. Washington, DC: USAID.

Van der Auweraert, P. 2013. "Institutional Aspects of Resolving Land Disputes in Post-Conflict Societies." In *Land and Post-Conflict Peacebuilding*, ed. J. Unruh and R.C. Williams. London: Earthscan.

Zongo, M. 2010. "Land Tenure and Migration in West Africa." Briefing Paper, Agence Française de Développement, Land Tenure and Development Technical Committee, Paris.

Chapter 8

Lessons in Resilience: Learning from the End of the Conflicts in Liberia, Sierra Leone, and Côte d'Ivoire

Study of three protracted conflicts in West Africa—the civil wars in Liberia, Sierra Leone, and Côte d'Ivoire—yields important lessons on the dynamics of resilience against political violence and civil war in the subregion. The conflicts overlapped in many respects: all concerned power sharing and identity and all were prolonged by access to minerals and natural resources. At the outset, all three conflicts were linked to control of power and the grievances of marginalized sociocultural groups (a combination of ethnic, age, and regional exclusion). All ended up being fueled by greed and the desire for self-enrichment of warlords and rebel leaders.

The factors responsible for bringing the three conflicts to an end were also similar. They included war fatigue, strong interventions by regional actors, backing from foreign forces, and the quality of leadership.

All three countries continue to face significant challenges as a result of many years of fighting. Some of the drivers of conflict around land and identity politics are still at play, although they are less active than before the conflicts. Institutions have been substantially strengthened, and economic activity promptly recommenced in Côte d'Ivoire and Sierra Leone, attaining record levels.

Although the conflict in Côte d'Ivoire was drawn out, it was much less bloody than the civil wars in Liberia and Sierra Leone. The civilian population was mostly spared, except in the last few months of the conflict, and the casualty count was limited to 3,000–5,000 people over the 12 years of war. The potential for reconciliation was therefore greater than in Liberia or Sierra Leone.

Descriptions of the Conflicts

The first civil war in Liberia began in 1989, following the invasion by the National Patriotic Front of Liberia (NPLF), led by Charles Taylor, from Côte d'Ivoire.

The roots of the conflict were closely linked to the dispute over Liberian identity that pitted freed slaves against indigenous communities (Dupuy and Detzel 2008) and the sense of marginalization of the latter. The conflict unleashed a major humanitarian catastrophe in the region, as an estimated 700,000 Liberians fled to neighboring countries.

The war dragged on for several years, partly as the result of ill-conceived diplomatic responses and constant splits among rebel groups. Several attempts were made to end the conflict through talks in neighboring countries. The first was the Cotonou Accord of 1993. Subsequent agreements followed the same framework but differed in key respects, notably the manner in which armed groups would share power. The Abuja Agreement of 1995 and its supplement in 1996 paved the way for elections a year later, which Taylor won before promptly reneging on key provisions of the peace agreement. The new civil war that ensued drew to a close only in 2003, with Taylor's exile, the deployment of troops from member countries of the Economic Community of West African States (ECOWAS), and a peace agreement.

The decade-long civil war in Sierra Leone, which ended in 2002, resulted in the deaths of an estimated 50,000 people and the displacement of two-thirds of the country's population. The roots of the conflict included a crisis of governance over many years that led to the decay and collapse of state services and the political and economic marginalization of the population.

The war was triggered by an uprising by rebels from the Revolutionary United Front (RUF), backed by Charles Taylor. Various attempts were made to secure peace, starting with the 1996 Abidjan Peace Agreement, which unraveled in 1997 following the overthrow of the government. A new peace accord signed in Lomé in 1999 granted amnesty to the rebels and included provisions to incorporate them into an inclusive government. It also provided for the deployment of a United Nations (UN) peacekeeping mission that would focus on the disarmament, demobilization, and reintegration of fighters. This effort failed after RUF rebels targeted UN peacekeepers.

The intervention of the United Kingdom in May 2000 finally turned the tide against the RUF. Following a six-month hiatus, the Abuja Ceasefire Agreement was signed on November 10, 2000. In May 2001, a more detailed and substantive agreement—the Abuja Ceasefire Review Agreement, or Abuja II—was signed. Facilitated by ECOWAS, it resulted in a breakthrough for peace. The agreement provided for disarmament of the RUF and the Civil Defence Forces (CDF) militias, as well as the restoration of state authority (Malan, Rakate, and McIntyre 2002).[1] A formal declaration announcing the end of the conflict was made in January 2002. The change in Sierra Leone's immediate neighborhood also played an important role in ending the conflict. International stabilization in Liberia, pressure on supporters of the RUF, and Guinea's backing of the campaign against the RUF improved the prospects for peace (de Waal 2009).

Once considered a beacon of stability in West Africa, Côte d'Ivoire experienced more than a decade of instability following a coup in 1999 (McGovern 2011). A number of structural factors formed the backdrop to the conflict, including the north-south divide, land ownership, and the politicization of citizenship and identity, all of which increased in salience following the death of President Félix Houphouët-Boigny in 1993 (Cilliers and Handy 2013). A military coup in 2002 led by officers from the north resulted in the bifurcation of the country, with the south controlled by President Laurent Gbagbo and the north controlled by the rebels. Neighboring countries made various attempts to introduce peace initiatives to unify the country—namely, the Linas-Marcoussis Agreement of 2003, the Accra III Agreement of 2004, the Pretoria Agreement of 2005, and the Ouagadougou Political Agreement of 2007. The peace process benefited from mediation by France, which facilitated the Linas-Marcoussis Agreement; the African Union (through former South African President Thabo Mbeki), which facilitated the Pretoria Agreement; and ECOWAS, which facilitated the Ouagadougou Political Agreement.

The first round of presidential elections, in October 2010, ended peacefully, albeit without a definitive victor. A presidential run-off in November 2010 between the incumbent Gbagbo and the challenger Alassane Outtara resulted in both candidates claiming victory and inaugurating themselves as president. The Special Representative of the United Nations for Côte d'Ivoire announced Outtara the winner based on an independent tally. The political crisis gave way to postelection violence that claimed an estimated 3,000 lives and displaced almost a million civilians. The conflict began to diffuse in April 2011, after forces loyal to Outtara captured Abidjan (Cook 2011).

Lessons Learned

Several lessons can be drawn from the three wars regarding the way peace was achieved and sustained. (These conflicts differed from the conflicts in Mali and Nigeria involving extremist groups. The lessons may therefore not be fully applicable to those settings.)

War Fatigue Helped Lead to Peace

Coupled with sanctions and pressure from foreign backers, fatigue contributed to infighting among the rebels in Sierra Leone, as commanders who had amassed great wealth expressed a desire to end the conflict and rejoin society (Davies 2002). The Liberian conflict also owed its termination in part to growing fatigue among combatants and the public at large. Growing public anger with the conflict came to a head when an estimated 100,000 Liberian demonstrators protested in front of delegates attending the Akosombo peace talks, expressing frustration with both the ongoing violence and the numerous failed peace accords (Adeleke 1995). Fatigue played an important role in galvanizing civil society, in particular women's groups. The final straw was the apathetic southern reception to the return of the Force Nouvelle from the north, demonstrating that the population as a whole wanted an end to hostilities, even if it meant surrendering to the rebels.

Regional Actors Played a Positive Role

In all three cases, regional actors, in particular ECOWAS, were central in securing peace. The increased risk of the spillover of conflicts, as well the need for stability to support growth and investment across the region, made the involvement of heads of states and governments essential in supporting stabilization in conflict-affected countries across the region. Interventions by ECOWAS were key to ending the three conflicts, first diplomatically and then militarily. Despite their occasional military weakness, which necessitated further interventions, ECOWAS troops were credited with the initial stabilization, the protection of civilians, and the defense of legitimate governments (Francis 2009; Olonisakin 2011).

In Liberia, ECOWAS became involved through the deployment of troops of the Economic Community of West African States Monitoring Group (ECOMOG) and the mediation of several sessions of peace talks. This initiative faced several challenges, the most serious of which was division among the ranks of member countries. Both Burkina Faso and Côte d'Ivoire—which had backed the uprising by Taylor and had longstanding differences with President Samuel Doe—strongly opposed intervention by ECOWAS. Despite the absence of a ceasefire, a group of countries led by Nigeria came up with a peace plan and deployed nearly 4,000 troops in Liberia. The death of President Doe, in 1990, eliminated an important obstacle to regional consensus and permitted the deployment of troops by Mali and Senegal to the ECOMOG mission (Adeleke 1995). ECOWAS took the lead in facilitating peace talks between the parties to the conflict. Despite political divisions, poor logistics, and disagreements over the mandate that marred its intervention, ECOWAS was critical to securing a political settlement.

Regional actors, including ECOWAS and the regional hegemon Nigeria, played a key role in preventing Sierra Leone from descending deeper into conflict during its civil war, particularly during the initial years of the crisis, when the international community was absent. Intervention took various forms, including the deployment of troops from countries claiming an ECOWAS mandate, the facilitation of peace talks and monitoring of peace agreements, and the imposition of sanctions and restrictions on conflict parties. Although ECOWAS was initially divided over whether to use military force, neighboring countries, led by Nigeria, deployed troops, defending their actions as in line with

ECOWAS's mandate (Goldmann 2005). The Organization of African Unity and the UN Security Council both subsequently mandated ECOWAS to restore constitutional order following the 1997 coup. Nigeria is also credited with lobbying for international community involvement in Sierra Leone, which led to the imposition of UN sanctions.

In its role as the regional hegemon, Nigeria received support from "enclave powerbrokers"—countries that took the lead in resolving conflicts within their immediate neighborhood. Guinea played an important role in mediation and peace initiatives in the Mano River Basin region. Côte d'Ivoire historically played an important role in peace initiatives in Francophone West Africa. Burkina Faso has been an important powerbroker since 2003; it was deeply involved in trying to resolve crises in Côte d'Ivoire, Mali, and Togo.

These examples illustrate resilience among countries in the region. Stability is not solely dependent on the actions of a single hegemon, it also relies on smaller countries expending their resources toward regional peace and stability (Musah 2009). ECOWAS mediated between the government and rebels in an attempt to resolve the 2002 political crisis in Côte d'Ivoire; in 2003 it dispatched 1,200 peacekeeping troops to replace the French troops manning the border between the warring parties. ECOWAS also helped set the agenda in the midst of the crisis triggered by the 2010 presidential elections (box 8.1). It swiftly backed the outcome announced by the Côte d'Ivoire election commission and endorsed by the Special Representative of the UN Secretary General, which recognized Outtara as president, while urging Gbagbo to abide by the results (Cook 2011). Both the African Union and the United States threw their weight behind the stance taken by ECOWAS, which rejected a proposal by Thabo Mbeki for a power-sharing agreement between Gbagbo and Outtara.

Inclusion of Civil Society Helped Make Agreements Take Hold

Civil society groups in Liberia were involved from the early stages of the conflict in trying to end hostilities. Civil society in Liberia was vibrant even before the outbreak of conflict, and more groups emerged during the conflict in response to state failure to provide services. Among the first to intervene were faith-based groups, such as the Interfaith Mediation Committee (IFMC), an amalgamation of the Liberia Council of Churches (LCC) and the National Muslim Council of Liberia (NMCL). The IFMC held talks with the conflict parties in 1990; its recommendations formed part of the ECOWAS peace plan (Atuobi 2010). Women's groups were also active (box 8.2), campaigning against wartime rape and advocating on behalf of women's issues. Local and international civil society groups worked to diffuse tensions at various points. In 1995, a coalition of civil society groups, including religious groups and labor unions, formed the National Coordinating Committee for Peace (NCCP). Its objective was to bring the combatants to the negotiating table through public pressure. Civil society

BOX 8.1

The Important Role of ECOWAS in Developing West Africa's Security Architecture

The tremendous progress made across West Africa in recent decades, in terms of both the institutionalization of conflict resolution frameworks and the continuing consolidation of democracy, has led to speculation among scholars that the subregion will eventually develop into a stand-alone security community (Bah 2005)—that is, a group of countries that subscribe to particular norms and values that together constitute a framework by which disputes can be resolved peacefully. When conflict broke out in Liberia and Sierra Leone in the early 1990s, ECOWAS faced a host of challenges, including logistical difficulties and lack of interstate cooperation. The lessons learned during these and subsequent interventions have helped shape its response to crises, such as the situations in Côte d'Ivoire in 2003 and Togo in 2005 (Arthur 2010).

A key development was the 1999 protocol on the Mechanism for Conflict Prevention, Management, Resolution, Peacekeeping, and Security, which laid the foundation for the establishment of six organs, including the early warning system ECOWARN. Another milestone was the adoption in 2008 of the ECOWAS Conflict Prevention Framework (ECPF), which seeks to stem potential conflict before it emerges. The ECPF functions through 14 components, which include governance, youth empowerment, and early warning; cross-border initiatives; and the ECOWAS standby force (Bah 2005).

ECOWAS has been a trailblazer in engaging civil society as part of its approach to conflict and peacebuilding. In 2003, it established the West Africa Civil Society Forum (WACSOF) as a platform through which civil society actors can contribute to discussions within ECOWAS.

Disagreements among member-states (over the questions of how to deal forcefully with "spoilers" and how to contend with the logistical, fiscal, and organizational constraints that undermined efficacy, for example) presented significant hurdles to progress. Despite them, ECOWAS continues to play a key role in maintaining peace in the subregion, as demonstrated in Guinea-Bissau and Mali. The organization also remains a central agent in mobilizing the international community to address the subregion's challenges.

---

also played a role in the August 1995 Bintumani Conference, which set elections for 1996. In particular, the Inter-Religious Council of Sierra Leone (IRCSL), which became an important vehicle for confidence-building measures between the government and the rebels, is credited with preventing religious schisms emerging as a consequence of armed conflict (Pham 2004).

These efforts notwithstanding, civil society groups were mostly marginalized from the peace processes during the first civil war in Liberia and at the

BOX 8.2

Women's Role in Peacebuilding in West Africa

Women have historically been heavily involved in matters of war and peace in West Africa. From priestesses and traditional peacemakers to praise singers and custodians of culture, women have worn the mantle of peace envoys in their communities for centuries. Examples include "queen mothers" in Ghana and in Yoruba land in Nigeria and "bondo" women in Sierra Leone.

As militias and insurgent groups, which are made up primarily of men, increasingly made decisions pertaining to conflict, women turned to grassroots peace activism. Their exclusion from formal processes meant that they looked to market associations, faith-based groups, guilds, and trade and intermarriage networks to protect their families and communities. Buoyed by success at the grassroots level, women agitated for representation at a more formal level, which led to their involvement as observers in the Sierra Leonean peace talks in Lomé and in the Ivorian peace talks; the inclusion of a gender framework in ECOWAS; and the nomination of Ruth Sando Perry as president of the transitional government in Liberia, nearly a decade before the election of Ellen Johnson Sirleaf as Africa's first female head of state. In Guinea-Bissau, women's groups launched an advocacy campaign that succeeded in bringing together various stakeholders in the wake of the 2004 electoral protests. The establishment of the Mano River Women's Peace Network (MARWOPNET) in 2000 marked a new level of engagement and success for women in regional peace initiatives, as its members joined forces and prevented a recurrence of conflict between Guinea, Liberia, and Sierra Leone.

Source: Alaga 2010.

---

beginning of the negotiations in Sierra Leone. The focus of mediation in Liberia and in Sierra Leone was on the armed groups. As a consequence, peace agreements (such as Sierra Leone's 1999 Lomé Accord) were flawed, as they reflected only the interests of combatants. Heavy lobbying by civil society organizations, and the dawning realization of their role as important stakeholders, led to their inclusion in the Accra peace talks in 2003. Civil society groups were also included in the power-sharing agreement that emerged from the talks, a fitting acknowledgment of their role in safeguarding peace (Fayemi 2004).

"Spoilers" Had to Be Eliminated from Power-Sharing Arrangements

Attempts across all three countries to reach power-sharing agreements with hardline leaders who had no real interest in peace were met with very little success. In the final analysis, spoilers (Charles Taylor in Liberia, Foday Sankoh in Sierra Leone, and Laurent Gbagbo in Côte d'Ivoire) and their followers had to be eliminated from the political pact for peace deals to hold. In Côte d'Ivoire and Sierra Leone, the intervention of foreign troops helped shift the balance of power decisively away from Gbagbo and Sankoh. By eliminating spoilers, these interventions contributed to the rapid restoration of security and development aid, which was critical in signaling the government's commitment to moving away from conflict.

Rapid Mobilization of Foreign Aid for Reconstruction and Development Supported Stability

The timely mobilization of aid following the end of conflict is crucial. It can help achieve the key priorities of economic recovery while preventing a relapse into conflict. In the three examples, quickly mobilized aid helped shore up stability. In Liberia, donors began mobilizing aid immediately after the end of the second civil war, in 2003, in a marked departure from the situation at the end of the first civil war, when Taylor ascended to power. Relations between President Taylor and major donors were strained for various reasons, including Liberia's role in destabilizing Sierra Leone. These poor relations affected both the amount of assistance and the means of disbursement (most aid circumvented the government). The situation improved dramatically with Taylor's exit from power (Sesay and others 2009). In February 2004, donors pledged $500 million to rebuild Liberia. The election of Ellen Johnson Sirleaf and the move by her administration to embrace donor-recommended reforms created the conditions for further support. At the G8 summit in 2007, donors committed to financing debt relief and to cover 90 percent of Liberia's debt under the Heavily Indebted Poor Countries (HIPC) initiative.

Delivery of aid in the wake of the conflict in Sierra Leone was swift because of the democratic legitimacy of President Ahmad Tejan Kabbah, which made engagement easier than in Liberia under Taylor (Sesay and others 2009). In 2005, a gathering of donors under the umbrella of the Consultative Group for Sierra Leone announced an $800 million pledge to help Sierra Leone reduce poverty between 2005 and 2007 (World Bank 2006). The United Kingdom took the lead in funding major reforms in governance, the security sector, and decentralization (Thomson 2007).

Aid was also rapidly mobilized for Côte d'Ivoire. Major development partners, including the International Monetary Fund (IMF) and the World Bank, approved debt relief.

Leadership Was Central to Sustaining Peace in the Medium Term

The role of leadership in sustaining peace has been central in all three countries, with a direct relationship between strong leadership and the actions of donors. Good leadership enabled the conditions that encouraged donors to increase their engagement.

President Sirleaf is credited with significant improvements in economic governance since the end of the conflict. In 2005, Liberia faced numerous economic challenges, from widespread corruption to high domestic and external debt, underscoring concerns of a relapse into conflict. In response, donors and the transitional government compiled the Government and Economic Assistance Programme (GEMAP), an ambitious program to improve Liberia's public financial management system, reform the civil service, and introduce anticorruption measures. President Sirleaf fully endorsed and began implementing GEMAP while also initiating other important reforms, the impact of which was seen in subsequent years. As a result, Liberia reached the "completion point" for the HIPC process. Liberia also climbed up the rankings of Transparency International's Corruption Perceptions Index, rising from 137th of 158 countries in 2005 to 97th of 180 countries in 2009 (Gujadhur 2011).

Some observers have attributed robust donor support in Sierra Leone following the end of the conflict to the leadership of President Kabbah (Sesay and others 2009). His excellent working relationship with the international community was premised on his democratic legitimacy; his many years' experience as an economist at the United Nations Development Programme; and policies, which included fostering reconciliation.

President Outtara has been widely praised for his economic stewardship following the end of the conflict in Côte d'Ivoire in 2011. He oversaw a number of reforms, including the empowerment of farms in the critical cocoa sector and the reduction of poverty in rural areas. The government also embarked on a major drive to improve infrastructure (Boutellis 2013). In recognition of reforms undertaken and progress made since the end of conflict, in 2012 the IMF and World Bank approved debt relief of $4.4 billion (IMF 2012). Côte d'Ivoire has enjoyed extraordinarily strong economic growth since the end of the conflict, with growth rates of 8.8 percent in 2013 and 9.0 percent in 2014 (Yembiline, Traoré, and Padilla 2014).

Note

1. The CDF was a paramilitary organization that fought in the civil war in Sierra Leone. It supported the elected government of Ahmed Tejan Kabbah against the RUF.

References

Adeleke, A. 1995. "The Politics and Diplomacy of Peacekeeping in West Africa: The ECOWAS Operation in Liberia." *Journal of Modern African Studies* 33 (4): 569–93.

Alaga, E. 2010. "Challenges for Women in Peacebuilding in West Africa." Policy Brief 18, Africa Institute of South Africa, Pretoria. http://www.ai.org.za/wp-content/uploads /downloads/2011/11/No-18.-Challenges-for-Women-in-Peacebuilding-in-West-Africa .pdf.

Arthur, P. 2010. "ECOWAS and Regional Peacekeeping Integration in West Africa: Lessons for the Future." *Africa Today* 57 (2) 3–24.

Atuobi, S. 2010. "State-Civil Society Interface in Liberia's Post-Conflict Peacebuilding." KAIPTC Occasional Paper 30, Kofi Annan International Peacekeeping Training Centre, Accra. http://www.kaiptc.org/Publications/Occasional-Papers/Documents /Occasional-Paper-30-Atuobi.aspx.

Bah, A. M. 2005. "West Africa: From a Security Complex to a Security Community." *African Security Review* 14 (2) 77–83. http://www.issafrica.org/pubs/ASR/14No2 /EBah.pdf.

Boutellis, A. 2013. "Côte d'Ivoire's Ouattara Puts Economic Recovery Ahead of Political Reconciliation." *World Politics Review*, March 19. http://www.worldpoliticsreview .com/articles/12799/Côte -d-ivoire-s-ouattara-puts-economic-recovery-ahead-of -political-reconciliation.

Cilliers, J., and P.-S. Handy. 2013. "Lessons from African Peacemaking." Paper presented at the Africa Mediators' Retreat, Oslo Forum Network of Mediators. https:// www.osloforum.org/sites/default/files/Africa-Mediators-retreat-BP-African%20 Peacemaking.pdf.

Cook, N. 2011. "Côte d'Ivoire's Post-Election Crisis." CRS Report for Congress, Congressional Research Service, Washington, DC. http://fpc.state.gov/documents /organization/156548.pdf.

Davies, V. A. B. 2002. "War, Poverty and Growth in Africa: Lessons from Sierra Leone." Paper prepared for Centre for the Study of African Economies (CSAE) Fifth Annual Conference, "Understanding Poverty and Growth in Africa," St. Catherine's College, Oxford University, March 18–19.

de Waal, Alex. 2009. "Mission without End? Peacekeeping in the African Political Marketplace." *International Affairs* 85 (1): 99–113. http://www.chathamhouse.org /sites/files/chathamhouse/public/International%20Affairs/2009/85_1dewaal.pdf.

Dupuy, K., and J. Detzel. 2008. "Appeasing the Warlords: Power-Sharing Agreements in Liberia." CSCW Policy Brief 4, PRIO, Oslo. http://www.prio.org/Publications /Publication/?x=7201.

Fayemi, J. K. 2004. "Governing Insecurity in Post-Conflict States: The Case of Sierra Leone and Liberia." In *Reform and Reconstruction of the Security Sector*, ed. A. Bryden and H. Hänggi, 179–206. Münster: LIT. http://www.apcof.org/files/5175_8.pdf.

Francis, D. J. 2009. "Peacekeeping in a Bad Neighbourhood: The Economic Community of West African States (ECOWAS) in Peace and Security in West Africa." *African Journal on Conflict Resolution* 9 (3).

Goldmann, M. 2005. "Sierra Leone: African Solutions to African Problems?" *Max Planck Yearbook of United Nations Law* 9: 457–515. http://www.mpil.de/files/pdf2/mpunyb _goldmann_9_457_515.pdf.

Gujadhur, V. 2011. "Postconflict Economic Governance Reform: The Experience of Liberia." In *Yes Africa Can: Success Stories from a Dynamic Continent*, ed.

P. Chuhan-Pole and M. Angwafo, 127–40. Washington, DC: World Bank. http://
siteresources.worldbank.org/AFRICAEXT/Resources/258643-1271798012256/YAC
_Consolidated_Web.pdf.

IMF (International Monetary Fund). 2012. "IMF, World Bank Back $4 Billion Côte
d'Ivoire Debt Relief." *IMF Survey Magazine*, June 26. https://www.imf.org/external
/pubs/ft/survey/so/2012/car062612a.htm.

Malan, M., P. Rakate, and A. McIntyre. 2002. *Peacekeeping in Sierra Leone: UNAMSIL
Hits the Home Straight*. Institute for Security Studies, Pretoria. http://www.issafrica
.org/uploads/Mono68Full.pdf.

McGovern, M. 2011. *Making War in Côte d'Ivoire*. Chicago: University of Chicago Press.

Musah, A. 2009. "West Africa: Governance and Security in a Changing Region." Africa
Program Working Paper Series, International Peace Institute, New York.

Olonisakin, F. 2011. "ECOWAS: From Economic Integration to Peace-building."
In *ECOWAS and the Dynamics of Conflict and Peace-building*, ed. T. Jaye, D. Garuba,
and S. Amadi, 11–26. Dakar: Council for the Development of Social Science Research
in Africa (CODESRIA).

Pham, J. P. 2004. "A Nation Long Forlorn: Liberia's Journey from Civil War toward
Civil Society." *International Journal of Not-for-Profit Law* 7 (1). http://www.icnl.org
/research/journal/vol6iss4/art_1.htm.

Sesay, A., C. Ukeje, O. Gbla, and O. Ismail. 2009. *Post-War Regimes and State
Reconstruction in Liberia and Sierra Leone*. Dakar: Council for the Development of
Social Science Research in Africa (CODESRIA).

Thomson, B. 2007. *Sierra Leone: Reform or Relapse? Conflict and Governance Reform*.
London: Chatham House.

World Bank. 2006. "Donors Pledge $800m to Fast-Track Poverty Reduction in Sierra
Leone." News Release 2006/177/AFR, World Bank, Washington, DC. http://web
.worldbank.org/WBSITE/EXTERNAL/COUNTRIES/AFRICAEXT/0,,contentMDK:
20739146~menuPK:258658~pagePK:146736~piPK:146830~theSitePK:258644,00
.html.

Yembiline, P., B. Traoré, and L. Padilla. 2014. "Côte d'Ivoire 2014." African Economic
Outlook. http://www.africaneconomicoutlook.org/fileadmin/uploads/aeo/2014/PDF
/CN_Long_EN/Cote_divoire_EN.pdf.

Chapter 9

Improving the Way Donors and Development Agencies Support Stability

Development policies are central to peacebuilding and stability efforts in West Africa. Economic and social development has a critical role to play in reducing tensions linked to grievances over unmet expectations, unequal access to resources, and perceptions of exclusion.

Governments often regard conflict and violence as taboo subjects for discussion with donors and development partners, out of fear that acknowledgment of risks may deter potential investors. Internal politics are also often off limits to donors. There is probably less reluctance to engage with these issues in West Africa than elsewhere in Africa, as a result of the involvement of the Economic Community of West African States (ECOWAS) in regional conflicts. Recognition of the strong developmental dimensions of conflict still often comes too late, however, as do attempts to mobilize the development resources and advice that accompany it. In Mali, for example, events foretold by many analysts caught development partners by surprise. In Mali, Nigeria, and elsewhere, only when the insurgency took on an unpredictable quality were efforts made to bring in more development aid to conflict-prone areas.

Part of the problem is the close association of fragility, conflict, and violence and the fact that fragility is seen as a measure of very poor governance. In fact, conflict and violence are prevalent in medium- and high-income countries as well, and subnational conflicts have occurred in France, Spain, and the United Kingdom. Many middle- and high-income countries have addressed urban violence and subnational tensions not only through political pacts and better security approaches but also through innovative development policies. Latin American countries, for instance, have recognized the development dimensions of conflicts and engaged with partners and donors on security and social inclusion programs. They have requested support from development partners in improving citizen security, combating urban violence, and reducing the incidence of subnational conflicts. As a result, these countries have realized important progress in these areas.

Integrating the Stability Dimension into the Planning of Development Policies

The g7+ group of countries recently caught the attention of policy makers with its insistence that fragility-affected countries carry out their own fragility and conflict risk analysis in order to inform their policies and dialogue with partners.[1] This step is a good one, but it should apply to all countries at risk of conflict and violence, not just states classified as fragile. Where conflict risks are relatively high, as in West Africa, solid conflict and violence risk analyses should undergird growth and poverty reduction strategies. Stability needs to be a clear objective and recognized as essential for sustainable long-term growth and poverty reduction. Viewing stability as a legitimate objective of development policy is likely the only way to reduce conflict and violence over the long term.

It is therefore essential to integrate the stability dimension into the overall planning of development policies in West Africa. Not all policies that support growth and poverty reduction will also support stability. Policies targeted at concentrating investments on growth poles, for example, can spur growth, but if not carefully designed they can also trigger conflict and major grievances. In countries where subregional inequalities are very high and generally associated with differences in ethnicity or religion, investing heavily in wealthier regions may reinforce inequalities and a sense of ethnic injustice. Policies that allocate community land to large development projects, as is the case in Sierra Leone, can trigger major conflicts with local communities that can easily escalate into national conflicts. Investment in extractives without institutional development to ensure that the population benefits from the revenues generated is a potential factor of conflict over the long term. To avoid risks, governments and partner organizations need to fully integrate the objective of stability into their investment policies, something that is still too rarely done.

Donors and development partners should not get entangled in the politics of the countries they support, but they should be well versed and cognizant of the political implications of their investments and the impact they may have on a country's political economy. If they are not, they can unintentionally invest in areas that can reduce stability. To avoid this outcome, rigorous political analysis ought to be integrated into conflict analysis and updated regularly. Fragility, conflict, and, for that matter, development are very often closely linked to power struggles; many programs and projects are still highly technical in nature, and many capacity-building efforts are disconnected from the political economy of development. In Mali, donor support for decentralization made significant technical progress in the few years before the uprising in the north, with improved systems for financial flows and procurement. However, because of the way in which local politicians influenced the delivery of projects and services on the ground, the programs were mismanaged—something most donors and development actors did not want to acknowledge. The frustration that ensued was very much at the origin of the conflict.

Much more attention should be paid to conflict risks in peaceful situations. Many conflicts continue to take governments and donors by surprise. They do so not because of a deficit of knowledge of local situations—there is a wealth of research on West African social and political dynamics—but because donors and development partners do not know how to handle conflict-risk issues or engage with governments over them and are therefore unwilling to acknowledge them in official documents and strategies. Conflict risks are usually not well analyzed or integrated into donor strategies. Governments would also benefit from better tools to ensure that information from the field and analysis undertaken by national research institutes finds its way to policy makers.

When peacebuilding efforts start with national dialogues or other official discussions, it is very important that donors be ready to act quickly to support governments, show their commitment to improving the situation, and demonstrate their readiness to tackle thorny issues. The examples of Liberia, Sierra Leone, and Côte d'Ivoire suggest that the rapid mobilization of donors can play a critical role in ensuring stability (see chapter 8). It is also important for donors to improve their coordination with peacebuilding operations and national dialogue efforts.

Supporting stability requires combined interventions in many areas, particularly good coordination between security sector reform, improvement of state institutions in general, and interventions in the social and economic spheres. Coordination between development actors, both nationally and internationally, and actors active in security sector reform and disarmament, demobilization, and reintegration is often weak (and in some cases nonexistent). Many elements of security sector reform—including wages and salaries, civilian oversight, budgetary control and monitoring of expenditures, and the rule of law—need to be part of the overall reform of the state in order to be effective (see chapter 6). Guinea-Bissau, for example, needs to create a pension fund for the military as part of overall efforts to manage civil service reforms. It is essential that actors involved in security sector reform and overall state reform talk to one another and work together to conduct activities such as public expenditure reviews.

The high level of interconnectivity between the various drivers of conflict in West Africa, as well as the centrality of institutions in managing tensions and violence, necessitates the integration of stability and security issues into development policies. Supporting stability and security requires policies that focus simultaneously on a variety of areas, involve a large number of actors, and integrate holistically into a country's overall development strategy. Promoting stability throughout the subregion will also require the scaling up of regional programs, so that cross-border issues can be addressed simultaneously in multiple countries. Although policy and program design should take account of each country's specific historical, cultural, and economic context, some approaches are applicable across countries.

Supporting Institutional Development

One fundamental area in which new approaches are urgently needed is the way in which donors and development agencies work with governments to improve institutions' ability to transform and adapt. The legitimacy and capability of state institutions is integral to stability (World Bank 2011). Sustained long-term effort is needed to transform institutions. Technical capacity building alone is largely insufficient to transform institutions; political will and the buy-in of the population and other stakeholders, such as the local authorities, businesses, politicians, and civil society, is fundamental to successful reform (Marc and others 2012).

Institutional development requires a very different philosophy of intervention than infrastructure projects. It needs to integrate trial-and-error approaches, investment in consultation and consensus-building efforts, support for building champions of reforms in countries, and careful monitoring of the impact of implementation in the field (Viñuela, Barma, and Huybens 2014). Investments should be planned over long periods of time, while incorporating flexibility and room for adaptation. Institutional transformations are not linear—they are usually messy and often very political in nature—but they are critical for stability. Ready-made technocratic solutions provided by donors rarely work; institutional transformations are highly context specific and thus need to be country led and based on internal consultation and consensus building (Viñuela, Barma, and Huybens 2014). Donors can play important roles, but ultimately solutions have to be elaborated locally. Internal processes for designing and implementing change are central to the dynamic of institutional transformations. Technical tools and innovations in the field of administrative organization are also important. Computerization of financial services and the use of cutting-edge information and communications technology can improve service delivery and increase transparency in government financial transactions, which increases the legitimacy of government. These measures will be effective, however, only if the political and cultural elements of institutional transformations are also implemented.

Using Development to Support Lagging Regions

Subregional imbalances, and the reality or perception among some groups that there is inequitable access to resources, are probably the most important and challenging issues facing the subregion. It is tempting to concentrate investments where the conditions for rapid development are best. Doing so in West Africa, however, risks exacerbating tensions. Lagging and peripheral regions require development. Private sector investment plays a leading role in the development of well-endowed subregions; development aid should be concentrated in lagging regions and focus on addressing perceptions of inequity in access to opportunities.

Lagging regions are not necessarily the poorest regions of countries in West Africa; they are regions in which perceptions of exclusion or marginalization are strong. Because lagging regions are often along borders, it may be useful to support cross-border economic exchanges and collaboration. There is a very strong political economy dimension to strengthening lagging regions with a view to ensuring stability.

Strengthening Local Governance

To promote stability, development partners need to complement investments in lagging regions with efforts to improve local governance. Investing in regions where local authorities lack legitimacy can be counterproductive for stability. In Mali, policies to support the development of the country's north without concurrent improvements to decentralization reinforced tensions and led to serious conflict. Efforts to support decentralization or policies of deconcentration represent one approach to this conundrum; they require greater citizen participation in local government, improved social accountability, transparency, and improvements in the quality of services provided locally. Another prerequisite is political openness at the local level. Efforts can be thwarted by perceptions that the central government's intention is to retain full control of local development and community initiatives.

Improving Land Management and the Management of Extractives

Unresolved land issues are a major source of instability in West Africa; efforts in this area are therefore essential. Sharper focus is needed on improving land titling systems, refining regulations that govern the use of community land, managing the use of land by pastoralists and agricultural communities, managing and improving grazing lands, and enhancing policies that affect land acquisition in urban areas or areas where extractive development or large-scale agriculture programs are in place. Many initiatives tend to be chaotic, because they lack a holistic approach to land management as well as proper regulation frameworks and institutions to implement policies. Donors often shy away from supporting land reform and management projects, which they view as very political and long term in nature and rarely in need of large-scale undertakings.

The boom in extractives discoveries has created both opportunities and challenges for several countries. A key challenge is the need to broaden the scope of governance in the sector to incorporate issues such as political bargaining at the local level, subnational dynamics, and the costs the industry imposes on communities. The extractives bonanza also has implications for subregional imbalances and lagging regions, which could affect stability. The windfall revenues from extractives offer an opportunity for addressing some of the challenges facing lagging regions.

Improving Prospects for Youth and Displaced Persons

The recent surge in growth has not created sufficient jobs to meet the demand of West Africa's labor market, leaving many youth with poor prospects for improving their livelihoods or finding their place in society. Most investments in extractives and urban service industries create very few jobs, and the extractives sectors is the source of little innovation.

The tremendous increase in the number of youth entering the market each year, with expectations for improved livelihoods, is a ticking time bomb. Although the youth bulge will not necessarily result in conflict, it will undoubtedly spawn an increase in grievances across Africa. Only by accelerating the development of informal activity and livelihood options can the demand for their labor be satisfied.

Low-income countries face a challenge in maintaining (much less increasing) the current levels of enrollment and the quality of education. But countries across the region will be unable to maintain their growth rates without increasing the size of their skilled labor forces. Significant investments in basic and technical education are required to increase stability.

These investments need to be accompanied by support for institutions that help youth develop a sense of confidence that they can have a future. Improving youth community activities, developing programs to mitigate drug use and petty crime in urban areas, and supporting youth integration into various state and nonstate institutions will all be central to creating a more stable West Africa.

Part of the solution to the issue of youth livelihoods lies in internal migration, within both states and the subregion. Improving the management of migrants is therefore an urgent priority. From providing identity cards and facilitating the issuance of birth certificates to enhancing regional policies that deal with migrants and developing a corpus of legislation to advance the conditions of migrants, these initiatives need to sit high on the regional policy agenda.

West Africa hosts a large number of displaced persons, in the Sahel and in the Mano River Basin region, as well as around conflict zones in Mali and northern Nigeria. Protracted displacement contributes to grievances and generates vortexes of instability while creating challenges for service delivery and poverty reduction.

Supporting Security Sector Reform and Strengthening Justice and the Rule of Law

Emerging security threats in West Africa in the form of trafficking, piracy, and terrorism have boosted the imperative for reform and improvement of the security sectors. A key obstacle is the insufficient connection between support to overall state building and security sector reform. Other hindrances to security sector reform include the fact that security is still regarded as an issue that has little bearing on development and that most security issues are kept under wraps. In many countries, the military continues to strongly influence politics.

Although corruption in the security forces remains high, donor policies rarely integrate development and support to security. The form of the emerging security threats necessitates greater integration of development and security dialogue and requires more opportunities for public discussion of issues.

Reform of the security sector needs to go hand in hand with improvement of justice and the rule of law, particularly because most security threats emanate from within countries' borders, from their own citizens. Reform of the formal justice systems is necessary but largely insufficient. Conflict management mechanisms, implemented with the involvement of local authorities, civil society, and communities, are essential in the medium term at the least.

Increasing Transparency, Strengthening Accountability, and Supporting Regional Institution Building

Partial democratization can create tensions and lead to violence. Political competition and the recourse to identity issues sit at the root of much election-related violence in the subregion. Meanwhile, the focus of politicians remains on controlling resources rather than building legitimacy (Williams 2011). Development partners need to support greater openness and the dissemination of information about public matters, help governments strengthen and develop the capacities of parliamentary and debating institutions, and support the development of social accountability mechanisms. More aid should be distributed to these important areas. Actively supporting genuine decentralization can go some way toward diffusing the negative effects of the "winner takes all" approach still prevalent in many West African countries.

The active presence of ECOWAS in peacebuilding has had a very positive effect on reducing the impact of conflicts in the subregion. It is the most effective regional institution in addressing conflict in Africa. Institutional development is nevertheless needed to improve its implementation ability. Greater support to ECOWAS and other regional institutions, such as the Permanent Interstate Committee for Drought Control in the Sahel (CILSS), is essential to address new challenges.

Note

1. The g7+ is a voluntary association of 20 countries that are or have been affected by conflict and are now in transition to the next stage of development (see http://www .g7plus.org/).

References

Marc, A., A. Willman, G. Aslam, M. Rebosio, and K. Balasuriya. 2012. *Societal Dynamics and Fragility: Engaging Societies in Responding to Fragile Situations*. Washington, DC: World Bank.

Viñuela, L., N. H. Barma, and E. Huybens. 2014. *Institutions Taking Root: Building State Capacity in Challenging Contexts*. Washington, DC: World Bank.

Williams, P. D. 2011. *War and Conflict in Africa*. Cambridge: Polity Press.

World Bank. 2011. *World Development Report 2011: Conflict, Security and Development*. Washington, DC: World Bank.

Index

Boxes, figures, maps, notes, and tables are indicated by *b*, *f*, *m*, *n*, and *t*, following the page number.

www.ingramcontent.com/pod-product-compliance
Lightning Source LLC
Chambersburg PA
CBHW071119280326
41935CB00010B/1062